NAGASAKI

THE MASSACRE OF THE INNOCENT AND UNKNOWING

CRAIG COLLIE

ALLEN&UNWIN

First published in Australia in 2011

Allen & Unwin
Sydney, Melbourne, Auckland, London

83 Alexander Street
Crows Nest NSW 2065
Australia
Phone: (61 2) 8425 0100
Fax: (61 2) 9906 2218
Email: info@allenandunwin.com
Web: www.allenandunwin.com

Cataloguing-in-Publication details are available from
the National Library of Australia
www.trove.nla.gov.au

ISBN 978 1 74237 289 1

Typeset in 12/16pt Bembo by Midland Typesetters, Australia
Printed and bound in Australia by Griffin Press

10 9 8 7 6 5 4 3 2 1

Contents

Maps

People featured in this book

Nagasaki

Dr Tatsuichiro AKIZUKI, 29, doctor, Urakami Dai-ichi Hospital

Chiyoko EGASHIRA, 35, teacher, Shiroyama Primary School

Sakue KAWASAKI, 10, adopted daughter of Mr and Mrs Takigawa

Sugako MURAI, 26, cook and nurse, Urakami Dai-ichi Hospital

Dr Takashi NAGAI, 37, radiologist, Nagasaki Medical College

Takejiro NISHIOKA, 50, publisher of *Minyu* newspaper

Mitsue TAKENO, 16, mobilised student, Nagasaki Arms Factory

Miwa TAKIGAWA, 49, housewife and community leader

Sumiteru TANIGUCHI, 16, postman

Koichi WADA, 18, mobilised student, tram driver,
    Nagasaki Tram Company

Tsutomu YAMAGUCHI, 25, draftsman, Nagasaki shipyard
    (seconded to Hiroshima)

Ukichi EGASHIRA, teacher and mobilised supervisor,
    Nagasaki arms factory (Ohashi)
Nurse Tsuyako FUKAHORI, head nurse, Urakami Dai-ichi Hospital
Yoshiro FUKUDA, 50, manager, Nagasaki arms factory (Ohashi)
Kyoto HASHIMOTO, mobilised student, Nagasaki arms factory
Nurse HASHIMOTO, Nagasaki Medical College Hospital
Chifusa 'Chi-chan' HIRAI, 16, a school friend of Mitsue Takeno
Akira IWANAGA, 25, draftsman, Nagasaki shipyard (seconded to Hiroshima)
Brother Joseph IWANAGA, Franciscan monk, Urakami Dai-ichi Hospital
Ryoko KAWASAKI, 8, adopted daughter of Mr and Mrs Takigawa
Kyobei MINAMI, 40, warden of Urakami Prison
Midori NAGAI, wife of Dr Nagai

Wakamatsu NAGANO, governor of Nagasaki Prefecture

Setsuko 'N-san' NAKAMURA, 16, mobilised student, Nagasaki arms factory

Father Saburo (Raphael) NISHIDA, Catholic priest, Urakami Cathedral

Haruko NOGUCHI, 12, tram conductor, Nagasaki Tram Company

Tatsu NOGUCHI, 13, tram conductor, Nagasaki Tram Company

Yoshini NOGUCHI, theology student, Urakami Dai-ichi Hospital

Junji SATO, 26, journalist, Domei News Agency

Kuniyoshi SATO, draftsman, Nagasaki shipyard (seconded to Hiroshima)

Professor SEIKI, Department of Pharmacy, Nagasaki Medical College

Mitsue TABATA, pregnant housewife

Torahachi TAGAWA, 40, foreman, Nagasaki arms factory (Ohashi)

Masuichi TAKIGAWA, 17, medical student, son of Miwa Takigawa

Sadako TAKIGAWA, 22, daughter of Miwa TAKIGAWA

Father Fusakichi (Simon) TAMAYA, 28, Catholic priest, Urakami Cathedral

Sakataro 'Oba-chan' TANIGUCHI, grandmother of Sumiteru Taniguchi

Taga 'Ji-san' TANIGUCHI, grandfather of Sumiteru Taniguchi

Tsuneo TOMITA, 21, pharmacy student, Nagasaki Medical College

Dr Susumu TSUNO, dean of Nagasaki Medical College

Tatsuro YAMAWAKI, 11, primary school student, twin of Yoshiro Yamawaki

Toshihiro YAMAWAKI, 14, mobilised student and older brother of Yamawaki twins

Yasuo YAMAWAKI, engineer, Mitsubishi Electric Corporation and father of
    Yamawaki twins

Yoshiro YAMAWAKI, 11, primary school student, twin of Tatsuro Yamawaki

Atomic Bomb Missions

General Leslie 'Dick' GROVES, director of the Manhattan Project

J Robert OPPENHEIMER, Director of Scientific Research,
    Manhattan Project

Major Charles SWEENEY, pilot, *Bockscar* and leader of second mission

Colonel Paul TIBBETS, pilot, *Enola Gay* and leader of first mission

Lieutenant Don ALBURY, co-pilot, *Bockscar*

Lieutenant-Commander Frederick ASHWORTH, weaponeer, *Bockscar*

Captain Kermit BEAHAN, 26, bombardier, *Bockscar*

Lieutenant Jake BESER, electronic countermeasures officer, *Enola Gay* and *Bockscar*

Captain Fred BOCK, pilot, *The Great Artiste*

Sergeant Ed BUCKLEY, radar operator, *Bockscar*

Sergeant Albert 'Pappy' DEHART, tail gunner, *Bockscar*

General Thomas FARRELL, Joint Chief, Project Alberta

Major Thomas FEREBEE, bombardier, *Enola Gay*

Sergeant Ray GALLAGHER, assistant flight engineer, *Bockscar*

Lieutenant-Colonel Jim HOPKINS, pilot, *The Big Stink*

Sergeant John KUHAREK, flight engineer, *Bockscar*
General Curtis LEMAY, chief of XXI Bomber Command
Lieutenant Fred OLIVI, third pilot, *Bockscar*
Captain William 'Deak' PARSONS, weaponeer, *Enola Gay* and Joint Chief,
    Project Alberta
Colonel Hazen PAYETTE, intelligence officer, Project Alberta
Rear-Admiral WR PURNELL, Joint Chief, Project Alberta
Dr Norman RAMSEY, Deputy Chief, Project Alberta
Dr Robert SERBER, scientist, Project Alberta
General Carl SPAATZ, Commander of US Army Strategic Forces
Sergeant Abe SPITZER, radio operator, *Bockscar*
Captain James VAN PELT, navigator, *Bockscar*

Japanese Leadership

General Korechika ANAMI, 58, Minister of War

HIROHITO, Emperor

Naotake SATO, 62, Japanese Ambassador to the USSR

Baron Kantaro SUZUKI, 78, Prime Minister

Shigenori TOGO, 62, Foreign Minister

Genki ABE, Home Minister
Lieutenant-General Seizo ARISUE, army Chief of Intelligence
Captain Mitsuo FUCHIDA, navy's Hiroshima investigation team
Field Marshal Shunruku HATA, army commander of south-west Japan
Baron Kiichiro HIRANUMA, president of the Privy Council
Koki HIROTA, former Prime Minister
Lieutenant-General Sumihisa IKEDA, chief of army budget planning
Marquis Koichi KIDO, 56, Lord Keeper of the Privy Seal
Prince Fumimaro KONOYE, 54, former Prime Minister
Shunichi MATUMOTO, vice-minister of Foreign Affairs
Hisatsune SAKOMIZU, 42, Chief Secretary of Cabinet
Prince TAKAMATSU, younger brother of Emperor Hirohito
Colonel Masahiko TAKESHITA, head of domestic affairs, Military Affairs Bureau
Admiral Soemu TOYODA, 60, Navy Chief of Staff
General Yoshijiro UMEZU, 63, army Chief of General Staff
General Otozo YAMADA, Commander, Kwantung Army
Captain Yasukado YASUI, navy's Hiroshima investigation team
Admiral Mitsumasa YONAI, 65, Navy Minister
Lieutenant-General Masao YOSHIZUMI, head of military affairs, War Ministry

American Leadership

Henry L STIMSON, Secretary of War

Harry S TRUMAN, President

James BYRNES, Secretary of State
Averell HARRIMAN, US Ambassador to USSR
General George C MARSHALL, US Army Chief of Staff

Soviet Leadership

Vyacheslav MOLOTOV, Foreign Minister

Joseph STALIN, General Secretary of Communist Party of USSR,
    Premier of USSR

General Aleksei ANTONOV, Soviet Chief of Staff
Lavrenti BERIA, Head of Security
Solomon LOZOVSKY, Deputy Foreign Minister
Yakov MALIK, Soviet Ambassador to Japan
Marshal Rodion MALINOVSKY, Commander, Trans-Baikal Front
Marshal Kirill MERETSKOV, Commander, First Far Eastern Front
General Maksim PURKAYEV, Commander, Second Far Eastern Front
Marshal Aleksandr VASILEVSKY, Supreme Commander of Soviet Forces in the Far East

Others

Private Allan CHICK, Australian POW, Fukuoka Camp 14, Nagasaki

Sergeant Peter MCGRATH-KERR, Australian POW, Fukuoka
    Camp 14, Nagasaki

Generalissimo CHIANG Kai-shek, President, Republic of China
Winston CHURCHILL, Prime Minister of Great Britain
Saiji HASEGAWA, foreign editor, Domei News Agency
Sergeant Jack JOHNSON, Australian POW, Fukuoka Camp 14, Nagasaki
Lieutenant Marcus McDILDA, P-51 pilot shot down near Osaka
Dr Yoshio NISHINA, physicist, developing Japanese atomic bomb
Tse-ven (TV) SOONG, Premier, Republic of China

Time differences

The time in Washington DC is 13 hours behind Tokyo. Moscow is 6 hours behind Tokyo and 7 hours ahead of Washington DC.

Tinian operated 1 hour ahead of Tokyo and its bombing missions remained on Tinian time even when they were over Japan. In this book, times in flight operations are described in Tokyo time, once they are in the air, to assist the reader grasp the chronology of events. Any US mission documents quoted, however, retain the time given in the document which will be Tinian time.

Because of the greater time differences, this approach is not used for Washington or Moscow. Paradoxical times (such as Americans having dinner at 7 a.m.) would be distracting. Time is given in local time in each case, but events are generally laid out in rough chronological order. This should ease understanding of the sequence of events. Where the time in two places is key to the understanding of events, both times are given.

Chapter I

Hiroshima, Monday 6 August 1945, morning

Fate is a plane high in the sky. Sometimes we hear it coming; some-times we don't. Sometimes we guess the significance of that sound; sometimes it eludes us. We listen to the distant drone in a sort of uncomprehending stupor. Fate is a lottery, after all. It is only with hindsight that we can appreciate the steps that should have been taken, usually long before, to redirect it. Mostly, by the time we hear the sound of our approaching fate it is too late to avoid the consequences.

This is the story of the days leading up to the release of a cataclysmic product of human technological ingenuity, heralded by the sound of a plane at high altitude above the humdrum daily grind of a city crippled by war and languishing in the swelter of summer. Dog days in a city that fate would soon overtake.

◆ ◆ ◆

On the bus that took them from the company-owned boarding house to within walking distance of Mitsubishi's Hiroshima shipyards, Tsutomu Yamaguchi realised he'd left his personal stamp—his *inkan*—behind. Dipped in red ink paste, the *inkan* was pressed on documents in lieu of a signature. Without it, Yamaguchi couldn't sign off on his departure paperwork. He told his two companions to go on and he would catch up with them at the shipyard. He got off and caught another bus back to their quarters. Smoke belched out of a wood-burning unit attached to the bus's rear end. That's how things worked after so many years of war. Making do with what was available.

On temporary transfer from Mitsubishi's Nagasaki shipbuilding works to its expanding Hiroshima operation, Yamaguchi and his companions, Iwanaga and Sato, were technical draftsmen working on a 5000-tonne oil tanker. The job done, they were ready to return home. The three had packed their bags early that morning. It was already a bright, clear summer day. They decided to go down to the workplace and farewell their colleagues of the last three months. The next day they would be on the train back to Nagasaki, to their families and friends on the southern island of Kyushu.

It was 6 August 1945. Japan had been at war with America and its allies since Pearl Harbor in December 1941. For the first six months the Japanese had surprised even themselves with the speed with which they drove through South-east Asia to the Dutch East Indies (now Indonesia) and Burma. But over the last three years all those gains had been slowly whittled away by the Allied counter-offensive. Having taken Okinawa after a bloody and costly battle, the Americans seemed poised to invade mainland Japan and bring Japan's dreams of empire to an inglorious end.

At this stage of the war, everything was in short supply. Life for the ordinary Japanese had become a grim struggle for survival, clinging to the forlorn hope of an improbable victory, pumped up by propaganda from Japan's various official sources. By 1945 there were no eggs, milk or coffee available in shops and very little tea. A bitter coffee-like brew could be made by roasting soybeans. Vegetables were the staple, mostly grown in backyard and communal plots. Many public areas, like school-yards and parks, had been turned over to market gardening. Petrol was virtually non-existent for the general public. There were no private cars. Buses and taxis burned wood for fuel and electric-powered streetcars still operated in many cities. Apart from them, the streets were filled with bicycles, pedestrians and a few military vehicles.

Since March, the Allied advance had moved close enough to Japan for regular formations of bombers to carry out massive firebombing raids on Japan's cities. The predominance of wooden buildings made these attacks particularly destructive. In the face of the grim reality of their lost imperial cause, the Japanese maintained a stoic resilience. Food might be scarce, but civilian and military morale held on doggedly.

U Ba Maw, prime minister of the puppet government of Burma, noticed the change in the people when he revisited Tokyo at that time. They were 'visibly subdued and disillusioned by events', he said, 'but most of them were as determined and defiant as ever'. Ba Maw was there during an American incendiary bombing of the city. He was struck by the Japanese capacity to endure. 'The result was quite literally a holocaust, a mass burning of one of the densest areas of the city. I saw the ghastly devastation the next morning. But there was no panic or self-pity or even audible complaint among the huge mass of victims. In fact some of them were able to express their happiness that the Imperial Palace had escaped.'

Throughout Japan, schoolchildren and other non-essential civilians had been evacuated to the country, but it wasn't systematically planned. Those who stayed behind were organised to combat fires, build shelters and work in factories and on gardens. Under bumbling leadership, the hopelessly inadequate home defence was ineffective against the scale of the aerial attacks. A system of air-raid alarms and shelters had been developed across the country. Alarms sounded almost every day, but so far Hiroshima had been spared from the attacks.

At 7 a.m. on 6 August, the Japanese early warning radar network detected US aircraft approaching from the south. The alert was raised and radio broadcasting stopped in many cities, including Hiroshima. The planes approached at high altitudes, but they were few and quite dispersed. By eight o'clock the radar operator in Hiroshima decided there were no more than three planes in the vicinity and the air-raid alert was lifted. Radio broadcast resumed, advising people to go to shelters if an American B-29 bomber was actually sighted, but these aircraft were assumed to be on a reconnaissance mission. Fuel was now in such short supply that Japanese fighter planes would no longer take off to intercept small groups.

Yamaguchi returned to his boarding house in the south-eastern quarter of the city. He either hadn't heard or had ignored the air-raid alert. As he took off his shoes, the elderly manager spotted his guest of the last three months and invited him to share a cup of tea. In the exchange of pleasantries, the 25-year-old Yamaguchi told how he was looking forward to seeing his family again. His son had been born just before he came to Hiroshima. He hadn't yet seen his new house. There was plenty to look forward to on his return home.

Another Nagasakian who had been away on business was already on a train home. A short, stocky man with a trim moustache, Takejiro Nishioka was in his mid-fifties, the publisher of *Minyu* (*People*), a Nagasaki daily. The intensity of recent American incendiary bombing had prompted newspaper editors in western Japan to look into emergency measures in case their printing plants were destroyed. The group had resolved to set up rotary presses in a cave shelter at a location in Nagasaki yet to be decided. The editors agreed to build the underground plant within a month, despite the shortage of labour and materials. The best labour source would be convicts, among whom they could expect some experienced coal miners, but this required approval by the minister of justice and the cooperation of prefecture governors. An order from the home minister would ensure the governors' support.

The well-connected and upright Nishioka was elected by the group to go to Tokyo to enlist the support of the two relevant ministers. His mission had been successful. He had the consent of both, but in discussions in Tokyo Nishioka realised they would need army labourers as well. These could be requisitioned through General Yokoyama, commander of army forces in Kyushu. In Japan, as elsewhere in the world, who you know can be as useful as what you know. Nishioka didn't know Yokoyama, but Field Marshal Shunroku Hata, army commander over south-west Japan, was a relative of Yokoyama and a friend of Nishioka. Hata had his headquarters in Hiroshima. The publisher decided to stop off there on the long train journey from Tokyo back to Nagasaki.

On 5 August there were no seats available on the scheduled west-bound service to Hiroshima, but Takejiro Nishioka was a man with connections. He used them to get on an overnight military train instead. It was expected to arrive at Hiroshima at eight o'clock in the morning, but the early air attack warning had delayed the train by twenty-five minutes. It was already 8.15 when it pulled into Kaidaichi on the outskirts of Hiroshima, 8 kilometres from the city centre.

On the same side of the city and close to the port, Yamaguchi had finished his tea and retrieved his *inkan*. Having put on his shoes, he set out once again for the shipyard, this time by streetcar. It went by a less direct route than the bus, going into the city centre and out again, but Yamaguchi was in no hurry. He walked the remaining short distance to the Mitsubishi Shipbuilding Company. Akira Iwanaga—his roommate in the boarding house—and Kuniyoshi Sato were already there chatting with workers in one of the large office buildings. Yamaguchi took off his jacket and rolled up his shirt sleeves. Another oppressively hot day was on the way. He crossed a short bridge over a creek. Walking past recently planted potato fields, he noticed a woman coming towards him wearing a black *monpe*, the shapeless uniform with gathered trousers that most Japanese women wore at that time. In that instant, Yamaguchi heard the faint drone of a plane high in the sky. He and the woman both looked up to see if they could spot it.

◆ ◆ ◆

8.09 a.m: thirty-year-old Colonel Paul Tibbets of the US Army Air Forces pointed his B-29 Superfortress over the Inland Sea towards the city of Hiroshima on Japan's main island of Honshu. The previous afternoon, he'd named the plane *Enola Gay* after his mother.

'We are about to start the bomb run,' Tibbets announced over the intercom. 'Put on your goggles and place them on your forehead. When the countdown starts, pull the goggles over your eyes and leave them there until after the flash.' The crew had been issued with arc-welder's adjustable goggles to protect them from the anticipated intense flash of the explosion.

There was no flak coming up, no sign of enemy planes. Co-pilot Captain Robert Lewis wrote in his in-flight log: 'There will be a short intermission while we bomb our target.'

Massive in the belly of the plane, as snug as the family St Bernard, lay a 4-tonne blue-black bomb called Little Boy. The name was not ironic—the American military is not much given to irony—but to distinguish it from its longer prototype. At 3.5 metres in length, it still wasn't short. The product of the top-secret Manhattan Project, the atomic bomb had been developed at laboratories in Los Alamos, New Mexico. It was assembled on Tinian, an island in the Northern Marianas group, which had been captured from the Japanese in the Allied advance through the Pacific. The Manhattan Project had been so closely guarded that the new US president, Harry S Truman, was unaware of its existence until he was promoted from vice-president on the death of Franklin D Roosevelt. Soon the whole world would know of it. A formation of three B-29s had taken off from Tinian, carrying the uranium-cored bomb capable of considerable but largely unquantified devastation. This type of bomb had never been tested.

Behind *Enola Gay* a second B-29, *The Great Artiste*, following 10 metres off its right wing, dropped back a kilometre or so. A third, the unnamed No. 91 piloted by George Marquardt, began circling to position itself to take photographs. The bombardier on *Enola Gay*, Major Thomas Ferebee, pressed his left eye to the Norden bombsight. At 8.13 + 30 seconds Tibbets said to him, 'It's all yours.' Then, over the intercom: 'On goggles.'

Ferebee's bombsight generated flight corrections in autopilot. The aiming point, the T-shaped Aioi Bridge spanning a branch of the flat Ota River delta over which spread the city of Hiroshima, came into the crosshairs.

'I've got it,' said Ferebee.

The bomb-bay doors swung open and a low-pitched continuous tone was sent through the intercom. In response the crew, except the pilots and Ferebee, pulled down their dark welder's glasses. The tone was also sent by radio to the other planes, giving them fifteen seconds' notice of the bomb's release.

At 8.15 + 17 seconds, the radio tone stopped abruptly, replaced by the sound of air rushing past the open bay. Little Boy dropped out rear first. It flipped and hurtled nose down towards Hiroshima.

Chapter 2

Hiroshima, Monday 6 August 1945

Major Charles Sweeney had the bulky build of the college footballer he once was, but with a face like a friendly bear and a self-effacing manner he wasn't intimidating. At the controls of *The Great Artiste* he watched *Enola Gay* lurch upward as its heavy payload fell free. Colonel Tibbets disengaged autopilot, banked 60 degrees to the left and dived into a 155-degree turn to gather speed. 'Bomb gone,' called Sweeney's bombardier, Kermit Beahan, and began his prescribed routine for the mission. The crew in Chuck Sweeney's plane heard the mechanical hum of pneumatic bomb-bay doors opening, followed by the roar of rushing air. Three cylinders slid into the air torrent. They looked like large fire extinguishers, but were aluminium packs with transmitters sending back data. A parachute opened behind each one.

Little Boy took 43 seconds to fall from *Enola Gay*, flying at 10,000 metres, to a preset detonation point 600 metres above the city. A cross-wind drifted the missile 250 metres away from Aioi Bridge. It detonated instead over Shima Surgical Clinic. Working like a gun barrel, a few thousand kilograms of high explosive propelled one piece of the unstable uranium isotope U-235 into another piece. A nuclear chain reaction was triggered when the two pieces pressure-welded to supercritical mass.

This bomb hadn't been tested because extracting U-235 from uranium ore is a laborious and expensive process. All the purified U-235 produced at that time, all 60 kilograms of it, was used in Little Boy. Exploding with a force equal to 12,500 tonnes of TNT, the temperature rocketed to over a million degrees centigrade, igniting the surrounding air and forming an expanding giant fireball. At the point of explosion, energy was given off in the form of light, heat, radiation and pressure. The light sped outwards. The shock wave created by enormous pressure followed, moving out at about the speed of sound.

In the centre of the city everything but reinforced concrete buildings disappeared in an instant, leaving a desert of clear-swept, charred remains. The blast wave shattered windows for 15 kilometres from the hypocentre or, as it's more colloquially known, 'ground zero'. Over two-thirds of Hiroshima's buildings were demolished or had interiors completely gutted, all windows, doors, sashes and frames ripped out. Hundreds of fires were ignited by the thermal pulse, generating a firestorm that rolled out for several kilometres. At least 80,000 people—about 30 per cent of Hiroshima's 250,000 population at the time—were killed immediately, but possibly nearer to 100,000. The exact number will never be known.

At the instant of detonation, the forward cabin of *Enola Gay* lit up. Tibbets felt a tingling in his teeth from the bomb's radiation interacting with the metal in his fillings. A pinpoint of purplish-red light kilometres below the B-29s expanded into a ball of purple fire and a swirling mass of flames and clouds. Hiroshima disappeared from sight under the churning flames and smoke. The tail gunner, Bob Caron, grabbed his Kodak camera and started snapping pictures. A white column of smoke emerged from the purple clouds, rose rapidly to 3000 metres and bloomed into an immense mushroom. The mushroom seethed turbulently as it rose on its smoke stem to 15,000 metres. Co-pilot Lewis wrote in his log, 'My God, what have we done?'

Chuck Sweeney had swung *The Great Artiste* in a hard-diving turn to the right. Those on board were pinned back in their seats. Sweeney had difficulty seeing through the goggles so he pushed them up. As he had straightened course, the sky was bleached a translucent white, 'brighter than the sun'. Light filled his head. His sight was returning when he heard his tail gunner, 'Pappy' Dehart, uttering gibberish over the intercom as they raced away from the bomb. The plane was hit with a violent force and bounced. Beahan yelled, 'Flak!' It was hit again with less force, but they were pressure waves from the explosion, not enemy flak. Data was coming back from the canisters that had been dropped. Scientists on board watched the blast-recording equipment with fascination and excitement. This was a new era in science, going who knew where?

In the third plane, physicist Bernard Waldman captured vision of the event on a special Fastax high-speed camera. He hadn't had time to test the camera in the air, so he counted to forty when he saw the bomb dropped and turned it on. In *The Great Artiste*, scientific observer Harold Agnew pressed a borrowed 16 mm home movie camera against the window and rolled his single spool of silent film. Beahan was so overawed he forgot to turn on a recorder to capture crew comments for posterity.

Navy Captain William 'Deak' Parsons was the 'weaponeer' on *Enola Gay* for that mission, the Manhattan Project's man on the spot. He sent a coded message back to Tinian to be passed on to their masters in the United States: 'Results clear cut successful in all respects. Visible effects greater than Trinity test [a bomb test in New Mexico]. Target Hiroshima. Conditions normal in airplane following delivery proceeding to base.' The mission had gone like clockwork. For those in the air the feeling was a mixture of elation and relief.

On the ground the experience was altogether different.

Looking up at the aircraft, Yamaguchi the naval draftsman had seen a small black object fall out. A white parachute unfurled, then another one. The distant engine's drone was the only distraction on this clear, hot day. In an instant, his eyes were filled with a blinding flash like a huge magnesium flare. All other sensory responses deserted him.

Like all workers at Mitsubishi, Yamaguchi had been drilled to respond to air raids. Instinctively he covered his eyes with his fingers, plugged his ears with his thumbs and dropped face-down on the ground. The woman he'd noticed in a black *monpe* ran in panic into one of the potato fields. Yamaguchi was hit with a shattering blast that rolled over him. It was like nothing he'd experienced before. The earth convulsed, lifting him like a lightweight baking tray half a metre in the air and a strong wind rushed underneath. He fell flat on the ground, dazed.

When he opened his eyes, Yamaguchi could see only darkness. Gradually texture and detail separated. He was in the middle of a black dust cloud in an opaque twilight. Through the gauzy light, small circles of flame were sprouting everywhere on leaves in the potato field. The woman in the *monpe* was nowhere to be seen. Yamaguchi became aware of a throbbing heat on the left side of his face and on his left arm. It felt like the heat was hovering just off his skin, which he noticed was severely burned. The dust was thinning, a mushroom cloud reared ominously over the city and he began to feel nauseous and faint. A desperate longing to be with his family in Nagasaki welled up within him. He craved the warm familiarity and comfort of home.

The injured draftsman stumbled across the potato field towards a tree standing bare in the middle, stripped of its leaves by the blast. He focused all his attention and flagging energy on the objective of getting to the tree. When he reached it, he slumped at its base. An intense thirst tortured him. All around were collapsed houses with burning timber.

He could see the conical hill that separated him from the shipyards where Iwanaga and Sato had been waiting for him. Four kilometres from the hypocentre, that hill had shielded the Mitsubishi plant from the full force of the blast. Just the same, windows had been blown out and ceilings had been pushed in. Broken glass and furniture had flown across the offices. Although there were some casualties among the 300 workers in the office building, they didn't include the two visitors from Nagasaki. Those able to move easily were told by the company watchman to go to the air-raid shelter in case there were further attacks. The two from Nagasaki went outside looking for Yamaguchi but their way was blocked by fires and broken bridges. They returned to the shelter in despair.

◆   ◆   ◆

At Kaidaichi on the eastern outskirts of Hiroshima, the publisher Nishioka had seen a strange 'lightning flash' from somewhere in the middle of the city. Soldiers ordered everyone off the train. Nishioka could see a billowing cloud climbing up from the city. Like others with him, he assumed there had been an explosion in an ammunition dump or a gunpowder store. The train's carriages were uncoupled, but the engine was continuing into Hiroshima. Nishioka used his authoritative manner and his connections to get permission to ride in the cab. His respectability was persuasive. It was the reason he had been chosen to go to Tokyo . . . and the reason that mission had been successful.

The locomotive didn't get far before it had to stop. The railway tracks were blocked with victims of the blast leaving the city on foot. Many had skin peeling from their faces and arms like a poster half torn off a wall; others walked slowly, murmuring, 'Water! Water!' Bits and pieces of burning material were spread all over the ground as if fed from a furnace below. It was starting to look like there had been something more catastrophic than a store explosion, but Nishioka had no idea what it could be. He hadn't heard any mass formation of bombers so it didn't seem likely to have been an air attack.

The publisher got to the north side of the city on foot, to Field Marshal Hata's headquarters on the lower slope of Mount Futaba. Elevation had helped buildings there escape the worst of the blast. They were knocked about but not incinerated. Hata's home adjacent to his headquarters did not appear damaged from the outside, so it seemed likely its occupant would be safe inside. At the entrance, Nishioka was met by an elderly officer whom he knew, although he couldn't recall his name. The officer's uniform was in rags. The civilian greeted the military man and enquired after Hata.

'I don't know whether the field marshal is alive or dead,' was the reply. Clearly something major and unimaginable had occurred.

Nishioka's side-trip had achieved nothing. There was no real prospect of locating his friend in the surrounding chaos. He decided to walk to a station and try to catch a train to Nagasaki. 'There was nothing I could accomplish under the circumstances in Hiroshima,' he explained later. 'The walk back, among innumerable dead and dying, the bleeding and skinless people, groaning and calling for water, was the most horrible, pitiable sight I have ever seen, even in a drawing of hell!'

◆ ◆ ◆

The Tokyo control officer, broadcasting scheduled programs from the transmission and monitoring centre of the Japan Broadcasting Corporation (NHK), noticed that his line to Hiroshima had gone dead. It was 8.17 a.m. He tried without success to re-establish transmission by using another telephone line. Elsewhere in the NHK complex, workers with earphones monitored regional broadcasts for defeatist comment. Shortly after seven, several stations stopped broadcasting so their staff could go to shelters when enemy planes were detected approaching southern Honshu. Broadcasts resumed with the all-clear. At a quarter past eight, Hiroshima's radio station went off air again without warning and didn't come back on.

Twenty minutes later, engineers in the Tokyo railway signal centre realised their main line telegraph had stopped working just north of Hiroshima. There must be a break in the line there, they concluded. Confused reports of a terrible explosion in Hiroshima were coming from railway stations outside the city. How that could affect a power line on the outskirts was not clear. There was no report from the main Hiroshima station and no response from there to a request for information.

Commander Okumiya, the Tokyo-based officer in charge of the navy's Homeland Air Defence, had a phone call from an officer at Kure naval base about eight thirty. Shortly before, there had been a 'terrible flash' over Hiroshima, 20 kilometres away, followed by a turbulent cloud column rising over the city. The Kure officer had been unable to reach Second Army headquarters in Hiroshima by phone. Okumiya asked if there had been an air raid and was told only a few B-29s had been seen.

The snatches of perplexing information coming in at various points were passed on to the Imperial Japanese Army's headquarters in Tokyo. Duty staff there tried to contact the military communications bunker in Hiroshima's castle, the nerve centre of Second Army under the command of Takejiro Nishioka's missing friend, Field Marshal Hata. All lines were dead. The completeness of the silence was puzzling. Headquarters staff knew that no large enemy raid had taken place and there was no sizeable store of explosives in Hiroshima at that time.

The Second Army's shipping depot at Ujina on the Hiroshima waterfront was far enough from the hypocentre for damage from the blast to not render it completely inoperable. Officers at the depot were able to get a message to the nearby naval base. It was similar to another report that came through from Lieutenant Hashimoto, a visiting navy communications officer. Hashimoto had been in the public toilet underneath Hiroshima railway station when the bomb exploded. Nonplussed by what he saw when he returned to the street, he ran to Kaidaichi and phoned a garbled report to Kure base.

Just before noon, Kure followed up its earlier telegram to Commander Okumiya with an eyewitness report that two B-29s had passed over Hiroshima at high altitude, followed by a searing flash and a huge roaring sound. Houses had collapsed across the city and fires had broken out. 'Everything is confused,' the message said. 'The fires and streams of refugees have made it impossible to get in touch with any place closer than Kaidaichi.'

In the wood-panelled office of the War Ministry, minister Korechika Anami, in a planning meeting with the army's Chief of General Staff, Yoshijiro Umezu, and its Budget Branch head, had also lost communication with the Hiroshima headquarters. Telegrams from the navy advised of a large explosion in Hiroshima and, a few hours later, of collapsed houses and widespread fires. General Anami called in the army head of intelligence, General Arisue. A young officer was dispatched by plane to investigate.

◆ ◆ ◆

About eleven o'clock, heavy rain with marble-sized droplets began falling in the north-west of Hiroshima from clouds created by the atomic blast. Called 'black rain', it was full of dirt, dust, soot and highly radioactive particles sucked into the air from the explosion. It was actually more a muddy colour than black, unpleasantly slimy like raining grease and leaving dark streaks and ingrained stains on clothes and walls.

On the south side of the city under his leafless tree, Yamaguchi escaped the downpour and was spared the danger, with his severe thirst, of drinking radioactive rainwater. Looking over and noticing a trench by a rifle range, he moved there for shelter. A woman lay in the trench groaning quietly. She was naked with dark red burns on her skin. She tried to get up but was too weak, mumbling in Korean to the whole world and to no-one in particular, 'Help me! Help me!'

In Japanese, she asked Yamaguchi, 'Am I going to die?'

He assured her she'd be okay. 'Stay in the shade of the trench,' he said.

They were joined by two students in black uniform, apparently unhurt. One looked at the injured draftsman with concern.

'You've got a serious burn, sir,' he said. Yamaguchi touched his own face lightly. The skin felt highly inflamed and about to peel; his burnt arm was black and swelling.

The student got a small glass jar from a bag he carried over his shoulder. It was medicine for burns, he said. His mother had fortuitously put the jar in his bag as he was leaving that morning for the factory where the students worked. Yamaguchi stoically refused the offer of help, but the younger man was insistent and put the ointment on his skin. It had a soothing sensation like lightly applied palm oil.

Still with no idea what had become of their fellow worker from Nagasaki, Iwanaga and Sato left their air-raid shelter. It seemed there would be no follow-up attack and the shelter was stifling. They found the company clinic, surrounded by ghostlike figures, some almost naked, many moaning in pain, skin covered with powdered cement so you couldn't tell which were men and which were women. Hair had been burned off those not wearing caps. These were workers who had been out in the open at the time of the blast.

By midday, Yamaguchi decided to move around the hill to the Mitsubishi office. The two teenagers had gone and the Korean lady was ominously quiet. Some of the fires had eased so it was now possible to pick a pathway through the debris. Along the side of the road lay several dead bodies. When Yamaguchi got to the temporary housing where his design section had been, there was nothing but collapsed and burning timber. The beach alongside was littered with dead Korean labourers.

As he shuffled towards what had been the company yard, survivors crowded around him and took him to the clinic. On the ground nearby, he saw charred bodies. Some had slight movements of the hands and feet, others were absolutely motionless. In front of the clinic, a medico put white ointment on Yamaguchi's arm and face, and wrapped bandages around the affected areas. The rudimentary medical attention, the concern of one human being for another, eased his sense of despair and unreality.

Treated and dressed, Yamaguchi was sent to join a group gathered in a nearby pine grove. Scanning the sea of strangers' faces, he was overjoyed to find his two colleagues from Nagasaki. His spirits lifted. The three from Nagasaki were together and had survived. Yamaguchi was given two small biscuits and some water, but he vomited after swallowing a piece of biscuit. Next to the three of them, office girls were crying because they couldn't go home. With the destruction of most of Hiroshima's bridges, there was no immediate way off the delta island on which Mitsubishi's shipyards stood.

◆　◆　◆

Just after midday, a reporter for Domei News Agency—the national agency set up as a foil for Reuters—arrived at a small studio at Hara on the northern outskirts of Hiroshima. Satoshi Nakamura was, at thirty-seven, an experienced local journalist. His home was in Hiroshima city, but as luck would have it he had spent the night with a friend some distance out of town. Reading the morning paper there, he was thrown to the floor by a force that shattered all east-facing windows. He had raced outside and saw a black cloud rising and twisting above Hiroshima.

As Nakamura cycled towards Hiroshima he was buffeted by a strong wind and a downpour of 'black rain'. His fingers gripping the handlebars were stained by dark residue in the sticky rain. At his destination, the reporter walked around the destroyed city with a notebook. He had no home now, but he was alive and there was work to be done. The first journalist to witness the devastation, he had nowhere to file his report.

Nakamura pedalled back out to Hara where NHK had a transmitter. The only operational line there was a phone connection to the Okayama transmitter, 140 kilometres further east. At 12.20 he dictated a short report to Domei's Okayama office: 'At approximately 0816 one or two enemy planes flew over Hiroshima and dropped a special bomb. Hiroshima is completely destroyed. Casualties estimated at 170,000.'

He had guessed the casualty figure by halving what was believed to be the city's population at the time. Half had been his impression of the level of dead and injured. It wasn't a bad estimate. When Nakamura later filed a second report, the Domei bureau chief challenged his earlier estimate. It couldn't be true that Hiroshima could be destroyed by a single bomb, he said. The reporter was ordered to correct his previous report; the army wouldn't accept it.

'The army are fools,' Nakamura shouted down the line.

◆ ◆ ◆

On the other side of the world, a portly army engineer waited anxiously in his general's uniform for news of the *Enola Gay* mission. His office on the eighth floor of the New War Building sat across the Potomac River from the Pentagon. Pacing near his desk, the general eventually rolled up his sleeves, took off his tie and loosened his collar. Such informality was out of character for General Leslie R Groves, military director of the top-secret Manhattan Project, but he was on edge for a reason. The mission was the acid test of three years of development under his leadership. A gifted military project director—he had overseen construction of the Pentagon—the abrasive and often tactlessly sarcastic Groves had the distinction of being equally disliked by both scientists and servicemen in the Manhattan Project. One of his subordinates has described him as the 'biggest sonofabitch I've ever met in my life, but also one of the most capable individuals . . . if I were to have to do my part all over again, I would select Groves as boss. I hated his guts and so did everybody else but we had our form of understanding.'

It was midnight in Washington DC, nearly four hours after the B-29 was scheduled to drop the new bomb. There had been no explanation of the lateness of any report from Tinian. Dick Groves was tense but didn't want to show it. He combined drive and organisational ability with blunt ruthlessness and self-confidence. It was important to him that he revealed no softness or weakness to his staff. But his greatest weakness was evident to all. Not yet fifty, he had a serious weight problem—not helped by his love of chocolate—that would eventually kill him.

Crossing the Potomac and walking into the New War Building's elegant Art Deco lobby of black marble, an army courier brought the report Groves wanted. In it, General Thomas Farrell, his man on Tinian, had repeated word for word Deak Parsons' message radioed from *Enola Gay*. Farrell had wired it via Manila where for some reason it had been held up. Groves read the document with relief and suppressed elation. He immediately called Colonel McCarthy, aide to US Army Chief of Staff, General George C Marshall. McCarthy, in turn, rang Marshall at home and passed on the news, to which the politely impassive general replied, 'Thank you very much for calling me,' and hung up.

Groves advised his outer office of the contents of the report. They had stayed late, waiting for the outcome of the mission. On hearing the news, they erupted with excitement, but they celebrated the triumph of the project, not their leader. There was no particular warmth towards him. Groves didn't join them but went back to his office. He drafted a report for General Marshall in the morning and lay down on a divan set up in his office. He fell into restless sleep.

◆ ◆ ◆

At the US Army Air Forces base on Tinian, preparations were under way by the base's mess cooks for a huge celebration. They knew the 509th Composite Group was returning from a successful mission that was the culmination of a highly classified project, but they had no idea what it was. It had to be more significant than the handful of three-plane raids to drop 'pumpkin' surrogate bombs on minor targets on mainland Japan, the limited action the group had seen so far and the subject of occasional jibes from other units on the base.

Hundreds of pies were prepared for a pie-eating competition. Hot dogs, beef and salami sandwiches, potato and fruit salads, all were on the menu for the big occasion ... whatever it was. There was free beer, up to four bottles per person—no ration card needed—and lemonade for those who preferred it. A jitterbug contest was announced. There would be a 'novelty act' (unspecified) and the appearance of a 'blond, vivacious, curvaceous starlet' (also unnamed). To top it off, a screening of a special movie, *It's a Pleasure* with Sonja Henie and Michael O'Shea. Clearly someone thought there was something to celebrate.

At three o'clock in the afternoon, local time, nearly six hours after it had lobbed Little Boy on Hiroshima, *Enola Gay* landed on Tinian's North Field Runway A. The crew had been in the air for over twelve hours and were wrung out. Hundreds of cheering servicemen lined the taxiway, many of them uncertain of the reason they were cheering although word was getting around swiftly with varying degrees of accuracy.

Tibbets swung the bomber onto the apron and cut its engines. Over two hundred people gathered around the plane: soldiers of all ranks, scientists, technicians, photographers, journalists, movie cameramen, several generals and at least one admiral. This was history. Everyone wanted to be a part of it. *The Great Artiste* and No. 91 held back and landed almost unnoticed on Runway B a short time later.

The hatch in the nosewheel well of *Enola Gay* opened. Colonel Tibbets emerged feet first. Others on board followed in quick succession. A voice called out, 'Attention to orders!' and the flight crew lined up on the tarmac. Guam-based General Carl Spaatz, Commander of US Strategic Air Forces in the Pacific, strode up to Tibbets and pinned a Distinguished Service Cross onto his flight suit, damp with sweat. Having got out of the plane with his pipe in his hand, Tibbets concealed the bowl in his left palm with the stem up his sleeve while the medal was fixed on his chest. The two men saluted each other. All and sundry began shaking hands and slapping backs.

The crew of *Enola Gay* were taken to the debriefing room for a two hour post-mission session. They were given a physical check-up and a medicinal shot of high-grade bourbon to fortify them. Geiger counters were run over their bodies, their clothes and the *Enola Gay*. The health risk of exposure to radiation was not well understood. It was probably the main concern of the check-up, the rest being primarily to disguise this. The level of radioactivity found was not considered harmful.

An informal gathering followed under the curved roof of the Quonset hut. Food, cigarettes, bourbon and lemonade were laid out on a table. The release of tension was palpable, both in those who'd flown to Japan and the support team who'd remained on Tinian. There'd been no certainty how well this mission would go and many reasons to fear it might be a disaster. But it wasn't.

Relief was in the air. 'Dutch' Van Kirk, the navigator, admitted the bomb was dropped seventeen seconds behind schedule. Hazen Payette the debriefing officer, formerly a Detroit lawyer, asked, 'So why were you late?' A wave of laughter spread around the table.

On a receipt for the uranium projectile brought to Tinian a few days before, Deak Parsons scribbled 'I certify that the above material was expended to the city of Hiroshima, Japan at 0915, at 6 August. Signed WS Parsons' and showed it around the room. Wherever they were, Tinian worked to Guam Army time, an hour ahead of Tokyo.

Spaatz gave a speech congratulating the crew, all of whom were later awarded Silver Stars. The session ended in the late afternoon. Some of the crew were completely exhausted by the events of the day. Some went to join the party the mess cooks had spent the day preparing, but they were too late. All the beer, sandwiches and salads were gone. The pie-eating competition was over. A winner of the jitterbug contest had been declared. No-one could recall who the curvaceous starlet was, or if there had even been one. All that was left was *It's a Pleasure*.

◆　◆　◆

By mid-afternoon, the Imperial Japanese Army was starting to piece together a picture of Hiroshima's bombing. It seemed that only three planes had been over Hiroshima when the bomb exploded. It seemed also that two of these planes didn't drop any bombs, pointing to the inescapable conclusion that only one bomb had caused the devastation that was now Hiroshima.

The army had a growing suspicion this might be an atomic weapon. Japanese Naval Intelligence had picked up in late 1944 that the Americans were working on the atomic bomb. More recent information was that the US government was buying up available supplies of pitchblende, the ore from which uranium is extracted. Although Japanese scientists working on their own atomic project did not believe a fission bomb would be produced in less than three to five years, there was a nagging feeling among the army people that the American program had progressed faster.

Editors of the five big Tokyo newspapers were summoned to the office of the Information and Intelligence Agency (IIA), along with a representative from Domei. The IIA was the government agency in charge of press and radio censorship. An army press officer told the group that they were to downplay their reporting of Hiroshima for the time being. 'We believe that the bomb dropped on Hiroshima is different from an ordinary one,' he said. 'However, we don't have adequate information at this stage. We will make some announcement when we have the proper information. Until we issue this report, you are to run any story on Hiroshima in an inconspicuous place in your papers as one no different from reporting an ordinary raid on a city.'

The army wanted to withhold critical details of the raid from the Japanese public for as long as possible. Its belief was that if they could keep the war going until the inevitable hand-to-hand battle with American soldiers on Japanese soil, the cost to America would be sufficient that it would be prepared to accept some conditions to Japan's surrender, rather than the unconditional surrender it was currently demanding.

The editors were not happy with their instructions, but there wasn't much they could do about it. The six o'clock news on the radio that evening gave the people of Japan their first inkling of the tragedy of Hiroshima ... except it didn't sound any worse than any of the other cities that had been firebombed since March. The first news item, as read, said: 'A few B-29s hit Hiroshima city at 8.20 a.m., August 6 and fled after dropping incendiaries and bombs. The extent of the damage is now under survey.' The item would have made no impression on Japanese listeners, except in Hiroshima where they would have wondered if there was another Hiroshima somewhere that had withstood a mild air attack. Certainly no light was shed on the cause of the conflagration in their city.

With evening setting in, Saiji Hasegawa left the Tokyo office of the Domei News Agency. To be on hand to orchestrate any rapidly developing news, Domei's foreign news editor stayed on weeknights at the nearby Dai-ichi Hotel. On his way out, he was told by the traffic department that two or three B-29s had attacked Hiroshima, causing a big explosion.

'Three planes can't do too much damage,' thought Hasegawa, and continued his walk to the hotel.

◆ ◆ ◆

Dick Groves didn't get to sleep for long. He was woken at four fifteen in the morning by a second message from General Farrell on Tinian, pumping up the description after speaking to the men on the bombing mission.

'One observer stated it looked as though the whole town was being torn apart,' the report said in part, 'with columns of dust rising out of valleys approaching the town. Due to dust, visual observation of structural damage could not be made. Parsons and other observers felt this strike was tremendous and awesome even in comparison with Trinity. Its effects may be attributed by the Japanese to a huge meteor.'

Groves made himself a pot of coffee and rewrote the report he'd drafted in the middle of the night. While it was being typed, he shaved and changed into a fresh uniform. A car took him across the river to the Pentagon. At 7 a.m., the time George Marshall habitually arrived at his office, an excited Groves was there to greet him with his report. It repeated Deak Parsons' initial in-flight message with additional information from the mission's return: 'Confirmed neither fighter or flak attack and one tenth cloud cover with large open hole directly over target. High speed camera reports excellent record obtained. Other observing aircraft also anticipates good records although film not yet processed.'

In fact, there was no high-speed film and never would be. The film from Dr Waldman's Fastax camera was ruined in the processing laboratory at Tinian, where a refrigeration unit broke down. Heat stripped the emulsion off the film, leaving it blank. In the end, Harold Agnew's borrowed 16 mm camera provided the only movie footage of the Hiroshima bomb, but it was some weeks before the project leaders found out that his film existed.

The two generals were joined in Marshall's office by General Henry 'Hap' Arnold, chief of Army Air Forces, and George L Harrison, assistant on atomic issues to Secretary of War Henry L Stimson. Hap Arnold had previously expressed the view to his deputy that the atomic bomb wasn't necessary because an invasion of Japan wouldn't be necessary. Firebombing and the naval blockade had left Japan desperately short of oil and with most of its factories destroyed. Its capacity to continue the war was fading, but now atomic destruction was a reality. The immediate concern of the men at the meeting was how best to get a message out to the world, including Japan, of just how lethal the new weapon could be. It was also important for the message to get to the Soviet Union.

A statement purporting to come from President Truman had been drafted a few weeks before. Its author, William Laurence, was a journalist on loan to the Manhattan Project from the *New York Times*. At that time, Laurence was on Tinian hoping to join a coming bombing mission as a high point in the inside story he was writing about the Manhattan Project. His draft statement had been tinkered with by Stimson, Groves and others. It described the attack on Hiroshima as just retribution for the attack on Pearl Harbor. 'The force from which the sun draws its power has been loosed against those who brought war to the Far East,' it said. It also referred to Japan's 'prompt' rejection—a somewhat ambiguous dismissal at a press conference—of an Allied ultimatum of unconditional surrender issued at the Potsdam Conference twelve days before.

At seven forty-five, Marshall used a secure scrambler telephone to call the Secretary of War at 'Highhold', his estate on the northern shore of Long Island. A lean patrician, Henry Stimson was a Wall Street lawyer before serving in the administrations of three Republican presidents. He returned in 1940 as Secretary of War to the Democrat Roosevelt, but didn't find Truman so much to his liking. A complex, quick-tempered personality, Stimson held conflicting and sometimes shifting views, priding himself on his probity where others saw paternalism and snobbery, and taking the moral high ground before having second thoughts ... and even third thoughts. He held himself out as an internationalist, while having a strong belief in American supremacy and the inferiority of non-white people and cultures. By 1945 the 77-year-old's health was failing. The recent Potsdam Conference had left him exhausted from Truman, Stalin and Churchill pressing for ascendancy at the same time as he grappled with the tension between morality and military necessity in development of the atomic bomb.

Stimson had not found it easy to maintain a consistent position on the necessity of the bomb, but the die was now cast. He offered his 'very warm congratulations' and urged that Truman, on board the USS *Augusta* on the way back from Potsdam, be notified as soon as possible. They agreed to release the president's pre-prepared statement at eleven o'clock that morning (midnight, Tokyo time).

Discussion about changes to the president's statement resumed after the call to Stimson. The words 'an important Japanese Army base' were added after 'Hiroshima'. Noticing Groves' elation, Marshall cautioned about sounding too triumphant. The Japanese, he said, must have suffered huge casualties. Groves had been accused of many things but pussyfooting wasn't one of them. 'I'm thinking less about Japanese casualties and more about the Bataan Death March [a forced march of Americans captured in the Philippines notorious for its brutality],' he said. In the corridor later, General Arnold, who'd previously thought the atomic bomb would be unnecessary, slapped General Groves on the back. 'I'm glad you said that,' he said. 'It's just the way I feel.'

◆　◆　◆

By mid-afternoon in Hiroshima, officials were encouraging Mitsubishi workers to make their way back to their homes. With the bridges to the shipyard's delta island apparently destroyed, the three visitors from

Nagasaki had to wait with others for a motor launch to get them to another part of the city. Workers, including the three, pushed onto the already crowded launch. From the moving vessel they could see the city burning. In the half-light, pillars of fire flamed brightly like a stage set for grand opera.

In the crush on board, Yamaguchi was separated from Iwanaga and Sato. The launch reached a landing at the army shipping depot and they disembarked in a smoky twilight. The men were caught in a throng of injured and uninjured and made their own way through the burning city. There seemed to Yamaguchi to be children everywhere, some running, many limping along the side of the road. Their hair was burnt; many were naked, but Yamaguchi heard no crying. He passed a group of primary school girls, their skin burnt so it was peeling off and hanging over their wrists like loose sleeves. Apart from panties, their clothes were burnt off. Many had been blinded and were being led by others.

Yamaguchi crossed a concrete bridge, one of the few still standing. The boarding house where the workers from Nagasaki had been staying was nearby. On the bridge were a number of burnt people. Some were dead. Unable to walk any further, some were lying down. None of them spoke. Yamaguchi's enduring memory of that journey was of the absence of human speech. No shouting; just the sounds of a city burning. The crackle of fire; the sporadic crash of timberwork falling in. Under the bridge, bodies bobbed in the water like sawn logs.

The boarding house was reduced to a rubble of splintered wood and shattered glass at the foot of walls that were still standing. The manager's wife was sitting on a small concrete block where the gate had been. In a dazed state herself, she didn't recognise Yamaguchi with his swollen and blackened face. Her husband was nowhere to be seen. Yamaguchi announced his name and she burst into tears.

Soon after, Sato and Iwanaga arrived at the wreckage of the house. They were subdued, exhausted by the extraordinary events of the day even though they'd escaped injury. No-one had much to say. There was too much that was still beyond explanation or understanding. Sato wandered inside the shell of Mitsubishi's company boarding house.

The ceiling had been forced down, the floor thrust up. Glass was embedded in walls opposite where windows had been. It was no longer habitable.

Sato and Iwanaga went to a nearby bomb shelter. The elderly woman had no intention of moving until her husband returned. Yamaguchi was worried about spontaneous fires breaking out. He wandered back to the beach and spent the night lying under a fishing boat, his bandaged arms and face burning with pain.

◆ ◆ ◆

The crew of *The Great Artiste* had been met by their ground crew and a waiting truck. They had been given their whisky shot and checked by two doctors, one a radiologist. A Geiger counter was passed carefully over each person. Along with the crew of Captain Marquardt's No. 91, they had debriefed in a separate Quonset hut from the *Enola Gay* crew. They had seen from a distance the throng gathered around *Enola Gay*, but hadn't known where its crew had been taken. Sweeney, Marquardt and their crews were not invited to join the gathering with General Spaatz. They were left to make their way across to the party prepared by the mess cooks for the rest of Tinian base. Clearly they were the B team.

At six o'clock, Chuck Sweeney walked to the officers' club after a quick shower. There was a wild celebration under way with a stash of bourbon that had been commandeered from somewhere, probably the medical department. Some of the crew of *Enola Gay* were in the milling crowd. After an hour, Sweeney felt exhaustion creeping up on him. He was planning to head back to his room when he noticed Colonel Tibbets over to the side motioning him across.

Through the racket of the surrounding party, Tibbets told Sweeney of the plan to drop a second bomb in a few days' time if it became necessary. Kokura, an industrial city on Kyushu, was expected to be the primary target. It had a huge armaments factory in its centre, unlike Hiroshima where the military–industrial plants were mostly on the outer fringes. Tibbets told Sweeney he was to command this mission. Not having combat experience, Sweeney was both surprised and gratified. He'd hoped to fly the instrument plane again, but knew his was only one of fifteen crews that had been trained for these missions.

'You'll use the same tactics,' Tibbets said. Sweeney thought: three unescorted B-29s at 10,000 metres preceded by a single weather plane might now be a formation the Japanese would recognise. However, Tibbets had recruited him into the delivery arm of the Manhattan Project and he regarded the colonel with both gratitude and admiration. Sweeney said nothing.

Two armoured casings in large wooden crates, the halves of a giant metallic egg, arrived under cover of darkness at Tinian Air Base that evening. They were now in the windowless bomb-assembly building, securely sequestered behind double fencing. Sentries in machine-gun posts added to their security. At the back of another building, armed guards watched over a small magnesium suitcase lying on a bench, a thermometer stuck in its side. The case's metal surface was warm to touch. Inside were two hemispheres of plutonium, separated by a thin sheet of gold foil. The hemispheres, together weighing 6.2 kilograms, were to be joined to form a sphere the size of an orange and placed in the centre of the assembled weapon.

The date and target were set: 11 August, in five days' time; and Kokura, the armaments manufacturing city.

Chapter 3

Nagasaki, Monday 6 August 1945

Japan's national exercises blared out from the upstairs balcony of the house where the Takigawas lived. Locals, mostly women and older men, gathered on the vacant lot next door as they did each morning to follow ritual callisthenics instructions coming from the Takigawas' smart wooden radio. A patriotic tune on piano provided timing while a Japanese military man called the moves in a high voice comically like a British sergeant-major. '*Ryo-hiji-o hidari-ni furu!* [Swing elbows left!] *Ryo-hiji-o migi-ni furu!* [Swing elbows right!] *Ryo-hiji-o hidari-ni furu! Ryo-hiji-o migi-ni furu!*' Healthy bodies and healthy minds, all for a stronger Japan.

Mrs Takigawa had taken her place at the front of this group from the neighbourhood of Komaba-cho, between the river and the railway line halfway up Urakami valley. Her two little girls were up front with her. So was Mrs Takigawa's eldest daughter, Sadako, already widowed by the war at twenty-two and left with a baby boy.

'*Migiude-o atama-no ue-ni age. Karada-o hidari-ni mageru!* [Right arm over head. Bend left!] *Hidariude-o atama-no ue-ni age. Karada-o migi-ni mageru!* [Left arm over head. Bend right!]' Bending in alternate directions in the warming sun, the women in their loose-fitting trousers, the

27

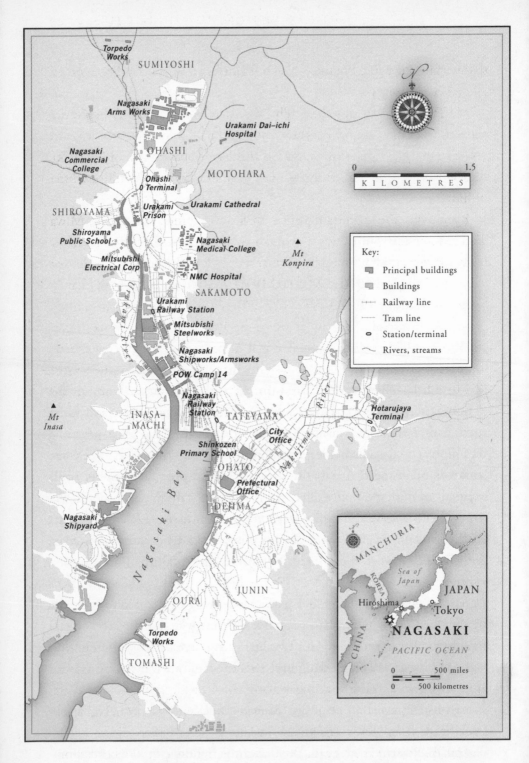

Nagasaki city, prior to the atomic bombing

traditional *monpe*, and the men in ad hoc uniforms of one kind or another, all moved in unison.

Mr Takigawa was not there. The absentee husband and father was a *gunzoku*, a civilian employee of the military, and was rarely given leave to come home. For some time stationed at the naval base north of Nagasaki, he'd worked a little closer for the last year, but his family still saw little of him.

Even with the uncertain future that now framed their lives, Miwa Takigawa at forty-nine was a woman to be reckoned with. Driven by plans for her children, she had earmarked each to be either a teacher or a doctor. They had reached that goal, were well on the way or had barely begun the journey. Her eldest son had qualified as a teacher but was already gone, a *kamikaze* pilot lost in action in the Philippines. Sadako had never worked, but had married a teacher as if to make up for that. Seventeen-year-old Masuichi passed the university entrance exam in fourth year of middle school, a year earlier than most. In a society that revolved around the military, he planned to be an army doctor. Much of his time not spent at Nagasaki Medical College was occupied with the local squadron.

The two younger girls attended the primary school, across the river, but were on school holidays. Ryoko was intended by her mother for a career as a teacher, whether the eight-year-old knew it and shared the ambition or not. Mrs Takigawa was a hard taskmaster regarding her children's education. She made them study hard and train hard. These days, she would be called *kyoiku mama*, an education mother.

Two years older than Ryoko, Sakue fitted in well with her mother's ambition for her. She shared it. Sakue wanted to be a doctor like her brother, Masuichi, whom she idolised. The ten-year-old already felt the calling from hearing about people injured in air raids. Although Nagasaki had so far been let off fairly lightly, she knew about the raids on other cities from adults' conversations. Sakue was a serious and curious child, eavesdropping on adult chatter as often as she could. She believed it was her duty to help these poor people in Japan's other cities.

Mrs Takigawa was larger than life, untiring in her pursuit of her responsibilities and beyond. Everything she did was with the grand gestures of the parish philanthropist. A country girl by upbringing, she had been strikingly fashionable before the war, often wearing high-heeled shoes and a wide-brimmed hat stylishly tilted. At the ceremony when Sakue entered primary school, her mother had worn Western clothes, unusual in the Nagasaki suburbs at that time. The little girl's new classmates had teased that her mother was a copycat of the empress. But Miwa Takigawa had been to Manchuria, an exotic overseas location. When the war started and she still dressed in style, she was accused of copying Americans. Sakue longed for her mother to discard the hat and come to school dressed in something unremarkable, but she never did.

Possibly because of her village origins, Mrs Takigawa took an interest in what everyone was doing, sometimes poking an unwelcome nose into their business. A few in the district regarded her as a busybody and were cautious of her. On the other hand, she was generous to a fault, cultivating potatoes and the Japanese radish daikon in a plot near the river and sharing them with the neighbourhood. At home, she did all the cooking and was a competent dressmaker, making clothes for other families as well as her own. When the young girls' clothes became moth-eaten, she mended them with cotton sewn in star shapes. Replacing clothing was not easy in wartime Japan and, in any case, little girls don't object to stars on their clothes.

Outgoing and assertive, it was unsurprising Miwa Takigawa became head of Komaba-cho's women's association. Providing the national exercises program to those around was part of her duty to her neighbours and to the nation. She believed implacably that Japan's fortunes would turn in its war with the Western colonial powers, that *kamikaze*, the divine wind, would blow and Japan would win. The emperor had said so. It was everyone's duty to keep in good health for this coming victory. '*Te-o koshi-ni. Karada-o ushiro-ni mageru!* [Hands on hips. Bend back!] *Te-o mae-ni nobashi. Zenkutsu!* [Hands stretched out in front. Bend forward!]'

◆ ◆ ◆

Nagasaki sits at the end of a long, deep bay. The Urakami and Nakajima rivers form two valleys in which the city lies and they are separated by a mountain spur. Except for these valleys and the area where they met, most of the city is hilly. At this time, a network of canals ran a few hundred metres inland from the mouths of tidewater streams. Small barges carried goods up these waterways. The main roads, railways and tramlines ran up the two valleys and round the edge of Nagasaki Bay. Elsewhere the roads were narrow and winding, zig-zagging up the steeper hills. They weren't built for motor vehicles and were used instead for carts pulled by animals or humans.

Quays and warehouses spread along the bay's edge near downtown Nagasaki. The streets behind were filled with shops and shoppers. Ferries carried people across the bay from the city to the industrial plants on the bay's western shore dominated by the cranes and gantries of its shipyards.

Another industrial area was the Urakami valley, the small villages of which had been swallowed by the expanding city. By the 1940s, Urakami was the progressive quarter of Nagasaki with broad streets and athletic fields. Development had also spread up the Nakajima valley where government and commerce were concentrated. The two valleys were the hub of the city's industrial and administrative power.

The Urakami valley was Nagasaki's land connection to the rest of Japan. The long road running through it had a name no more colourful than Route 206. A railway line, bringing people and goods from elsewhere on the island of Kyushu, ran alongside it to Nagasaki's main station.

Nagasaki had grown since it was founded by the Portuguese in the sixteenth century and the Dutch later established a port there. As Japan moved onto a war footing, the port prospered. Much of the personnel and supplies for fighting in central and south China moved through it. But Nagasaki was unable to maintain its predominance. Distant from its sources of supplies and cut off on its own peninsula by mountainous terrain, it was declining as a port by 1945. Other centres progressed at Nagasaki's expense. It had ceased as a coaling port when facilities were built nearer to the coal mines.

Nagasaki had grown into virtually a one-company town, not that unusual in a country where powerful business conglomerates (*zaibatsu*) were predominant. Mitsubishi was one. Set up as part of the shipyards,

Mitsubishi Electrical Equipment Works had operated separately since 1923, producing heavy electrical equipment. The Mitsubishi Arms Factory was established in 1917 in the lower Urakami valley. Another weapons plant was built during the war at the other end of the valley. The Mitsubishi Steel Works, near the arms factory, produced steel plate for shipbuilding. As the war progressed, small industries and private shops struggled and fell by the wayside. Mitsubishi took up the slack, so that by 1945 over 90 per cent of Nagasaki industry was owned by Mitsubishi. Nagasaki's Mayor Okada and Wakamatsu Nagano, Governor of Nagasaki Prefecture, were both Mitsubishi men.

◆ ◆ ◆

After a short walk from the home he shared with his wife and eleven-year-old daughter, Torahachi Tagawa arrived at the newer Mitsubishi weapons factory. It was seven o'clock on 6 August 1945, a date that would become emblematic for Japan, although Tagawa had no way of knowing that on this clear summer morning. By then forty, he had been with the arms company since he was sixteen, working his way up to foreman. He began his working week by leading employee warm-up exercises, the customary start each morning at the factory. At Tagawa's command, workers turned to the north-east and bowed deeply in the direction of the Imperial Palace, praying for the emperor's divine guidance in the war. The foreman saluted the works director and presented a summary of the day's rollcall given him by work unit heads when he arrived. There were more absentees than usual.

A process was in place for dealing with absentees. Mitsubishi's security section would call at the employee's house to find out if there was an acceptable reason for their absence. Sickness required a doctor's certificate. If they had no valid reason for being away, workers would be brought forcibly to the factory. For several months now, the company had resorted to whipping habitual absentees. Sometimes Tagawa himself administered the stick. It was something he neither disliked nor enjoyed, just an onerous responsibility that came with the job of foreman as the factory struggled to maintain its output.

Tagawa supervised 510 workers at the factory, producing 91-type torpedoes. In 1941, when production started, the output was 300 torpedoes a month. For over a year now, that productivity had been difficult to maintain. Their skilled workers had been conscripted. Drafted unskilled workers and students from the Patriotic Corps were filling the gap left by their departure, but they didn't have the experience or skill necessary to keep up output.

Up in an office overlooking the yard in which the exercises took place, the deputy director of the Ohashi factory faced an accumulation of these wartime problems. With his slick, combed-back hair, round face, thick horn-rimmed glasses and toothy grin, fifty-year-old Yoshiro Fukuda looked like a Japanese bureaucrat who wasn't fazed by anything. In actuality, the whole burden of keeping the plant operational was getting him down. Lack of fuel and lack of transportation plagued the factory's operations. The foreman of the metal forging department had told him the works couldn't be kept on full production. Their coal supply was exhausted. The head of supply assured him a shipment would arrive on Wednesday afternoon, two days away. It remained to be seen whether Shibata's assurance would amount to anything. Yoshiro Fukuda had heard it all before and it was playing havoc with his health. Mounting anger and frustration had given him a stomach ulcer.

The factory whistle sounded, announcing the start of the shift. Having completed the morning drill, foreman Tagawa went to his office to prepare paperwork for upcoming projects, most notably a new top-secret rocket engine. Senior manager Fukuda sat in his office with the recurring pain of his ulcer for company, worrying about who was going to let him down next. He was pretty sure it would be the coal supplier.

◆ ◆ ◆

Father Tamaya had been told that the senior priest wanted to have a word with him. Wandering around the grounds of Urakami Cathedral in the early morning sun, he looked for Father Nishida without success. As the day got hotter, he decided to try the cool interior of the cathedral instead.

Fusakichi Tamaya had adopted the saint's name Simon. A visiting priest at the cathedral, he was there for six weeks from his church on Kuroshima, a small island in a bay north of Nagasaki. Urakami Cathedral had become steadily more understaffed as its priests were called into the army. The 28-year-old Tamaya had been turned down for military service because of a heart valve condition. He was able to fill the more pressing gaps in the archdiocese without the risk of being taken away to the war. However, the looming defence of the homeland against the anticipated American invasion might change even that. Kyushu was expected to be the first point of attack

Although reluctant to leave his flock on Kuroshima, Father Simon wasn't averse to a temporary transfer to Nagasaki. It happened to be his home town. Born into a large family, one of ten children, he'd gone to a primary school in the Urakami valley, later attending Nagasaki Theological College and a Tokyo seminary. Assigned to the church in Kuroshima three years before, his reputation as a priest with an affinity with children might ring alarm bells these days. Then, it was seen as a feather in his pastoral cap.

Nagasaki is the Roman Catholic capital of Japan, with some 70 per cent of the country's Catholics living there at that time. It has had a chequered history since its founding.

The missionary St Francis Xavier converted some of the feudal lords to the *kirishitan* religion in his two years there. The Jesuit intriguing that followed attracted the unwelcome attention of the shogun Hideyoshi, who ordered the crucifixion of twenty-six Catholics in Nagasaki, six of them Europeans. In the brutal campaign of persecution that followed, thousands of Christian converts across Kyushu and other parts of Japan were killed, tortured or forced to renounce their religion. Catholics went underground as *kakure kirishitan* (hidden Christians), although the ruling regime continued to allow limited access to Nagasaki for European traders, particularly the English and Dutch, who had no interest in religious conversion.

Following the Meiji Restoration in 1868, restoring imperial rule as Japan opened to the West, Roman Catholicism resurfaced and flourished. A Romanesque cathedral—formally named St Mary's Cathedral, but known by all as Urakami Cathedral—was constructed on the patch of land where, during the years of persecution, interrogated villagers had been forced to tread on an icon of the Virgin Mary. The Catholics of cosmopolitan Nagasaki have had to fight hard for their religion, maintaining it through a long struggle. It is cemented deeply in their soul.

Where the hilly ridge of Mount Konpira starts to climb out of the Urakami valley, the cathedral sat on a prominent rise overlooking the houses of the faithful. Terraced gardens were stepped up the slope behind and around. Closely packed wooden cottages gave way to farmhouses and patches of uncleared forest between the cathedral and the Franciscan hospital a little further up the valley.

At this time of the year, despite the depredations of war, the Catholic community was preparing for one of the Holy Days of Obligation. The feast day for the Assumption of Mary, the celebration of the Virgin Mary's rise to heaven at the end of her earthly life, was coming up on 15 August. It was preceded by fourteen days of fasting and increased attendance at confession, a busy time for the two clergy at Urakami Cathedral.

Father Tamaya was scheduled to leave this peaceful setting and return to Kuroshima the following day, the Tuesday. He expected to pack his meagre belongings into his sole bag that evening after seeing his family for the last time for a while. In the meantime, the visiting priest sought out Father Nishida and found him in the back of the cathedral building.

Nishida had a favour to ask. Would it be possible for Tamaya to hold off his return to Kuroshima till later in the week, preferably Friday? The young priest was willing to agree. Although he felt the need to get back to his own parishioners, he recognised the demands on the main church in such difficult times. He would leave instead on Friday, 10 August.

◆ ◆ ◆

Two girls made their way down the steep stone-paved lanes of Junin and joined the long queue of workers at the Senba-cho tram stop. Mitsue wore a rayon blouse and the serge *monpe* she had made from a kimono her grandmother gave her. An armband proudly proclaimed her as part of the Prefectural Girls' High School Patriotic Volunteer Corps. Mitsue Takeno lived with the widowed Mrs Hirai and her sixteen-year-old daughter, Chifusa, whom everyone called Chi-chan. The two girls were in fourth year at Nagasaki Girls' High School but, like all teenage school-girls at this stage of the war, they no longer went to school. Mitsue had been drafted to work at the Nagasaki arms factory's Mori-machi plant. Chi-chan was working at the foundry next door.

Mitsue came from a village on the islands off the coast north of Nagasaki. Her father was supervisor of netting operations at a fishing and seafood processing business there. Initially she had lived with an aunt in Nagasaki, but after the aunt fell ill Mitsue boarded with her school friend, Chi-chan, who lived closer to their school.

The small wooden-walled tram to Urakami was packed. With the two schoolgirls on board, it rocked its way up the valley. Mitsui got off the tram first. On one side of the stop stood long saw-toothed rows of factory buildings; on the other, wall-to-wall small houses. The skinny girl—so thin that people called her *senko* (incense stick)—walked with other shuffling workers down the road to her factory, past air-raid shelters dug into the rock wall. The obligatory air-raid hood and dark cotton pouch holding a first-aid kit were slung diagonally over her shoulders and chest so their straps crossed to form an 'X'. It was the style of the times as the Japanese people withstood the aerial assault on their homeland.

In a first-floor workshop of the weapons factory, Mitsue filed tiny parts of torpedoes, surrounded by clanging industrial din and the pungent smell of machine oil. Heavy cranes moved back and forth overhead; a grinder spewed out sparks. A machine nearby hammered out metal pieces. In the middle of the workshop, Mitsue was one of five girls sitting at a long work table filing nuts and bolts to remove imperfections from the casting process. Their benchtop was dark with fine lead dust. A large crane moved up and down through a square hole in the floor alongside, carrying heavy loads between floors. A wire safety fence had been erected around the opening. Below, men could be glimpsed working on a large cylindrical object. The girls understood their factory produced torpedoes and submarines, but this was the nearest they got to seeing either.

Four of the five girls at the table were from Mitsue's school. One was her best friend, Setsuko, who lived with her family near the arms factory. The fifth girl at the table was from a different high school. A loner, she worked in silence. The four from Nagasaki Girls' High seldom spoke to her.

The schoolgirls often sang a random selection of popular songs over the relentless workshop clatter. They always included the song of the Students' Corps.

Young cherry trees we are
With flowers still in bud,
To their full height yet to grow,
But ready are we to sacrifice our young lives
For the need of our country.
To the holy cause is the Students' Corps dedicated.
Our hearts are afire with patriotism.

In the middle of the industrial din it didn't matter how good or bad their singing was. No-one could hear them anyway.

◆　◆　◆

At nine that morning, Tsuneo Tomita started work as he had for the last three weeks, digging an air-raid shelter behind the Pharmacy Department. The 21-year-old was a third-year pharmacy student at Nagasaki Medical College. At the beginning of July, some of the third-year lectures were called off so the manpower could be used to build shelters. Now that all their classes had been abandoned, these students were expected to continue their studies at night as best they could. First- and second-year students were working in factories or in the city.

The students dug with hoes and picks as they worked their way deeper into the shelter they were constructing. The solidly built Professor Seiki led the digging while students in shorts carried the earth away. The once immaculate college grounds had drifted into disrepair. Gardens had been taken over by weeds; lawns were dug up to grow sweet potatoes.

Most of the students lived outside the city and had been coming into Nagasaki each day, but not Tsuneo. He lived with his family nearby, but spent much of his time hanging around with friends anyway. Some of the class had left to join the military. Some of those remaining were helping build the new dugout; the rest were busy setting up vegetable gardens in the college grounds.

On 1 August, Nagasaki was raided by aircraft from an American carrier, a relatively mild attack compared with the blanket incendiary bombing some of the other Japanese cities had endured. When the siren had sounded, Tomita had gone up on the hillside with a friend. They watched in chilled fascination as seven low–flying planes flew over the ridge and dropped bombs near the hospital and the medical school. Three students were killed in the attack and more than ten seriously injured. After this raid, the students were on duty at the college day and night, sleeping now on raised platforms in the classrooms.

Less than a kilometre away, under the command of Kyobei Minami, a group of Nagasaki men worked for Japan's war effort with far less commitment than Tsuneo Tomita and his fellow students. Forty-year-old Minami was Warden of Urakami Prison. He was also a family man, living in the prison residence with his wife and two children. While the commitment of the students to the war effort was sometimes muted, that of Minami's charges was non-existent to all intents and purposes.

Each day at early morning rollcall, 200 of the prisoners under his supervision were given the same choice: they could volunteer to work for the Fatherland Defence Corps on whatever task the corps assigned to them that day, or they could stay inside the prison grounds and make uniforms.

A third of the prisoners chose to stay in the prison for the day and work there, alongside twenty-five prisoners who had no choice because they had life sentences. Some of the smarter ones had figured out that a bombing raid was more likely to target the shipyards, where the prisoners were usually sent, than the prison. Self-preservation was behind their decision, although the previous week's raid raised questions about its reliability. If the hospital, why not the prison?

The two-thirds who volunteered to work for the Fatherland Defence Corps did so mostly for a change of scenery, to ease the cabin fever. Setting out at seven thirty in their green work clothes and peaked caps, under the watchful eye of the warden and twelve guards, they marched in ranks for 2 kilometres down Route 206. At the Mitsubishi foundry, their task was to make screws for coastal defence craft and torpedo boats being assembled at Mitsubishi's shipyards. In the foundry offices, Warden Minami would while away the day catching up on paperwork he brought with him.

◆   ◆   ◆

At the end of the prisoners' daily march was another labour group, contributing to the war effort with even less enthusiasm than Urakami Prison's inmates. One hundred and ninety-four Allied prisoners of war (POWs) were held in Fukuoka Camp 14, sandwiched between Mitsubishi's iron foundry and the railway line. A hundred and fifty of them were Dutch; twenty-four were Australian.

The Dutch had been brought from Java to Nagasaki in 1943 to work in the shipyards around the bay. Australian and British prisoners had arrived a year later, transferred from the outskirts of Batavia (now Jakarta) to bolster the dwindling Japanese labour force. Conscription had emptied Japan's factories, and student replacements were insufficient and not very productive.

That the newer arrivals were there at all was a small miracle. With a cargo of sugar, pumpkins and POWs, the *Tamahoko Maru* had arrived off the coast of Kyushu in the middle of the night to be torpedoed amidships by an American submarine. On board were 772 prisoners of war, including the Tasmanians Peter McGrath-Kerr and Allan Chick. Eight hundred repatriating Japanese were in the aft section.

McGrath-Kerr was down in the forward hold, preparing to come on deck, when the merchantman was struck. Water poured through the opened hatchway, coming up from below at the same time. The iron ladder was jammed with men desperately trying to get out. McGrath-Kerr didn't bother to try to push his way through them. Instead, he floated up to the ceiling as the hold filled with water. Lights in the hold went out, adding to the confusion. The Australian pulled his body along the roof beams until he hit the hatch's rim. Hauling himself around the ledge, he was able to float up through the hatch.

The ship sank in less than two minutes at a steep angle. Only those near the hatch opening had any chance of getting away. It was already under water and sinking fast when McGrath-Kerr escaped through the opening. Unable to swim, he was propelled rapidly upwards anyway, losing his trousers in the rush. All he could recall was the thought, 'It's taking a long time to drown.'

He struck his head against a floating timber hatch cover and crawled on top. In the moonless night, the chorus of people's panicked shouting in Japanese as well as English was unnerving. Someone floating by threw McGrath-Kerr a pair of Japanese trousers. His timber raft was disintegrating. The Australian was pulled across to an overturned lifeboat by Jack Johnson, another Australian POW. Six others joined them, clinging to it until morning.

Chick, also down in the forward hold when the *Tamahoko Maru* was struck, had no memory of how he got out. He remembered being in water and expecting to drown. Having 'given up the ghost', he came to in the sea, clinging to a wooden float with an English POW, a Japanese guard and one other.

A destroyer, looking for the American submarine during the night, had picked up a few survivors. Everyone else had to wait until dawn to be picked up by a whale chaser. The Japanese guard was rescued from Allan Chick's float early in the morning, but the rest had to wait for another boat which stood 20 metres off the float. Chick, a Tasmanian fisherman before the war, was able to swim across to it.

The captain of the destroyer made survivors on his ship jump into the water and swim to the rescue boat. An Australian POW who couldn't swim drowned in that transfer. Of the *Tamahoko Maru*'s 772 prisoners, 213 were rescued; 85 Dutch, 72 Australians, 42 British and 14 Americans. Once on board, Japanese and POWs were moved to opposite ends of the whaler. It was past midday by the time Peter McGrath-Kerr, one of the last to be plucked to safety, was retrieved from his upended lifeboat in the ocean.

The rescued POWs were left on a wharf. There was no thought of escape. A bedraggled European was unlikely to go unnoticed stealing through a Japanese city. They waited several hours until trucks came and took them to an open area alongside a railway line. Marched into an enclosure, they were given clothing, made to sign forms—including an undertaking not to escape—and fingerprinted.

Next door had been a cotton spinning mill with brick walls on all sides, a suitable site for a prison camp. Every alternate saw-tooth roof had been taken out to make a series of corridors with dormitory compart-ments built of pine between them. Roofs of corrugated asbestos sheeting were supported by a steel girder framework. The former cotton factory was now Fukuoka Camp 14, but it became overcrowded with the ad-ditional inmates. Their first job was to construct extra barracks buildings to accommodate the increased numbers.

The newcomers were not allowed to mix with the Dutch POWs already there, but as they were mostly Javanese who didn't speak English this didn't matter much. There was little friction between the POW groups, although the white Dutch expatriates, used to servants, could be high-handed.

Shipbuilding work had dropped off with a materials shortage caused by the Allied naval blockade. The Australians were made to work instead in the foundry next door to the camp. A carbon arc furnace there poured metal castings for a range of metal shipping parts, going up in size to propellers and cylinder-blocks for marine diesel engines. Pneumatic hammers knocked out the moulded metal pieces. Allan Chick was given a mallet to break off the spurs left behind on the castings. McGrath-Kerr was mostly occupied cleaning out the sand-filled cores in preparation for the next casting.

There was a temptation for minor sabotage of the Japanese war effort by finding weaknesses in the casting and making them worse. Some grabbed the opportunity. Others had the more arduous job of loading a steel trolley with scrap metal from a heap and hauling it to the furnace to shovel it in. Among the metal were pieces marked 'NSWGR' (New South Wales Government Railways).

Civilians took charge of the POW work gangs after they were marched the 300 metres from camp to foundry. Japanese workers there were older men, beyond conscription age. Two women, one with a baby in a sling on her back, mixed cement with shovels. Women were also unloading coal from barges, in baskets hanging each end of a pole. The surrounding noise was the same industrial cacophony as schoolboys and girls endured elsewhere in the foundry and in the machine shop next door. The prisoner workers caught sight of these young 'volunteers' from time to time with their patriotic armbands, their paper sunshades and their breeches with black cashmere socks and suspenders on the outside. Among these distant passing workers was Mitsue Takeno's friend Chi-chan.

By mid-1945, foundry work was petering out. The Japanese started to transfer prisoners to northern Kyushu to work in the coal mine at Fukuoka Camp 5-B. McGrath-Kerr had put his hand up when asked who could repair motor vehicles. Working on old motor tricycles, he was among the 200 who remained in Nagasaki. Chick continued working in the foundry with its considerably reduced workload. With his small build, he might have been thought more suited to foundry work than coal mining.

There had been small bombing raids on Nagasaki in April and July. In the first, a single B-29 had dropped a bomb on a large harbour ferry while passengers were boarding, killing 129. Time-bombs dropped along the wharf area had paralysed activity there for four days as the army tried to defuse them. On 20 July, a small formation of A-26s had targeted the dock area, burning a warehouse and damaging a workers' dormitory. The morning raid of 1 August involved twenty-four B-24s. McGrath-Kerr watched as the planes flew overhead, saw their bomb-bay doors opening and their bombs dropping out. He could see if any were coming their way. Afterwards, he counted twenty-three bomb craters around the camp. A Dutch POW had been killed in the raid when the entrance to one of the shelters collapsed. It was only because most of the barracks were empty by that stage that more in the camp weren't killed.

After that, foundry work was limited. Because there'd been complaints about the lack of shelter from the aerial attack, prisoners were now building an air-raid shelter in the side of the hill nearby. Others were repairing a bridge over Mifune Canal with bamboo and ropes. The bridge allowed access to the new dugout, but it had been damaged in the raid five days before.

Air-raid warnings had become a daily occurrence. When the sirens screamed, prisoners were herded into a shelter with Japanese workers and they sometimes got talking. They didn't have much language in common, but a few on each side had a smattering of the other's words. Hand gestures did the rest. The workers said that if Japan was invaded the people would fight to the bitter end. Civilians were being taught to make petrol bombs and to fight with sharpened poles.

This wasn't good news for the Allied prisoners. They had heard rumours that the war was coming to an end and had noticed the increased presence of American aircraft in the sky. They were apprehensive about surviving an invasion of Japan, knowing the Japanese would fight to the finish. It wasn't clear what would be done with the POWs during this last-ditch stand. Their state of mind was a confused mix of faint hope, resignation and stubborn defiance.

◆ ◆ ◆

The Noguchi sisters hid behind the Ohashi terminal's toilet block in their tram conductors' uniforms, crying privately. They were the two eldest of eight children of a dirt-poor farming family from southern Kyushu. Tatsu and Haruko had been scooped up by the tram company's agents, who trawled rural areas recruiting labour to replace workers lost to the military and Mitsubishi's better-paying factories. As the oldest child, it was thirteen-year-old Tatsu's responsibility to supplement the family's meagre income eked out from a traditional rural subsistence life. Twelve-year-old Haruko had come with her, but the job was proving hard physically and emotionally.

Koichi Wada, a driver with the Nagasaki Electric Streetcar Company, observed the sobbing girls from a distance. He had noticed the Noguchis, small even for their ages, moving in their uniforms through the crowded trams, dwarfed by the passengers. Most of the time, they were lost in the crowd. Koichi was fascinated by these young and pretty uniformed waifs, but he had never spoken to them. That was not considered a proper thing for an eighteen-year-old student to do.

The job of conductor was not easy. The streetcars, made of timber and small by today's standards, had a capacity of forty passengers. Factory workers and mobilised students had priority. Since there were no buses in Nagasaki, the trams were packed much of the time. People who didn't have priority would jump on regardless and it was the conductor's responsibility to deal with them, but the principal job was to sell tickets, get the money, and punch the tickets in the crowded public vehicles. Pulling a rope hanging from its upper end, they had to re-position the tight-sprung pole from one overhead wire to another when the tram tracks diverged or converged.

The Noguchi girls lived in the company's dormitory for female workers, a five-minute walk across the river from Ohashi. Apart from the physical hardship of the job, they were often bullied by the senior female conductors. The older sister, Tatsu, was just hanging in there. She had little option if her family was to be fed. But it had already become too much for the younger Haruko. Sometimes she went out with her sister and the pair of them functioned as a single conductor; other times she hung around Ohashi terminal.

A mobilised student from Nagasaki Commercial College, Koichi Wada had started as a conductor, but was now working as a driver. It was hard physical work with its hand-operated brake, turning a heavy metal wheel to stop the tram. Like the Noguchis, he was the breadwinner for his family in Maruyama on the south side of the city. Koichi lived with his grandparents and his younger sister, Chiyoko, aged fifteen. Their mother had died in childbirth in 1937, his bank-clerk father from tuberculosis later that same year. Since then, Koichi and Chiyoko had lived with their father's parents who had once run a profitable business supplying fruit to restaurants, but now in their late sixties they were too old to work, even in the desperate labour market of war-torn Japan.

Tram employees worked nine days in a row, one a double shift, and then had a day off. But the company paid its mobilised student workers, unlike Mitsubishi's factories. All Mitsubishi gave its student workers was a small bread roll at the end of the day. On the other hand, it paid its adult labour better than the tram company, so many tram workers moved to the factories.

The first shift had to arrive at work before the cars started running at 5.30 a.m. That morning, Koichi was at Hotarujaya tram terminal in time to eat a quick breakfast he'd brought with him. He had pressed his *inkan* on the work sheet, showed his name plate and joined the line of drivers. After getting a brake handle and his streetcar number for the day, he walked across to the depot and climbed into the driver's seat. The day was spent, until mid-afternoon when his shift ended, plying the route up the Urakami valley to Ohashi, round the circuit in the business district and up the Nakajima valley to Hotarujaya.

Tram work gave the student a mobility that appealed to his youthful restlessness and his sense of the times. It was in the course of pausing before the return journey from Ohashi that Koichi had come across the distressed Noguchi sisters. They were still behind the toilet block when it was time to start his scheduled run back down the valley.

◆　◆　◆

Sakue and Ryoko had dressed up their tricycle with a white head bandanna someone had 'borrowed' from home. Inscribed with the word '*kamikaze*', the divine wind which would turn around Japan's fortunes in war, it turned the toy into a tank for the purposes of the afternoon's play. Driving it up and down the street in front of the Takigawa house, the children met the imaginary invading enemy with the same ferocity and effectiveness that the sharpened bamboo sticks of their neighbourhood home defence exercises would surely mete out to the Americans when they came.

The children's game was a means of denying the intuition of some, like ten-year-old Sakue. Reading between the lines of the adult conversations she overheard, she had an inkling that Japan was losing the war, but knew that no-one was allowed to say so. Everyone expected an American force to land on Kyushu sometime in the not-too-distant future. The official line was that this would be a fatal miscalculation. The invaders would be driven back by the patriotic fighting spirit of the Japanese people and of the military charged with their protection.

The two girls took turns riding the tricycle, along with their friends. Sakue and Ryoko had only the one three-wheeler to share between them, but no-one else from the neighbourhood had one at all. Everyone took their turn on it to ensure the enemy was routed.

They used to play hide-and-seek and *hanaichi-momme* (a competition of rock-paper-scissors), but by mid-1945 these games had been put aside. Now, air-raid drills and sheltering when the sirens rang out occupied their day. There was little time and never enough children around to play the games they had enjoyed so much in less threatened times.

The girls' nephew, Tamashii, had already made his sacrifice for Japan's cause in the war, although he didn't yet know it. The one-year-old's name means 'patriotic spirit', a product of the vogue of the time for parents to give their children victory-related names. A popular slogan proclaimed: 'If we have *nihon tamashii* [patriotic Japanese spirit] we will win the war.' The son of Maseru and Miwa Takigawa's eldest daughter, Tamashii had never known his father, killed in action and the ashes never brought home. The widowed Sadako had moved back with her parents, bringing with her a single memento of her husband and Tamashii's father: a graduation speech rendered by a calligrapher on parchment. It had been framed and placed on the Takigawa family's Buddhist altar.

Tamashii was often left in the care of the young girls during the day, especially since they had been virtually living in the air-raid shelter since the 1 August attack. The shelter was damp and full of mosquitoes, but air-raid warnings had become so frequent that they had to spend a lot of time there just the same. Young children were sent immediately to the shelters while adults stood by with fire-fighting and emergency rescue equipment. On this Monday, however, Sadako had taken Tamashii with her to work with her mother on the vegetable garden Miwa Takigawa had established beside Urakami River.

Sakue and Ryoko came inside in the late afternoon. Sadako was already mending some of the family's older clothes. Elsewhere in the house, Mrs Takigawa was chairing a meeting of the local women's association, all part of the busy schedule of a community leader. Sakue's evening chores were to take vegetables to various neighbours and polish the rice. Because of the husks, brown rice doesn't expand on boiling like white rice does. Sakue and Ryoko put the family's ration in an empty *sake* bottle and pounded the husks off with a bamboo stick, a long and tedious job.

◆　◆　◆

Among the pots and pans and other utensils in the spacious basement kitchen of Urakami Dai-ichi (First) Hospital, Sugako Murai prepared an evening meal for patients, monks and medical staff. That night it was a stew of brown rice and vegetables grown in the hospital grounds— pumpkin, eggplant, potatoes and sweet potato. The evening meal was always served to patients at 4 p.m. and to others when they could take a break from their duties. As a result of food shortages, the hospital was increasingly relying on its own produce and was able now to provide only two meals a day, the other at eleven in the morning. It was always rice and vegetables, but they were good-sized serves.

Lately the hospital's cook had been thinking she'd like to return to nursing. She liked the company and camaraderie of the kitchen—Franciscan Brother Iwanaga coming in to assist when he could get away from the myriad tasks he did around the hospital, and five or six volunteers from the neighbourhood coming regularly to help out clearing tables, collecting bowls from bed-bound patients and washing up in the large kitchen sink—but Sugako was getting restless. She'd reminded the head nurse recently that she'd been trained as a nurse.

Sitting on Motohara Hill, the hospital overlooked Urakami valley from its eastern slopes. Before the war, it had been a Franciscan monastery and theological college. Most of the teacher priests were Canadian and had been interned when the war started. As with nearby Urakami Cathedral, many of the younger priests had been conscripted.

The military had shown an interest in taking over this solid brick building of three storeys, and had inspected it several times. With a number of tuberculosis patients in the region, the monks had converted the college to a sanitarium. It was a smart move. The military lost enthusiasm for appropriating a building that housed a contagious disease.

About seventy tuberculosis patients were accommodated on the upper floors of the hospital, which doubled during the day as a clinic for local midwives. Consulting rooms for out-patients were on the ground floor. Specialised medicine was no longer available at that stage of the war. The best the Franciscans could offer was two reliable meals a day of vegetables and rice.

◆ ◆ ◆

As Dr Nagai walked home from Nagasaki's medical college, where he was head of radiology, he heard the bells of Urakami Cathedral ring out the Angelus as they did every evening at six o'clock. It was a welcome sound after the persistent air-raid alarms that now filled their lives. A few field workers nearby went down on their knees in distant and silent prayer.

A convert to Catholicism, these simple acts of piety filled Takashi Nagai's heart at a time when dark clouds were ever present. Apart from the grim prospects for Japan in the war in which they had been immersed for years, he had been diagnosed two months earlier with leukemia. His white blood cell count was 108,000. The normal count is about 7000. Safety standards for those working with X-rays were poorly developed at that time, so the cancer was probably caused by radiation exposure at work. Dr Nagai was given three years to live.

After completing his medical studies and serving in China twice, once in the Manchurian Incident in 1931 and returning as a military doctor to Shanghai in 1932, Takashi Nagai was now, at thirty-seven, a family man. As a student, he had boarded with the Moriyama family, hereditary leaders of a *kakure kirishitan* group in Urakami. In 1934, he had married Midori Moriyama, who had influenced his conversion to their faith.

Life for the strongly built Nagai had been good until the diagnosis . . . apart from the war. With relentless American air strikes against cities across the nation, authorities were pressuring those city-dwellers not engaged in essential war work to evacuate to rural Japan. Takashi and Midori had proposed their two young children go to the country with their grandmother, but they'd made such a fuss about it that the Nagai parents had put the plan on hold.

On the evening of 6 August, Takashi Nagai heard a report of a new bomb that had devastated Hiroshima. There was little detail, but it worried him nonetheless. He had a feeling the dangers of the times were ratcheting up. The move to the country was revived, not as a proposal but as a decision. Midori would take the children and their grandmother to a house in Koba the next day. Dr Nagai would brook no argument. There was none.

◆ ◆ ◆

Koichi Wada walked home from Hotarujaya tram terminal in the late afternoon warmth to his home in Maruyama. At that time, Maruyama had a reputation as the 'pleasure quarter' of Nagasaki. Koichi felt ashamed to say he lived there, so he'd tell people he was from Koshima, further up their valley and far more salubrious. The walk took about an hour, down one valley packed with small cottages crawling up the slope, around the end of a hilly ridge and up another valley. Above the built-up areas he could see the terraced patches worked by local market gardeners, growing sweet potatoes, radishes and other vegetables.

Koichi was preoccupied with the subject that now dominated his and so many other minds: relentless, nagging hunger. Although he was earning cash as a streetcar driver, it didn't extend much beyond his family's meagre ration entitlements. His younger sister, working in an office in the business district as a mobilised student, earned nothing—not even a bread roll—and their grandparents weren't working. They had been well off when they operated the fruit distribution business, and earlier in the war were able to barter their kimono collection to supplement their food supplies, but the kimonos were running low and the black market now wanted cash as well.

Koichi had befriended some of his work colleagues who'd come in from the country to find work. From time to time, when he and a rural friend had the same day off, they would visit the friend's family and come back with local produce from the region. Now the young tram driver was supplementing that irregular supply. He'd been up the hillside and noted gardens with produce ready to eat. At night, sometimes alone, sometimes with an accomplice, he'd sneak back to those gardens and pinch a few vegetables. Only a couple were removed from any one garden. The space left behind was covered with leaves.

They didn't bring bags because that might attract attention. Covered with dirt, the stolen food was stuffed into pockets, taken home to be secretly cleaned and eaten raw. They couldn't cook their booty because that would be noticed and questions would be asked. If their families knew they had stolen vegetables, the mortification and shame would be unending. Eating the stolen food didn't put an end to hunger. It didn't leave them gorged or even satisfied, only less hungry—but that was sufficient to justify their actions to themselves.

On this mild summer evening, Koichi Wada was aware of a couple of gardens ripe for picking. He'd noticed also that after a few clandestine visits some of the spaces were becoming obvious, but he didn't think further about the implication of this for his own security. Driven by his pangs, he came back after dark and stealthily entered the garden. He came by himself this time, but was no longer alone. Either because he too had noticed the gap in his row of produce or because Koichi's luck had run out, the garden's owner was in shadow at the edge of his market patch, observing but unobserved. He came rushing after the intruder, shouting angrily across the small rectangle of soil that was his livelihood.

Running as fast as he could, the younger Koichi managed to elude his pursuer, but his pulse was racing by the time he was confident he had got away. He decided it was only a matter of time before he could be in big trouble and resolved there and then to give up his secret life of petty crime. Without him, his family had no source of income. He had no idea how the law dealt with vegetable thieves and no wish to find out. He wasn't really a criminal anyway, just a young man constantly hungry like everyone he knew. Yes, there had been an element of youthful excitement and adventure about it, but he would now pursue other avenues to put an end to the hunger.

◆　◆　◆

And so another day in the war-weary southern Japanese city drew to a close. Monday, 6 August 1945 wasn't significantly different for the people of Nagasaki from any other day up to that point. It was to become a day of great significance to Japan and to the world, as it turned out, but there was little in Japan's radio news and evening newspapers to suggest that. People continued their austere existence, constantly hungry, constantly doing without just about everything. For the most part, they still believed in the cause, although harbouring unspoken doubts about the outcome, while their leaders pursued a war they repeatedly insisted would be won in the end.

Chapter 4

Moscow, Sunday 5 August 1945, evening

Joseph Stalin had returned to Moscow from the Potsdam Conference on the evening of 5 August. He met with senior officials and discussed, among other things, the war in the Far East and the possibility of the United States using the atomic bomb. The General Secretary of the Communist Party of the Soviet Union—and Premier as well since 1941—was a worried man. A cat and mouse game was being played between the two emerging superpowers and Stalin was determined to prevent the Soviet Union being the mouse.

The strongman of the USSR, Joseph Stalin appeared anything but. Short at 5 feet 4 inches (1.63 metres), his thin build was buried under a loose jacket, overcoat or military uniform. Childhood smallpox had left him with a withered left arm and a pockmarked face. His teeth were discoloured, his moustache coarse and streaked. He spoke haltingly with a heavy Georgian accent. But contrary to his reputation in the West as a stereotype tyrant, he seldom lost his temper. Stalin was an astute negotiator, and respected by his adversaries for this skill.

Leadership of the Allied powers had changed, losing some of its manageability in the Russian's view. Despite their different ideologies and competing global interests, Stalin had regarded the patrician

Roosevelt as a partner in shaping the coming post-war world, even when the American president was scheming behind his back. That was just politics. The pugnacious Churchill was a third partner in the global political team. But Roosevelt had died and Churchill now led His Majesty's Opposition in Britain. By the end of Potsdam, the Soviet leader was the only one of the 'Big Three' still in power. Still, he wasn't convinced things were going his way.

The Big Three at the time—Stalin, Roosevelt and Churchill—had met in February at the Black Sea resort of Yalta. They had principally hammered out a process for dealing with Germany's imminent surrender, but Roosevelt was also looking ahead to the concluding stages of the war with Japan. He worried that the inevitable invasion of Japan's home islands might be as costly in American lives as the capture of Okinawa had been. Soviet entry into the war could ease the cost. It would tie up Japan's Kwantung Army in Manchuria and possibly draw further troops away from the American assault, thereby reducing Japan's ability to resist the attack. The Kwantung Army had been a formidable force. The Allies were unaware how much it had been bled to reinforce the Japanese military elsewhere.

In a secret protocol attached to the Yalta agreements, the USSR undertook to enter the war against Japan within three months of a German surrender. At the time, the Soviet Union was abiding by a neutrality pact it had signed with Japan before Pearl Harbor. In return for the Yalta undertaking, Roosevelt and Churchill agreed that, following the defeat of Japan, Russia would get back the southern half of Sakhalin Island and the Kurile Islands. They also agreed to Soviet use of ice-free Port Arthur (now Lushun) and the China Eastern railway, all in Manchuria, although no-one had told the Chinese. All these spoils had been in Russian hands before the 1904 Russo-Japanese War.

Germany had surrendered on 7 May and the clock was ticking.

On 5 April, the Soviet government had announced it would not be renewing the Soviet–Japanese neutrality pact when it expired in 1946. Russia was ostensibly still keeping to the current agreement but in reality, with its troops no longer occupied on its western front, the Red Army had been mobilising in the Far East since May. The eastern front was at the end of a single long railway line, the Trans-Siberian. Rapid deployment was difficult, but battle-hardened soldiers from the European war and armaments were being moved across Siberia at a rate of up to thirty trains a day, mostly at night and assembling away from the border and the railway line, beyond the gaze of passing prying eyes.

Fourteen hundred new T-34 medium tanks were railed from the Ural tank factories rather than bringing older tanks from eastern Europe with their operators. On top of these, America supplied Sherman tanks under Lend-lease, shipped in June to Vladivostok under non-US flags. Along with them came clandestine shipments of US trucks, fuel and food supplies. By the beginning of August, the eastern front was 1.5 million troops strong, supported by 5000 tanks and nearly 5000 combat aircraft.

The operation was a remarkable feat of planning and almost obsessive secrecy. Headquarters of Marshal Aleksandr Vasilevsky's Far Eastern Command was set up in eastern Siberia on 5 July. All senior commanders came there under false names and more junior ranks. Vasilevsky himself travelled as Colonel General Vasil'ev, and his two field leaders, Marshals Malinovsky and Meretskov, were Colonels General Morozov and Maksimov respectively.

Japanese diplomatic couriers on the Trans-Siberian Railway had noted movements of men and equipment, but this was dismissed by Japan's army intelligence. It assumed that the USSR would minimise its casualties by holding off until after the US invasion and would not mount a winter offensive ... if it was going to mount an attack at all. Some clung optimistically to the view that the Soviets would honour the neutrality pact.

In late July, an intelligence colonel reported that Soviet tanks and reconnaissance forces were moving along the Manchurian border and did not appear equipped to sit out the winter. He guessed the Red Army might be planning to attack as soon as August. The colonel was ignored by the army hierarchy.

◆　◆　◆

While the Soviet Union was busily preparing to enter the war, a section of the Japanese leadership was trying to find a way out of it. Baron Kantaro Suzuki had been appointed prime minister in April 1945 to bring this about because his predecessor had not been strong enough to stand up to the military. Suzuki had confirmed it was the emperor's wish, but he had to balance this instruction against the possibility of those opposed to peace moves attacking or even assassinating him. As a result, he publicly advocated an increased war effort while trying, through diplomacy and any other available means, to negotiate with other countries to end the war.

At seventy-seven years of age and a former admiral, Baron Suzuki was thought to be 'too venerable to be effective'. He was not an inspiring leader. Deaf and given to drowsiness, he was hard to pin down on any issue. He was apt to preside benignly over the process of government and then go along philosophically with whatever happened. As far as his own opinions were concerned, he would contradict himself from one day to the next. On the issue of negotiating an end to the war, the balancing act he felt obliged to perform meant sometimes he seemed in favour of it, sometimes he seemed undecided.

Unlike the other Axis powers or the Soviet Union, Japan had no single all-powerful ruler. Even the emperor was constrained by protocols and conventions. Commanders of the army and the navy and diplomatic and government leaders all held differing views that had to be heard. All issues were to be decided collectively after discussion and consultation. The nation's leadership muddled its way towards finding a formula to end a war in which nearly everyone knew it was facing defeat.

Suzuki ordered Hisatsune Sakomizu, the Chief Secretary of Cabinet, to survey Japan's fighting capabilities. Were they sufficient to continue the war? By the end of May, Sakomizu had reported that Japan could not continue. The inability to produce enough aircraft, drastic losses of ships, food shortages and the growing anti-war sentiments of the people all added up to that conclusion.

In May, the Supreme Council for the Direction of the War, Japan's inner cabinet of six, began discussing ways and means of extricating itself from the war, including using Russia's 'good offices' to mediate with the Allies. In the course of these debates, the Supreme Council divided into two factions, one for finding a way to end the war, the other for continuing the war, at least for the time being. The Japanese leadership couldn't agree on what was an acceptable outcome to request Russia to pursue.

Following the surrender of Germany in the European war, War Minister Korechika Anami proposed an imperial conference to decide whether Japan should prolong its war. The minister and the military were urging continuation of hostilities, but Anami was not opposed to discussion. At no time did he obstruct positive peace steps taken by Prime Minister Suzuki or Lord Keeper of the Privy Seal, Koichi Kido. On one occasion the War Minister told Kido he would not support his peace initiative but would not oppose it 'too vigorously'. Anami's position, with firebrand officers watching his every move, required a delicate balance.

Prime Minister Suzuki asked a former prime minister, Koki Hirota, to sound out the Soviet Ambassador in Tokyo about USSR willingness to approach America on Japan's behalf. Yakov Malik was staying in a resort town two hours' drive from Tokyo. It wasn't until 3 June that Hirota went there and feigned accidentally bumping into the ambassador. They dined and talked. The Russian undertook to speak to Moscow, but the Soviet Foreign Minister, Vyacheslav Molotov, was never very interested.

While Hirota's discussions with Malik dragged on interminably, Ambassador Naotake Sato in Moscow was instructed to set up a meeting between a Japanese emissary and the Soviet leadership to propose a Russian approach to its Anglo–American allies on Japan's behalf. From the outset, Sato expressed doubts about the likely success of this venture.

On 22 June, Emperor Hirohito called a conference of the six Supreme War Council members. It was the first time he had taken the initiative during the conflict. He told the gathering it should have a plan to conclude the war, not just a plan to defend the home islands. He wanted to know when the special envoy would go to Moscow. The equivocal reply was that members hoped it would be before Stalin went to

Potsdam. The prime minister told Chief Secretary of Cabinet Sakomizu after the conference, 'Today the emperor said what everyone has wanted to say but was afraid to say it.'

The imperial conference agreed to send a delegation led by Prince Fumimaro Konoye to Moscow. Ambassador Malik was reportedly ill in Tokyo and the discussions with Hirota were not progressing. Three weeks later, his patience wearing thin, the emperor asked Foreign Minister Shigenori Togo, 'As it is now early July, should not our special ambassador be dispatched to Moscow without delay?' Soon after, Hirohito called in Konoye and secretly instructed him to accept any terms he could get and wire these terms direct to him.

On instruction from Tokyo, Ambassador Sato contacted the deputy to Russia's foreign minister. Solomon Lozovsky wanted more details of the mission before Minister Molotov could give a response. Sato was told by Togo to explain that the mission's aim was: (1) to ask Russia to intercede with the US to bring about an end to the war, and (2) to improve relations between Russia and Japan following the USSR decision not to renew the neutrality pact. Lozovsky replied on 13 July that since Stalin and Molotov were about to leave for the Potsdam Conference no answer could be given until they returned to Moscow.

◆　◆　◆

US strategists were anxious to reduce the cost of an invasion of the Japanese home islands. They'd been prepared to make concessions to the Soviets to achieve that, but a new card had appeared in the American hand. The development of the atomic bomb offered a different strategy should its coming test prove successful. The bomb might force a Japanese surrender without the need to invade at all. If the Soviet Union had not entered the Pacific war by that stage, the Americans reasoned, Stalin would be in a weaker position to make in Asia the sort of territorial gains he had made successfully in the aftermath of the European war. Stalin saw it differently, of course. At one point, he remarked that while Russia had been ravaged by Nazi assault, the Germans hadn't even broken a window on American soil.

Now America seemed destined to have the atomic bomb. Born out of a small research program in 1939, the Manhattan Project began in 1942 under the Manhattan Engineer District of the US Army Corps of Engineers and grew as a joint American-British-Canadian project. The location was chosen in part because it was near to Columbia University, a centre of early nuclear research. Army Chief of Staff George Marshall appointed General Groves (as he then became) as project chief. He in turn appointed as director of scientific research the American physicist J Robert Oppenheimer.

Naïve from a protected childhood and given to melancholia, Oppenheimer came from a wealthy non-practising Jewish family in New York. A chain-smoker and workaholic attracted to Eastern mysticism, his past association with Marxism was thought by some to pose security problems, but Groves was convinced Oppenheimer had the brainpower required for the project. He was prepared to stick his neck out over it. Groves had to fight to appoint his man and he prevailed, but in doing so he had to agree that his scientific director would remain under surveillance. Groves and Oppenheimer were never personally close but operated successfully through mutual respect.

As the atomic bomb was becoming a reality by early 1945, it was perceived differently by the various players in the US structure. To the military, this bomb was no more than a better firebomb. It was more explosive, more efficient and required fewer bombers, but it didn't represent a new era in weaponry. As a result, it wasn't put under the stringent lines of authority that might be prescribed for a revolutionary development. Henry Stimson, the Secretary of War, had a quite different view. To him the Manhattan Project was not to be considered simply in terms of a military weapon but as a 'new relationship of man to the universe', on a par with the Copernican model of a sun-centred solar system or the laws of gravity.

A secret high-level advisory group that included Stimson and the future Secretary of State, James Byrnes, made recommendations for proper use of atomic weapons. It never questioned whether the bomb should be used on Japan. It assumed it would be and debated only where it should be dropped.

A sub-committee within the Manhattan Project recommended targets. Its first deliberations were about the type of target. A small military objective carried a risk that the costly weapon—two billion American dollars had been spent on its development—might be wasted with poor aiming. The preference was to use it on a large urban area so it could destroy large numbers of closely built wooden frame buildings and Japanese civilians. The Target Committee recommended detonation at altitude to achieve maximum blast damage. The preference was also to use it on a relatively undamaged city. The problem with a city already devastated by firebombing was that people might not notice much difference.

Five cities were proposed as targets: Kyoto, Hiroshima, Yokohama, Kokura and Niigata. The armed forces were instructed to exclude these cities from conventional firebombing. Groves and the scientists wanted a 'clean' background so they could assess the effect of the bomb. They wanted visual targeting without cloud cover so they could photograph the resulting damage. A clean target also had the better 'shock value' against the enemy.

People in Hiroshima eventually became aware that their city was not being subjected to the incendiary attacks of other cities. A rumour spread that President Truman's mother had been imprisoned in Hiroshima Castle, that the American military had been instructed to spare the city while she was there.

Groves' first choice was Kyoto. It was largely untouched by bombing and was psychologically important to the Japanese. Its surrounding mountains would focus the blast and increase the bomb's destructive force. Stimson had visited Kyoto in the 1920s. He knew its status as Japan's intellectual and cultural capital and considered its destruction to be barbaric. Stimson argued for Kyoto to be dropped from the list and eventually won President Truman over to his view. Kyoto was dropped and replaced with Nagasaki in a 25 July directive.

Stimson was concerned that America's reputation for fair play and humanitarianism might be damaged by targeting urban areas. His colleague, George Marshall, had a similar view. Marshall believed the bomb should be used first on military targets and only later on large manufacturing areas after first warning the surrounding population to leave. In the end, both men's views were ignored. On 25 July, General Thomas Handy issued on their behalf an order to General Carl Spaatz, Guam-based commander of US Army Strategic Air Forces.

The command was to 'deliver' the first 'special bomb' as soon after 3 August that weather permitted visual targeting. The target was to be selected from a list of four provided: Hiroshima, Kokura, Niigata and, added that day, Nagasaki. Additional bombs were to be delivered on those targets as they became available.

Spaatz had told Handy, 'If I'm going to kill thousands of people, I'm not going to do it on verbal orders. I want a piece of paper.' Now he had one. He passed on the orders to Tinian.

The sub-committee had decided not to specify military–industrial areas as the target since they were scattered and, apart from Kokura with its huge munitions factory in the middle of the city, generally on the suburban fringes. Air crews were left to select their own target to maximise the bomb's effect on the city as a whole. The greatest impact would be achieved by aiming at the centre of a city where the population was densest.

It wasn't clear how the mass killing of civilians would drive the Japanese to capitulate. Japan's cities had been firebombed since March, setting a precedent for targeting non-combatants without any surrender resulting. Stimson had to settle for persuading himself that the project was not intentionally targeting civilians in the face of clear evidence to the contrary.

◆ ◆ ◆

The Soviet Union was conducting its own research to develop an atomic bomb. Some of the project's knowledge came from classified information supplied by people within the scientific team at Los Alamos. German-born British physicist Klaus Fuchs had been passing information to Soviet intelligence since 1941 and was transferred to Los Alamos in 1944. Theodore Hall, like Fuchs a long-time communist, made contact with the Soviets in 1944 while at Los Alamos. Many others have not been publicly identified and some probably remain unknown even to American counter-intelligence. Most provided information to the USSR for ideological reasons, not for money. Most were unaware that others were doing the same thing. Many Americans at that time were sympathetic to communism or even members of the American Communist Party.

Information coming to the Kremlin through espionage agents was first evaluated by Stalin. He knew about the Manhattan Project and its purpose long before Harry Truman. Despite the extensive intelligence received from within Los Alamos, the Russian leaders—Stalin, Foreign Minister Molotov and chief of Soviet security Lavrenti Beria—didn't anticipate at that stage the role the atomic bomb would come to play in international politics. They thought Soviet scientists were fantasising and, perhaps because it was volunteered, suspected that much of the intelligence from America might be 'disinformation'.

◆ ◆ ◆

To many of the US strategists, the certainty that either invasion or the atomic bomb would be necessary to bring about Japan's surrender seemed to be waning, despite the enemy's apparent dogged determination to continue the war. The Imperial Japanese Navy was virtually non-existent after the Battle of Leyte in the Philippines and bombers were reducing Japan's cities to ashes. How long could they go on? America's strategic planners started looking ahead at how they would deal with a capitulated Japan. One of the contentious issues, they all knew, would be what to do with the emperor.

Joseph Grew, an ambassador to Tokyo in the 1930s, was now under-secretary in the State Department. Letting the emperor remain, he argued, would help stabilise a defeated Japan. In any case, the occupation wouldn't continue indefinitely and Japan could restore the emperor once it ended. Grew still favoured using the term 'unconditional surrender', however, to avoid any suggestion that the American people lacked the will to continue the war. Stimson and Marshall too took the view that the formula of unconditional surrender should be modified, but then was not the time to do it for undisclosed 'military reasons'.

Elsewhere in the American structure, views on the emperor issue were equally divided. The military's Joint Chiefs of Staff favoured retention of the emperor to control the Japanese armed forces after surrender. The State Department's advisers, on the other hand, were opposed to it. They saw retention of the emperor as appeasement and leaving the roots of Japanese militarism intact. Joseph Grew's contrary views had been influential with Truman until the July appointment of James Byrnes as Secretary of State. Byrnes preferred to form his own opinions.

In the end, Truman's personal dislike of Hirohito (although they'd never actually met) and the possible backlash from the US public were probably the main reasons for the president not making a statement about the post-war role of the emperor. Americans were hostile to Hirohito and wanted him dethroned. A Gallup poll in June 1945 found 33 per cent wanted the emperor executed as a war criminal, 11 per cent wanted him imprisoned. Only 7 per cent favoured his retention even in a puppet role.

What the American public didn't know, but its leadership knew, was that Japan was actively seeking an end to hostilities, even though it didn't yet have unanimous cabinet support. The cables in June between Tokyo and Moscow—between Foreign Minister Togo and Ambassador Sato—had been intercepted and decoded by Henry Stimson's War Department. Togo had indicated that the emperor had expressed an interest in ending the war through negotiation. Two cables shortly before the Potsdam Conference confirmed there were divisions within the Japanese government but that Hirohito was actively pursuing peace if the surrender terms could be modified. Stimson and the Secretary of the Navy, Forrestal, had full information on the intercepts and Truman had certainly seen the most important ones. The president would refer to them in conversation at Potsdam. Although principally about the aftermath of the European war, Potsdam would prove pivotal to the final stages of the war with Japan.

Chapter 5

Potsdam, 16–29 July 1945

Harry S Truman, the 33rd President of the United States, arrived at Potsdam with some trepidation. An inexperienced hand at foreign affairs, dependent on the expertise of his advisers, he had not previously met either Stalin or Churchill. He admitted to his wife his dread of facing the two political giants. For moral support, the new president brought his poker buddies across the Atlantic with him on the USS *Augusta*, drinking and playing cards into the night. At the end of the ten-day journey, Truman settled into the 'Little White House' at Babelsberg, between Berlin and Potsdam on Berlin's south-western outskirts. The Little White House was not white, in fact, but yellow. Its former occupant, a German movie producer, was by then in a Russian labour camp.

In the early morning of 16 July, while the Potsdam Conference was setting up, the atomic bomb was tested in the New Mexico desert. A plutonium implosion device rigged on a tower, it was detonated in the Jornada del Muerto (Journey of the Dead) Valley, near Alamogordo. The test was code-named Trinity and was a resounding success, although it was a different type of bomb from the uranium-based weapon that would be used on Hiroshima.

Truman came to Potsdam with his new Secretary of State, James Byrnes, as principal adviser. The secretary of war wasn't part of the official US delegation at Potsdam, ostensibly for health reasons, but Stimson made his own way there anyway. He was already in Babelsberg when news of the Trinity test came through in a secure cable from General Groves. Stimson walked over in the evening to the Little White House to pass on the news personally to Truman, but with the report from Groves clouded in cryptic language it didn't make much impact on the president. It goes unmentioned in his memoir. Four days later, when an expanded and unambiguous follow-up report came from Groves, Truman finally showed a glimmer of excitement. 'The Japs will fold before Russia comes in,' he predicted.

Stalin's arrival at Potsdam was delayed by a minor heart attack which had been kept secret. He came to the Little White House on 17 July and had lunch with Truman, who noted that Stalin looked you in the eye when he spoke to you. The Russian leader was in good humour despite his health scare, cordial and polite.

The next day Truman had a private meeting with Stalin at the conference and secured from him a promise to enter the war against Japan and to work towards a liberated Manchuria open to international trade. Truman was so pleased with himself he wrote to his wife saying he'd got what he came for and had outfoxed the 'smart as hell' Stalin. As the Soviet leader had already promised at Yalta to enter the war—indeed, was anxious to do so—it was hardly a major breakthrough, although Truman and Byrnes may not have been given a full account of the Yalta agreements. Roosevelt had seldom confided in his vice-president. Truman clearly did not yet see the atomic bomb as removing the need for Russia to enter the war against Japan.

The Potsdam Conference was held in the ivy-draped Cecilienhof Palace, a two-storey brownstone country estate. It had been used as a hospital during the war and had been refurbished for the conference by the Russians, in whose occupied territory Potsdam stood. Geraniums had been planted in the courtyard in the shape of a giant red star.

Stalin impressed the new American president with his wry humour. Asked why he refused to give Russia its share of the German fleet,

Churchill explained that the fleet should be destroyed or shared, but since weapons of war were abominable the captured vessels should be sunk. Stalin responded, 'Then let us divide the fleet and Mr Churchill can sink his share if he wishes.'

Through intelligence coming from Los Alamos, the Russians kept abreast of the Manhattan Project's progress. The first report of an imminent bomb test reached Stalin as he was leaving for Potsdam. On either 20 or 21 July, Soviet intelligence informed him that the test had taken place successfully. Stalin believed it would still be some time before the new weapon would be used against the enemy, but Stimson advised Truman on 22 July that the weapon could be delivered earlier than expected. Truman was 'intensely pleased', according to Stimson, and was probably just starting to appreciate the strength of this card in his hand.

Brimming with new-found confidence, Truman and Byrnes wanted to see the effect on Stalin of the suggestion they had a new unspecified weapon. Truman spoke to the Soviet leader after a plenary session on 24 July. He mentioned casually that America had 'a new weapon of unusual destructive force' but didn't say it was an atomic bomb. According to Truman's memoirs, Stalin said he was glad to hear it and hoped they would make 'good use of it against the Japanese'. However, Truman seems to have embellished the story by the time he wrote it. The British Foreign Secretary, Anthony Eden, was standing a few metres away from the two leaders. He wrote in his memoirs that Stalin nodded and said 'thank you' without further comment. Within earshot was VN Pavlov, the interpreter who translated Truman's remark. His recollection is that Stalin merely nodded without saying anything.

In discussing the exchange later with Byrnes, Truman commented on Stalin's lack of response and wondered whether the Russian had fully grasped the significance. Stalin had, of course, but it wasn't news to him. After the session he told Vyacheslav Molotov about Truman's remark. 'They're upping the ante,' commented Molotov. Stalin laughed and said, 'Let them. We'll speed up our work.'

On his return to Moscow, the Soviet boss directed all USSR resources to be made available to break the American monopoly of the bomb.

Development of the new weapon was incorporated into the next five-year plan for the Soviet economy. Stalin gave Lavrenti Beria, chief of Soviet security, extraordinary powers to marshal everything necessary to the project, although it had to remain in strict secrecy under control of the Central Committee. The arms race was off and running.

◆ ◆ ◆

On the afternoon of 24 July, the chiefs of staff of the armed forces of America, Britain and Russia met at Potsdam. Each brought his retinue of advisers with him. General Aleksei Antonov announced that Soviet troops were being consolidated in the Far East in readiness for an assault on Japanese forces in Manchuria in late August. It was dependent on completion of negotiations with China over the terms of the Yalta agreement. Stalin had told Truman that the USSR would enter the war by mid-August. If Truman had not been aware of the terms agreed in Yalta, he now was.

The Soviet plan, Antonov told his fellow chiefs of staff, was to occupy Manchuria and the Liaotung Peninsula, with its strategic port of Port Arthur. They would withdraw after the defeat of Japan. General Marshall, in turn, assured the Russians there was no US intention to move into the Kuriles or Korea. The USSR had not expressed an interest in the latter, but it would logically move into Japanese-occupied Korea after Manchuria. Stalin's greater concern, however, was that Japan might capitulate before Russia entered the war, providing the US with an excuse to withdraw from the Yalta agreement because Russia hadn't been able to keep its side of the bargain. On the other hand, if the Red Army already occupied territories covered under Yalta, the negotiation would play to a different tune.

The American strategists assumed the Soviets would enter the war when negotiations with Nationalist China had resolved the Yalta issues. Talks between Soviet Foreign Minister Molotov and Chinese Premier TV (Tse-ven) Soong had been suspended while the former was at Potsdam. Truman and Byrnes cabled Nationalist leader Chiang Kai-shek advising not only that he resume negotiations after Potsdam, but also that they did not see the need for him to make any concessions to the USSR.

Stalling the Chinese negotiations might delay the Soviet assault on Manchuria. The atomic bomb now had two benefits in forcing an early surrender by Japan. It would forestall the need for an American invasion planned for November. In addition, it would preclude Soviet entry into the eastern war and its advance through China, joining the occupation of Japan. That was not a prospect Truman welcomed. As a bonus, the atomic bomb would demonstrate to the Soviet Union America's expanding military capability. The Cold War was at the embryo stage.

◆ ◆ ◆

Further cables between Japan's Foreign Minister Togo and Ambassador Sato during the Potsdam Conference were intercepted by US intelligence. They indicated the only condition Japan was seeking was preservation of 'our form of government'. In other words, the emperor.

Potsdam went into recess for three days to allow Churchill and British Foreign Secretary Eden to return to Britain for the outcome of the British general election. A 25 July cable from Tokyo instructed Sato to meet anywhere with Molotov during the recess. He was to make clear that 'we should like to communicate to the other party [the US] through appropriate channels that we have no objection to a peace based on the Atlantic Charter [a 1941 blueprint for the world after World War II]'. The only sticking point was the demand for unconditional surrender. Like previous cables, it too was intercepted by American intelligence.

Towards the end of Potsdam, Stalin told Truman of a further message from Sato repeating that the mission of Prince Konoye would 'convey to the Soviet government that it was exclusively the desire of His Majesty to avoid more bloodshed by the parties engaged in the war'. Stalin had told Truman at the beginning of Potsdam of the initial Japanese approach. The Soviet leader was all for fobbing off the Japanese to allow Russia time to enter the war. The message couldn't have been clearer to the US president by now. Encouraging Russia to enter into surrender discussions with Japan could solve his two concerns: the bloodshed cost of a land invasion, and Soviet entry into the war. However, Truman showed little interest in pursuing the Japanese feelers. He agreed that

Russia should give a definite negative response and thanked Stalin for telling him.

◆   ◆   ◆

Two major pronouncements by the Allies came out of the Potsdam Conference, one regarding Germany (generally called the Potsdam Proclamation), the other Japan. The Potsdam Declaration to Japan would have a profound impact, both on the concluding stages of the war with Japan and on international affairs in the post-war era for several decades—and in each case not necessarily to anyone's advantage. It would create an excuse for using the atomic bomb on Japan, by demanding a positive, specific and unequivocal response or else suffer enormous devastation by unspecified means. Ironically, the declaration itself was equivocal. The long-term effect of the declaration by America would be to drive a wedge of mutual suspicion between itself and the USSR that would become the Cold War. The stand-off between the two superpowers would last at least until the collapse of the Soviet Union in 1991, if not longer.

The Potsdam Declaration had been drafted by Joseph Grew and Henry Stimson, but it was polished by Jim Byrnes, Grew's new boss. Byrnes worked with British delegates on the final version of the declaration of terms to Japan, deliberately excluding the USSR. Grew and Stimson had included an option to 'include a constitutional monarchy under the present dynasty if it be shown to the complete satisfaction of the world that such a government will never again aspire to aggression'. It was struck out by Byrnes on Truman's insistence. Article 6 began, 'There must be eliminated for all time the authority and influence of those who have deceived and misled the people of Japan into embarking on world conquest.' Article 12 now required the establishment 'in accordance with the freely expressed will of the Japanese people a peacefully inclined and responsible government'. In this form of words the status of the emperor was ambiguous. Did he come under Article 6 or Article 12?

The declaration promised 'prompt and utter destruction' if Japan continued hostilities. This meant little to a nation destroyed daily by incendiary raids. There was no mention of the atomic bomb.

On 24 July, Truman, Churchill and senior military people met and approved the final draft of the Potsdam Declaration. Churchill suggested modifying 'unconditional surrender' so Japan could make a show of some saving of military honour. This would still leave all the crucial points intact and might result in a speedier surrender. 'I don't think the Japanese have any honour after Pearl Harbor,' was Truman's curt response.

A copy of the declaration was sent to Chiang Kai-shek in China through US Ambassador Hurley in Chungking, the temporary National-ist Chinese capital in the west China mountains. There was no reply or acknowledgement from China, causing some concern in Potsdam. White House staff wired Hurley that if Truman had not received a reply from Chiang in twenty-four hours he would release the declaration with or without Chiang's signature.

The delay was no more than could be expected in a world at war. First, traffic volume had delayed transmission through Hawaii. The copy was delivered by Hurley to Premier Soong that evening, but his brother-in-law, Chiang Kai-shek, was in mountainous terrain across the Yangtze River. The next day, Hurley went by ferry to Chiang's resi-dence at Yellow Mountain. While they were there, Chiang was visited by Dr Wang Shih-Chieh, soon to replace Soong as Minister of Foreign Relations. Both agreed with the draft except for one change: Chiang wanted to be listed above the British PM to help him with perceptions at home. The telephone at Yellow Mountain was out of order. Hurley had to return to Chungking before he could contact Potsdam with Chiang's response.

With the time zone difference, the Chinese endorsement was received on 26 July. At nine twenty that evening, the joint declaration was issued from Berlin in the names of President Truman, Generalissimo Chiang Kai-shek and Prime Minister Churchill (who ceased to be prime minister that same day with Labour's Clement Attlee victorious in the British election). It was released in a radio broadcast rather than through diplomatic channels. An announcement on shortwave radio from San Francisco was the first to be picked up in Tokyo. It was the early morning of 27 July (Tokyo time).

The Russians were not invited to sign the declaration even though they had agreed to enter the war in August and were eager to join the ultimatum to Japan. When they were shown it on the night of 26 July they immediately asked for its release to be delayed so they could study its wording. Byrnes replied that it had already been made public.

Of the three Americans—Truman, Byrnes and Stimson—only Byrnes left Potsdam with his strategy for the final stages of the war with Japan unaltered. Truman arrived at Potsdam with the main objective of getting Russia into the war, but left believing the US no longer needed the Soviet Union. Stimson arrived believing knowledge of atomic power should be shared with the world (including the USSR) to avoid a post-war arms race. Within three days of experiencing what he regarded as repression by the Soviet police state, he changed his view. Nothing should be shared with the Soviet Union, he had decided, until they espoused freedom of speech and enacted a bill of rights. However, the liberal traditionalist Stimson had been largely sidelined at Potsdam by Truman and particularly Byrnes, reduced to little more than messenger boy and occasional adviser.

◆ ◆ ◆

The first senior member of the Japanese government to read a transcript of the Potsdam Declaration was Foreign Minister Togo's vice-minister. He advised Togo that Japan should accept the terms as stated. It would be sheer folly to do otherwise. He had started drafting a Japanese acceptance. A driving force in the peace faction, Togo was a different personality to the prime minister. Unfortunately, he was also outspoken and arrogant, often contemptuous of other people's opinions.

'Wait. It won't be as easy as you think,' was the foreign minister's dismissive comment. 'The army will never accept the ultimatum as it now stands.' The vice-minister was instructed to 'make a careful study of the legal aspects of the declaration'. It would produce an interpretation that required a considerable degree of wishful thinking.

Togo had a morning audience with the emperor, reporting on nego-tiations with Moscow and the Potsdam Declaration. The minister was concerned about the consequences if Japan rejected the declaration. He was still pursuing Soviet mediation to bring about an end to the war and Japan should wait for the outcome of that before deciding its position on the declaration.

At ten thirty, the Supreme War Council met. Togo felt the Allies had softened their demand in the earlier Cairo Declaration for 'the unconditional surrender of Japan'. Now they called for 'the unconditional surrender of all Japanese armed forces', which he read as loosening the demand. His view was that the Potsdam Declaration should not be rejected until its ambiguities were clarified, particularly in relation to the status of the emperor. An adviser to Navy Minister Yonai had noticed that Stalin was not a signatory to the declaration. It was assumed, incorrectly, that the USSR had chosen not to sign with the intention of remaining neutral. This offered some hope that Russia might be prepared to intercede with its allies on Japan's behalf.

Navy Chief of Staff Toyoda, a hardliner, argued the Potsdam Declaration would reach the Japanese people sooner or later. The government should issue a statement that it could not consider agreeing to the terms as they stood, rather than risk appearing to be intimidated by it into no response. Prime Minister Suzuki and Foreign Minister Togo objected to this. It was agreed that for the time being the Japanese would hold off a formal response to the Potsdam Declaration until they had a Soviet reply to their request for mediation.

The issue of how to inform the Japanese people of the declaration was discussed at length in a full cabinet meeting that afternoon. Togo argued that the government should make no announcement until it decided its position. As it has already been broadcast, asserted one minister, the Japanese people will get to hear of it before long. They should be told about it first by their own government. It was agreed in the end that the Potsdam Declaration should be released to the public in summary form, without comment by the government. The Information and Intelligence Agency should instruct the press to minimise its publicity.

Immediately after, there was a routine meeting for information exchange between the government and the military high command.

Togo made the tactical mistake of absenting himself from the meeting, with other business to attend to. One of the military men proposed rejection of the Potsdam Declaration. The inner cabinet, without Togo, hastily re-assembled in an adjacent room. War Minister Anami and army and navy chiefs of staff Umezu and Toyoda now insisted that the government denounce Potsdam. Navy Minister Yonai was overruled. Prime Minister Suzuki agreed to announce publicly that the government would ignore the Potsdam Declaration.

Late in the afternoon, Suzuki held a press conference. Reporters asked for a response to the Allied demands and were told the Japanese government intended to ignore them. Suzuki used the word *mokusatsu*, meaning not 'worthy of comment'. *Moku* means 'to be silent' and *satsu* means 'to kill', together 'to kill with silence'. It can also mean 'no comment', which Suzuki subsequently claimed was the meaning he intended with the word, although that was contrary to the reconvened cabinet decision.

The next day's papers picked up on *mokusatsu* and added their own editorialising. 'Laughable Surrender Conditions to Japan' headlined *Yomiuri Hochi*. 'The Government Intends to Ignore [*Mokusatsu*] It', said the more restrained *Asahi Shimbun*. At four o'clock that afternoon Baron Suzuki held another press conference to discuss the Allied ultimatum. He dismissed it as a rehash of the Cairo Declaration, saying the government considered it of little importance. He added, 'we will simply *mokusatsu* it', but made no attempt to explain the sense in which he used the word. Suzuki went on to say the government was determined to continue the war until victory was won.

Togo was livid when he heard about Suzuki's statements to the press. He protested that they were inconsistent with cabinet's decision, only to find there had been a subsequent cabinet decision. However, the genie was out of the bottle. It was not possible to retract Suzuki's words. There was nothing Togo could do. Monday's newspapers reported Suzuki's comments extensively. They were picked up by the world's press and, in America particularly, the word 'ignore' became 'reject'.

The infuriated foreign minister continued to pursue his determination to find a solution to Japan's predicament. He cabled Ambassador

Sato in Moscow: 'What the Russian position is with respect to the Potsdam Declaration made by England, America and Chungking is a question of extreme importance in determining our future counter-policy . . . we should like Your Excellency to have an interview with Molotov as quickly as possible.'

Sato, meanwhile, looked through Russia's newspapers for reports about Potsdam, concluding that the Soviet Union would not agree to act as a go-between. As instructed, he called again on Deputy Foreign Minister Lozovsky in the late afternoon of 30 July. The Russian was non-committal but said he would tell Molotov that Sato was seeking an urgent reply to Japan's request. Sato tried once again to convince Tokyo that the USSR had no intention of intervening on Japan's behalf. He cabled Togo that evening, 'I believe that Stalin feels there is absolutely no necessity for making a voluntary agreement with Japan. On this point I see a serious discrepancy between your view and the actual state of affairs.'

Three days later, Togo was adamant. 'The most urgent task which now confronts us,' he responded, 'is to persuade the Soviet Government to accept the mission of our special envoy. His Majesty, the Emperor, is most profoundly concerned about the matter and has been following develop-ments with the keenest interest. The Premier and the leaders of the army are now concentrating all their attention on this one point . . . I urge you to do everything possible to arrange an interview with Molotov at once.'

This cable, like the others, was intercepted by American intelligence. With the reference to leaders of the army, the US could have drawn the conclusion Japan's peace initiatives now had the unanimous support of its leadership. If it did, it made no attempt to follow that up. As it happened, however, it was untrue . . . as Togo knew full well.

On the same day, a Washington memo to the president reported contact with a Japanese group in Switzerland. They had described the Potsdam Declaration as an 'astute document which left a possible way out', especially the term 'unconditional surrender of the Japanese armed forces'. They cautioned that the US should not take too seriously what was said over Tokyo radio. It was mostly propaganda to maintain morale in Japan. A real reply would come soon through official channels.

◆ ◆ ◆

While the Japanese leaders struggled to agree on their response to the Allies' ultimatum, the Potsdam Conference pressed on to its concluding stages. On 29 July, Molotov visited Truman. Stalin had a cold, he said, and Molotov would be representing him at the conference that day. Truman suspected Stalin's 'cold' was actually disappointment with the UK election result. The second of Stalin's three cornerstones of the international diplomacy partnership had been replaced, leaving only himself of the original Big Three.

Molotov wanted to meet first to ask if the allies in the Far East war would be prepared to request Soviet entry into the war on the basis of an expected Japanese refusal to accept the Potsdam Declaration. The Soviet concern was with the appearance of breaching its treaty with Japan. A request from allies would take the sting out of that. The US president suspected the proposal was intended to make Russia's entry into the war appear decisive to victory.

The president consulted with the British and with Byrnes. There was a concern about the US asking another government to violate a treaty. Truman later responded directly to Stalin. When a Soviet–China agreement was reached, he proposed, the US would send a letter advising that Articles 103 and 106 of the recently drafted, but not yet formally ratified, United Nations Charter authorised Russia's entry into the war. Truman privately anticipated the war would be over before that point was reached.

Stalin had appointed Marshal Vasilevsky as Supreme Commander of the Soviet Forces in the Far East on 1 August after the Potsdam Declaration had been released without Soviet input or endorsement. The Soviet High Command, *Stavka*, ordered the formation of three fronts by the Red Army in the Far East, one on the north-western border of Manchuria, the other two down its eastern side. On 3 August, Marshal Vasilevsky and his Chief of Staff, Colonel-General SP Ivanov, reported that the Far East fronts would be at maximum concentration about fifty kilometres from the border within two days. Vasilevsky was now able to pull the invasion day forward to 9 August.

Stalin had been polite and cordial at Potsdam because it was required, and firm when it was needed. He hadn't particularly taken to the new American president, whom he dismissed as a 'petty shopkeeper'. He certainly wasn't Roosevelt. Although the atomic bomb had never been mentioned explicitly, it had a discomforting presence nonetheless. Stalin recognised Truman's 'sly adviser', the new Secretary of State Byrnes, as practising what would come to be known as atomic diplomacy, the use of nuclear strength to leverage political outcomes. The only response to this—apart from buckling to it—would take the two emerging super-powers down the dangerously reckless path of escalation to 'mutually assured destruction': MAD. Joseph Stalin couldn't have foreseen such specific outcomes; nevertheless, he was not happy.

Chapter 6

Nagasaki, Tuesday 7 August 1945

It was the middle of the night in Japan when Harry Truman had lunch on board the USS *Augusta*. The ship was by then south of Newfoundland, four days out from Plymouth on the way home from the Potsdam Conference. The president had joined the crew of *Augusta* for lunch in their mess hall. The officers ate in their wardroom elsewhere in the vessel, but Truman was a homespun Democrat. A lunch with the sailors was good for business. James Byrnes, Truman's Secretary of State, was also on board and dining at another table in the mess hall. A Southern lawyer of humble origins, Byrnes was a good behind-the-scenes political worker. He would have understood Truman's political gesture and may even have suggested it.

The president's meal with the ordinary folk was interrupted by the arrival at his side of Captain Frank Graham of White House staff with a cable and a map in his hand. The map was of Japan with Hiroshima circled in red pencil. Up to that point, Hiroshima was just another Japanese city with a difficult-to-remember name. The cable was from Henry Stimson.

From the Secretary of War

To the President.

Big Bomb dropped on Hiroshima 5 August at 7.15 PM Washington time. First reports indicate complete success which was even more conspicuous than earlier test.

Truman jumped to his feet jubilantly and shook the aide's hand. 'Captain,' he said, 'this is the greatest thing in history.'

Graham was told to take the cable across to the secretary of state. Truman sat down and lapsed into silence, lost in thought. His company at the table watched discreetly, too distracted to make conversation. Clearly something important had happened.

A few minutes later a second, more detailed report arrived. It was a paraphrase of Captain Parsons' first coded message back to Tinian. Truman read it and went over to Byrnes at the nearby table. 'Jim, it's time to go home,' he said. He picked up a glass and fork off the table and rapped the glass sharply. The room went silent. The president told the sailors about the new weapon, telling them of the American lives it would save by shortening the war. It was his first rehearsal of the spin. The announcement was greeted with cheers filling the room.

Truman and Byrnes went down to the officers' wardroom, a broad smile on the president's face. He told them, 'We have just dropped a bomb on Japan which has more power than twenty thousand tons of TNT. It was an overwhelming success. We won the gamble.'

At 11 a.m., still 6 August in Washington (midnight in Tokyo) and about the same time as the president was lunching off the coast of Canada, radio stations in America were broadcasting a prepared statement from President Truman. Truman listened to it on the ship's radio. The American public was told that the United States had dropped an entirely new type of bomb, an 'atomic bomb', on the Japanese city of Hiroshima. Just as importantly, the rest of the world including Japan was informed. Between the lines there was a message there for the Soviet Union, for Stalin and his cronies and advisers.

The presidential statement began:

Sixteen hours ago an American airplane dropped one bomb on Hiroshima, an important Japanese Army base. That bomb had more power than 20,000 tons of TNT. It had more than two thousand times the blast power of the British 'Grand Slam' which is the largest bomb ever yet used in the history of warfare.

The Japanese began the war from the air at Pearl Harbor. They have been repaid many fold. And the end is not yet. With this bomb we have now added a new and revolutionary increase in destruction to supplement the growing power of our armed forces. In their present form these bombs are now in production and even more powerful forms are in development.

It is an atomic bomb. It is a harnessing of the basic power of the universe. The force from which the sun draws its power has been loosed against those who brought war to the Far East.

The United States and Great Britain, the statement continued in less muscular prose, had pooled their scientific knowledge in a secret research project spanning five years and involving thousands of workers, few of them knowing what they were working on.

We have spent two billion dollars on the greatest scientific gamble in history—we won ... We are now prepared to obliterate more rapidly and completely every productive enterprise the Japanese have above ground in any city. We shall destroy their docks, their factories, and their communications. Let there be no mistake; we shall completely destroy Japan's power to make war. It was to spare the Japanese people from utter destruction that the ultimatum of July 26 was issued at Potsdam. Their leaders promptly rejected the ultimatum. If they do not now accept our terms they may expect a rain of ruin from the air, the like of which has never been seen on this earth.

The broadcast was picked up by the Domei News Agency, which operated a large monitoring station outside Tokyo. Nearly fifty workers there, many of them *Nisei* girls born in the USA, listened to shortwave radio broadcasts from American stations. At one in the morning, the chief of the monitoring room was told that all US stations were broadcasting a press release by President Truman. The weapon that had been dropped on Hiroshima had been described as an 'atomic bomb'.

The supervisor immediately rang his own superior, Saiji Hasegawa. Domei's foreign news editor was still asleep in the Dai-ichi Hotel. At first irritated at being wakened and having no real idea what an 'atomic bomb' was, he quickly recognised the importance of what he was hearing. Hasegawa hurried across to his office. He read the transcripts that were starting to come through, then reached for his telephone and called the chief secretary of the Japanese cabinet, then living in an office on the third floor of the prime minister's official residence.

Rubbing the sleep out of his eyes as he answered his bedroom telephone, Hisatsune Sakomizu rapidly became wide awake as he listened to the news editor's story. He knew from the jumble of reports the day before that the Americans had used a new weapon of some sort. On hearing it was an atomic bomb, a possibility that had been in the wind for a while but was thought still to be some time away, he saw an opportunity to bring to fruition what he and his political faction had been desperately trying to engineer: an end to the war. He asked for copies of Truman's statement to be sent to himself and to the War and Foreign ministries.

The cabinet secretary called his prime minister to pass on the news. If it were true, Japan could not continue a war against an enemy that had such a weapon. It would be unable to defend itself. But this could offer a formula for the war faction to end the war without loss of face. It would not be necessary to blame the military for Japan's inability to continue the conflict under these circumstances. Blame would rest on the bomb or the failure of Japan's scientists to match Allied progress in developing it. It was the perfect excuse. The cabinet secretary proposed calling a meeting of the cabinet that afternoon. Prime Minister Suzuki agreed.

Meanwhile Hasegawa had phoned the Foreign Minister, Shigenori Togo, a driving force in the peace faction. By the time Sakomizu phoned him with the news he had already got from the Domei editor, Togo too could see the opportunity that identification of the type of bomb presented. He was all for a cabinet meeting as soon as possible.

◆ ◆ ◆

Otto Frisch was deep in thought in his Los Alamos room when a colleague opened the door to pass on the sensational news that had just come to hand. Hiroshima had been destroyed with a single atomic bomb. It was estimated 100,000 had been killed. The Jewish Frisch had fled the looming horror of Nazi Germany in 1933 and, ten years later, had joined the Manhattan Project. He was still very conscious of all that Europe had been through since he left. The sight of friends rushing to book tables at La Fonda Hotel in Santa Fe to celebrate the killing of so many people disturbed him.

That evening, Robert Oppenheimer, the sensitive, cultured humanist, made a speech in a Los Alamos lecture theatre. He walked through the cheering scientists in the auditorium, pumping his fists in the air. The responsibility of leading the Los Alamos team had given him a new confidence and a new personality. The mumbling researcher had become a demagogue. He told the crowd his only regret was that he hadn't developed the bomb in time to use it against the Germans. The audience cheered in its delight. For some time now, the community at Los Alamos had worked and lived in a bubble.

Across the Atlantic, the discoverer of nuclear fission, Otto Hahn, had been interned near Cambridge since the end of the European war, suspected of working on the German nuclear project. 'I thank God on my bended knees that we did not make a uranium bomb,' he said when he heard the news.

◆ ◆ ◆

Joseph Stalin didn't like the official apartments in the Kremlin. They were too vast and ornate for his rustic Georgian tastes. Even when he worked late, he preferred to go to his *dacha* (country villa) to sleep. It was secure enough there within a double perimeter fence and patrolled by

Russian wolfhounds. Twenty-five kilometres out of Moscow, the *dacha* was built for Stalin after the suicide of his wife in 1932.

Shortly after five in the afternoon of 6 August—midnight in Tokyo— Stalin heard news of the bombing of Hiroshima. He cancelled his evening appointments and went out to his *dacha*. His daughter, Svetlana, was there. At nineteen, she was already married but her husband was not with her. Her father refused to have any contact with him. Svetlana's memoir notes 'the usual visitors' came out in the evening. 'The usual visitors' included Molotov, Beria and Malenkov of the powerful State Defence Commit- tee. They sat in the *dacha*'s dining room, discussing the implications of the dawn of the atomic age—although they didn't yet recognise it as that— until late. Stalin was a night owl.

The atomic bomb may not have made much impact on the Russian public—the newspapers *Izvestiia* and *Pravda* both carried a brief report summarising the Truman statement well back from page one—but their political leaders felt it keenly. Stalin believed that with Hiroshima the old political equilibrium he had forged with Roosevelt and Churchill was destroyed. It was depressing. There was a new reality in the world's power politics which threatened Russia. Its hard-fought victory over Germany was 'as good as wasted'. The Soviets saw themselves as much a target of the Hiroshima bombing as Japan and they were right. To them it was atomic blackmail against the USSR, a 'threat to unleash a new, even more terrible and devastating war'.

More to the immediate point was the belief that Japan would quickly surrender in the face of threats of further atomic annihilation of its cities. Russia had not yet launched its invasion of Manchuria that was to be its insurance policy for the Yalta agreements. That opportunity, it seemed, had slipped away.

◆　　◆　　◆

After a sleepless night in a Hiroshima air-raid shelter, Akira Iwanaga and Kuniyoshi Sato returned to the ruins of their boarding house. Sifting through the rubble that once was their home, the Nagasaki visitors retrieved the bags they had packed the morning before and headed across the city to Koi railway station in the west. A dust cloud kept the sky dark. Sewing machines and bicycles lay burning on the ground. There were dead animals and corpses along every road and in the rivers. The smell of smoke and death hung in the air. At one point where a bridge had collapsed the men waded through a river, pushing their way through floating bodies.

Down by the beach in the early morning gloom, Tsutomu Yamaguchi crawled from under his fishing boat shelter, still agonisingly aware of his burns. He had not eaten for a day, his only sustenance being water leaking from broken pipes. Uncertain what to do, he wandered aimlessly until he overheard that a train was leaving Koi station for Nagasaki in the afternoon. In his pain, it never occurred to Yamaguchi to go back to the boarding house and look for his packed bag. He meandered towards the station, past blackened bodies lying in the streets. One was burnt to the bones in its lower half, with charred heart and organs exposed above. Yamaguchi's brain was numb from the constant pain and the horror. His listless body moved forward like an automaton. His ordered universe gone, his destination was the only thought he could retain.

He tried to cross the river with its carpet of dead bodies by crawling over the corpses on his hands and knees. A body sank under his weight and Yamaguchi slid into the water, painfully wetting his burnt skin. Getting back to dry land, he walked upstream until he found a bridge with a single beam still spanning the river and inched his way to the other side. Men were stacking truckloads of bodies in piles there. The corpses were doused in oil and cremated. Black oily smoke rose to join the dusty haze.

The last bridge in Yamaguchi's westward journey was a railway trestle. He had to balance painfully on a narrow steel rail high above the water. Near Koi station a crowd had gathered silently around an aluminium capsule said to have been dropped by parachute at the same time as the bomb. The bystanders craned their necks and pushed politely to get a better view of the artefact dumped in their midst. Uncertain that it wasn't another bomb, two policemen tried unsuccessfully to keep the crowd at bay. Nearby a woman sang a lullaby to a dead baby. Another lay naked at a shelter entrance, her breast torn apart. A baby played alongside her dead body. In the eerie silence the woman's lullaby sounded like it was being piped in from some other place, as if it was coming from the speakers of a public address system. The singing was the only human voice that had registered in Yamaguchi's hearing since the overheard conversation about the train to Nagasaki.

◆　◆　◆

The great coral ridge of Tinian had been half-levelled to become a US Army Air Forces base of six runways, each 3 kilometres long and ten lanes wide. Hundreds of planes stood beside the runways in long rows. From the air it looked like a giant aircraft carrier with B-29s taking off every quarter-hour. Nature had capitulated to human engineering.

Cleared of its native population by the Spanish after a 1670 massacre of missionaries, the land had been used for grazing and as a leper colony before being sold to Germany. Japan seized the Marianas Islands, except for Guam, at the outbreak of World War I. With a 1922 mandate from the League of Nations, the Japanese government leased Tinian to grow sugar cane and build two sugar mills, the labour force growing rapidly to 18,000 Japanese and Korean workers.

In July 1944 the US captured Tinian, although pockets of enemy soldiers remained hiding in the jungle. A year later, they had ceased to be much more than a nuisance. Japan had built four airstrips on the island; they were extended and enlarged for American bomber use. North Field No. 3 was used for many of the firebombing raids and was now to be used for atomic missions as well. When Idlewild Airport (now JFK) opened in New York in 1947, it was the largest commercial airport in the world. Its peak was half the capacity of Tinian's North Field No. 3.

The team of Project Alberta, the bomb delivery component of the Manhattan Project, had been on Tinian since mid-June. Deak Parsons, who had been second in command to Oppenheimer at Los Alamos, was in charge. The Tinian joint chiefs were Parsons, General Thomas Farrell deputising for General Groves, and Rear-Admiral WR Purnell as the navy's nominee, with little to contribute in practice. Four air-conditioned steel arch rib huts had been constructed on the project site, with two special pits fitted with hydraulic lifts for loading assembled bombs into the aircraft.

The project's engineers, scientists and technicians rose on 7 August at six in the morning. In the routine they had established for themselves, they breakfasted at seven and got straight down to the day's work. The day after Little Boy was dropped on Hiroshima, the team began assembly of the next bomb, the plutonium-cored Fat Man, in the air-conditioned steel hut known as 'the shed'. The workers there didn't call the weapon they assembled a bomb. It was always 'the gadget'.

The nickname for the new bomb had come from Project Alberta scientist Robert Serber, after the character in *The Maltese Falcon* played by Sidney Greenstreet. Serber, a fan of hard-boiled detective novels, had previously given the name Thin Man to Little Boy's predecessor, after another Dashiell Hammett novel. When the plutonium bomb was developed in its own casing, the original dual-purpose casing was substantially shortened and its name changed. Either Serber didn't have a Hammett reference for that one or conjuring names for bombs had been taken over by someone else. The bombs are often said to be named after Churchill and Roosevelt, but Americans don't name their bombs after British politicians. Nonetheless, correspondence regarding the bombs was written as if the references were to the two leaders in order to mask its true content. To conceal the delivery of components of Fat Man, for instance, correspondence might describe sending the belongings of the Fat Man as if they were actually Churchill's.

Originally Groves had planned for the second bomb drop to be five days after the first. His reasoning was that it should be soon enough to convince the Japanese that mass production of the weapon was possible, but enough time for them to consider surrender and act on it. That date would be 11 August. Norman Ramsey, Parsons' civilian deputy at Tinian, concluded by the seventh that the date could be brought forward to the tenth. He told Colonel Tibbets, who replied that it would be even better if Fat Man could be readied for a 9 August drop. Five days of bad weather were forecast to follow that day. Ramsey would match Tibbets' 'can-do' approach. They might have to cut a few corners, but he would tighten the schedule by two days.

Chuck Sweeney's plane, *The Great Artiste*, was still fitted out with instrumentation for measuring the blast effects at Hiroshima and special gear for dropping the recording canisters. There wasn't now enough time to remove that equipment and install it in the plane of Captain Fred Bock, whose crew was to fly the instrument plane in the second mission. Instead, Sweeney's crew would fly Bock's plane, *Bockscar*, and Bock would pilot *The Great Artiste*, already fitted out.

Fat Man was assembled under the supervision of Lieutenant-Commander Fred Ashworth, who would be weaponeer on the second mission. It was more complicated than for Little Boy and carried greater risk. Little Boy had been armed by Deak Parsons while they were flying towards Hiroshima, but the plutonium bomb would have to be armed and live when it was loaded on the plane. A crash at take-off would obliterate not only the B-29 carrying Fat Man but much of the island of Tinian as well.

Assembly of Mark III combat unit F31, Model Y 1561, as Fat Man was formally named, began with the fuses. Four sets were installed for insurance. One was timed to detonate at 43 seconds, barometric and radar detectors would fire at 600 metres (1890 feet), and a fourth fuse would be triggered on impact at ground level. If one fuse failed, there were still three calibrated to fire at or near the planned height.

Assembly technicians trod on eggshells. Over 5000 pounds of high explosive were packed around a nickel- and gold-coated sphere of plutonium the size of a cricket ball. A pea-sized ball of polonium and beryllium at its centre would initiate the chain reaction that would become a nuclear explosion. Baby powder was rubbed on parts of the 'gadget' to reduce friction during installation. The shed had a rubberised floor grounded by a copper wire grid to prevent the possibility of sparks or an unexpected heat source. Personnel wore rubber shoes and moved cautiously about the shed interior as if trying not to wake a sleeping baby.

◆　◆　◆

Sixteen-year-old Sumiteru Taniguchi left his grandmother's small wooden house on the hilly green slopes of Mount Inasa at about seven thirty. Along with his older sister and brother, he'd lived with his maternal grandmother and step-grandfather, affectionately known as Oba-chan and Ji-san, since his mother died when he was one. His father had gone to Manchuria to drive locomotives. For some time, Sumiteru had been the only one of the three siblings still living with their grandparents. His brother had followed his father to Manchuria, where he worked for the military as a radio operator. His sister had moved to Fukuoka and worked in a local post office. She had married and moved in with her husband's family in northern Kyushu. Now she had a child, but her husband had gone to war, so mother and child were staying in Nagasaki with her grandparents and younger brother.

Dressed in the 'national uniform' of khaki tunic, breeches and puttees and wearing a peaked post office cap, Sumiteru walked down the lanes and steps to the pier. A crowded early morning ferry took him across the bay to Ohato, from where he walked in the stream of anonymous office workers up to mid-town, to the main post office opposite city hall and the fire station.

Sumiteru had worked for the post office for the past two years, since leaving school at fourteen. He had not been particularly studious and, in any case, his grandparents were too poor for the cost of continuing at school. The young postman didn't get much out of schooling anyway. Militarism was in full swing and education was focused on physical training. It was wartime and they were instructed to build their bodies. They were made to work on construction of their new school. Carrying sand for building workers got them in good physical condition, but had no educative value. He was happy to leave.

Even after he left school, Sumiteru had to join drill exercises. A police officer or a military man instructed them in how to remove the ceiling to prevent incendiary bombs lodging under the roof. They were shown how to confront the Americans if they landed in Japan, making spears from bamboo, and how to pierce enemy soldiers with them.

The post office was a good place to work. In the mail and telegraph delivery section, they'd sort the mail in the morning and do deliveries in the afternoon. Because most of the older men had been called up, postal workers were mostly teenage boys and girls, and women. The boys were sent by bicycle to the outlying residential areas of the hilly city. Female postal workers delivered to downtown areas of Nagasaki and the lower end of its valleys.

Later in the morning, Sumiteru rode up Route 206 to the upper Urakami valley on his red post office bicycle. A black mailbag with a metal clasp hung off a bar on the front. Tucked into a saddlebag was his lunch box to have on the way, and a tyre repair kit. Most of the roads in the valley were unsealed, especially in the far reaches Sumiteru serviced, and punctures were frequent.

Pedalling up the valley kept him in good shape. When the gradient got too steep, he would sling the bicycle on one shoulder and climb on foot. Coasting at speed back down the streets and lanes coming off the hillsides, the wind rushing past Sumiteru's face was exhilarating. The enjoyment of the outdoors was what made the post office such a good place to work.

◆　◆　◆

When the theological college in Urakami was converted to the Urakami Dai-ichi Hospital, the Franciscans asked the Catholic Dr Nagai from Nagasaki Medical College to help out. He did so for a while, but soon found he couldn't spare the time from his university duties. Asking around, the hospital approached Dr Takahara, who had a private hospital in the city. As he had a large number of patients, he transferred some to Urakami Hospital, along with a young doctor who was sick the day he was supposed to start work. Dr Tatsuichiro Akizuki came instead and stayed.

In the hot Japanese summer of that August in 1945, Dr Akizuki was glad he was working in the hospital. It was cool inside its wards and offices. Elevation allowed the buildings to pick up any breeze that blew off the sea and up the Urakami valley. The number of doctors at the

Catholic hospital had been whittled away by the war as they were called up. All that remained were a few elderly doctors, along with Dr Akizuki as medical director. He too had been called up. It was shortly after he arrived, but he had a history of pleurisy. After three days of military drill, he was excused from service and returned to the hospital. Dr Akizuki now had the tubercular cases to attend to, along with some patients referred there by Dr Takahara.

Air-raid sirens rang out daily. The attacks were most frequent at night, between eleven and midnight. The siren would be followed by the approaching drone of a formation of unseen aircraft like a swarm of hornets. Mostly the swarm would pass by Nagasaki—the drone would grow and recede— and on to who knew where. Patients went to shelter in the basement at eleven each night. The next morning they would wonder which city had been hit the night before. It had become a daily routine.

Routine was the grim order of their lives by that stage of a war that had become increasingly desperate. Despite their situation, the people remained defiant and routine was a way of expressing it. Dr Akizuki's custom was to rise at six thirty, wash, and eat a simple breakfast made by his mother. His parents had moved into a farmer's house near the hospital, evacuating from the city where his father still worked at the law courts. Taking the one-kilometre walk to work, the doctor would arrive at the hospital at an early hour, around seven thirty, and get some of his paperwork out of the way while he sipped a cup of tea. He was a dedicated and fastidious doctor, but he was not a gregarious man. Generally eating alone at work, his reserved nature was often read by others as aloofness. About eight thirty he would start looking at patients.

Akizuki usually grabbed the opportunity to read the morning paper with breakfast. On Tuesday, 7 August, a headline in the local paper caught his eye. Not a particularly conspicuous article, but the wording disturbed him: 'New Type of Bomb Dropped on Hiroshima. Much Damage Done.' A 'new kind of bomb', he mused, not an incendiary bomb; and 'much damage' instead of the usual description of slight damage no matter how destructive the bombing might have been. Something had changed and it unsettled the doctor.

Junji Sato was also reading between the lines of the day's news reports. The 26-year-old reporter at Domei's Nagasaki bureau had heard an announcement from the military's Tokyo headquarters in the break between morning and evening transmission. The report said Hiroshima had been raided the day before by a small number of American B-29s inflicting heavy damage. A new type of bomb had been used. Details were under investigation. Sato had been in the news business long enough to know the military generally understated the reality in their reports. If they used an expression like 'fairly heavy damage', that probably meant devastation. If that could be achieved with a small number of aircraft, it was a worrying development.

Sato leant back in his stately surrounds and pondered the implications of his insight. The Domei bureau had been installed a year before in a room of a European-style red-brick house in the Nakajima valley. It was the home of a wealthy local businessman and his family. Early in 1945, the family had moved to the country and Domei had expanded to use the entire two-storey mansion with its distinctive 2-metre-high windows.

Sato's boss Yamanaka, the managing editor, was the stereotype of a senior journalist. Two metres tall, corpulent and demanding, he was a heavy drinker. He ran what was in essence an arm of the military propaganda machine. Press privilege allowed him to buy *sake* and tobacco at low official prices rather than at the prevailing market price in a time of scarcity.

Domei was the political and military arm of Japanese communications, publishing 'permissible' news and operating as a government link. When there were difficulties relaying messages between Tokyo and the regional governments, telegrams were sent through Domei's channels. The Nagasaki bureau was in contact by military telephone with the Nagasaki Fortress Command and also had a line through to its own Fukuoka office. Domei's network tentacles ran in many directions.

The agency also provided news bulletins to the general public, but with the war not faring well censorship was stricter than ever. Government and military directives were attached to most reports that were fed through the network. The Information and Intelligence Agency had merged the four Nagasaki newspapers, including Takejiro Nishioka's *Minyu*, into the one Nagasaki paper, the *Nippo*. People only heard or read what the powers deemed suitable unless, like Sato, they knew how the system worked. Then they could draw inferences like the one that now worried the young journalist.

◆   ◆   ◆

Mitsue and Setsuko, the two high school girls working in the torpedo factory workshop, were as thick as thieves. Mitsue's pet name for Setsuko was N-san (Miss N, her surname being Nakamura) and N-san called her friend the more usual Takeno-san. Japanese tend to use surnames rather than given names, even for friends. The girls would retreat each day at lunch break to a corner and talk about the things young women talked about, mostly about boys since they were never allowed to talk to them. Their chitchat was punctuated with giggles and gasps of astonishment.

For the last few weeks, they'd talked endlessly and conspiratorially about T-kun, a middle school boy working in the factory. The girls put their personal things in drawers in the work table. Once, Setsuko took a large photo out of the first-aid kit she kept in a drawer. Holding it against her chest, she teased, 'It's T-kun's photo. Want to take a look?'

'How did you get it, N-san? Let me see!'

Setsuko handed over the photo, beaming mischievously. She laughed at her best friend's disappointment when she saw it. It was not T-kun at all, but Kazuo Hasegawa, a popular movie star of the time.

A few days before, T-kun had stopped coming to work at the factory. The girls had no idea what had become of the object of their schoolgirl crush, but that day Setsuko had overheard a conversation she was dying to share with her friend. T-kun had volunteered for the Patriotic Junior Corps, it seemed. He had gone to Manchuria. Although he filled their lives for a brief period, the girls had never spoken to him and he had never spoken to them.

Takeno-san and N-san chattered on. The girls had gone to a photo studio a few days before, on a day off from work, and had a photo taken of them together. They had two prints made, one for each of them, the only memento either had of their friendship. They'd gone back to Setsuko's house that afternoon, but no-one was home. Mitsue's friend told her that her mother was actually her stepmother. Her real mother had died when she was very young, something Setsuko had never mentioned before.

Just before they were called back to work, Setsuko handed Mitsue a piece of paper on which she'd written a poem.

My little cosmos, you gentle flowers,
You are as slender as my mother in heaven.
The humming of the bees flying around you.
Is as sweet to me as the voice of my mother.

Setsuko seemed to get on well enough with her stepmother, but she couldn't replace her own mother.

◆ ◆ ◆

The Yamawaki twins, Yoshiro and Tatsuro, spent the day at home. In their final year of primary school, they had been on holiday since 20 July. Living in a large house with a large garden, lots of toys and books and four younger brothers and sisters, there was plenty to do.

The twins' younger brothers and sisters were actually the children of their father's second marriage. Their own mother had died of an illness when the twins were two. They had grown up with their father's new wife as their mother. Yasuo Yamawaki was a senior engineer at the Mitsubishi Electric Corporation near Urakami railway station in the middle of the valley. The family lived in relative privilege at the foot of Mount Inasa on the western side of the Urakami River estuary.

The four youngest were fully occupied that day. With the help of a day nanny, Mrs Yamawaki and the youngsters spent the day packing their bags, debating what they should take and what they needn't take. With increasing air-raid activity around Nagasaki in the last week or two, they were evacuating to the nearby prefecture of Saga where their mother's parents lived.

Mr Yamawaki had to go to work, so he was staying behind in Nagasaki with the three older boys. The twins' older brother, Toshihiro, was a mobilised middle school student working with the armaments factory at its relocated facility in the tunnel at Tomachi down the eastern side of Nagasaki Bay. Yoshiro and Tatsuro would soon be returning to school, but they were principally staying behind because someone had to look after the house during the day. If it got hit by a firebomb the twins were on hand to put out the fire. Ceilings in the house had been removed, as required by the authorities, so that an air-dropped napalm canister couldn't break through the tile roof and lodge above the ceiling where the fire would be harder to get to. Like most homes, the Yamawakis' had a concrete tank outside filled with water for fire-fighting.

As usual there were air-raid warnings that morning. The family went to a shelter built in their garden, but there were no attacks. The twins spent the rest of the morning with their picture books and magazines. They had few friends in the neighbourhood and their friends from school, across the river in the middle of the city, lived nowhere near them. Although there were schools around where they lived, family tradition decreed all the Yamawaki children would be educated in the commercial district.

Yasuo Yamawaki's father, the twins' grandfather, had been director-general of Nagasaki's customhouse, a position within Treasury. His sense of status had determined that his grandchildren should attend school near the government offices he frequented. The twins first went to a Buddhist kindergarten, with maids taking them to the ferry wharf at seven each morning, then to their current school at Shinkozen. Because they didn't go to a local school, they were thought snobbish by boys in the neighbourhood and picked on by local bullies. To make matters worse, their father wouldn't allow local children into their garden. The twins had each other for company whether they liked it or not, but they were happy to spend their day doing things together.

The magazines the boys read were often an extension of Japan's news-paper reporting of the war, bringing a pictorial version to new readers. Yoshiro and Tatsuro had already been told at school that, although Japan was a small country, it would win as it did when the Mongols invaded—

or attempted to—in the thirteenth century. The divine wind that blew Kublai Khan's ships around then would ultimately drive the enemy back now. History had become the handmaiden of national propaganda.

Pictures that had appeared in the press reappeared in the boys' favourite magazines: General Yamashita interrogating the Englishman, General Percival, after the fall of Singapore; Zero fighters pouncing on an enemy warship and splitting it in two; Japanese soldiers planting the Rising Sun flag on some newly occupied territory. There was no shortage of these pictorial adventures full of promise for the nation. Unbeknown to the boys, they were already hopelessly out of date.

Yoshiro and Tatsuro read newspapers as well, promoting the same message: numbers of enemy planes shot down; territory Japanese forces had captured; enemy ships sunk. Prisoners of war brought to Japan after some years in camps in South-east Asia or the Pacific were reported to be coming from a recently captured territory. There was only good news to be read. Withdrawals were 'strategic'; air-raid damage was 'minimal'. Nonetheless, the twins were warned by their parents that if they spread rumours to the contrary, the military police would come and get them. At the age of eleven, you don't have the critical faculties to read between the lines of such reports. It was a strange warning. They never heard any rumours to the contrary to spread.

◆ ◆ ◆

Each neighbourhood organised its own air-raid drills for local children. The Takigawa girls, Satsue and Ryoko, were part of a group from a few neighbouring blocks. An older man supervised the drill in the street on this Tuesday morning. He had run the exercises a few times before but Sakue didn't know who he was. He didn't introduce himself, just appeared, called the waiting children together and commenced the drill.

On other days they might rehearse resistance to invasion with their bamboo sticks, but this day was scheduled for air-raid responses. They started by practising running to the shelter. The man shouted out 'Warning issued,' and the children ran. When they came back, he shouted 'Enemy plane,' and they hid themselves. They practised falling prone on the ground, having been told that when bombs were dropped they should fall face-down where they stood. Otherwise the blast could pop their eyes out. They were instructed to cover their eyes.

Besides the shelter, which was twenty minutes' running distance away, there were small tunnels dug closer to home. You could go in one side and out the other. The day's drill included practising running into them during an air attack. 'Enemy plane,' the supervisor shouted.

Sakue had only her imagination to instruct her on the experience of an air raid. She hadn't seen much of the 1 August raid, having spent its duration in the shelter. She visualised bombs dropping around her, throwing plumes of dirt in the air, and imagined her eyes popping out and hanging on stalks. It seemed to the young girl they had spent the whole wartime trying to find out how to protect their lives, yet still little had happened from the air.

While the young girls were being instructed in how to cope with one aspect of the war, their mother and older sister were dealing with another. That morning, they were busy establishing a new vegetable patch on the edge of the playground at the girls' school at Shiroyama, located on the western side of the valley across the river from Urakami Prison. Nearby, the girls' teachers tended market gardens they had established on the school grounds for the same purpose. The various groups of working women (for the most part) would stop and chat from time to time. The camaraderie of all performing a socially useful function was a good distraction from the daily struggle of life in wartime Japan.

The staff of Shiroyama Primary School came to school every day, even though it was summer holidays. The sports fields, apart from the athletics track, were being used to grow sweet potatoes. What had once been flower gardens were now vegetable gardens. Like her teaching colleagues, Chiyoko Egashira spent the whole day there doing gardening chores to keep the school's war effort as efficient and as productive as they were able. There was fertilising and weeding to be done and vines to be turned. In the former flower gardens and any vacant areas they could find, they grew turnips, daikon and broad beans. Chiyoko felt with keen pride that the school was like a model for ways to increase food production.

Chiyoko Egashira was thirty-five years old. Her husband, Ukichi, worked at the Ohashi plant of Mitsubishi's Nagasaki arms factory, the workplace where Yoshiro Fukuda was deputy director and Torahachi Tagawa was a foreman. Like his wife, Ukichi was a teacher. He had taught at Nagasaki Commercial School, a short distance from Shiroyama Primary, but was now assigned as part of the war effort to supervising a group of mobilised students at the weapons plant.

The Egashiras had five children. Takashi, the eldest, was a mobilised student working near Ohashi for a transport and shipping company affiliated with the navy. At the other end was Naomi, the baby. On this day, as she often did, Ukichi's mother was looking after Naomi while her daughter-in-law spent the day cultivating the school's sports fields and flower beds after a frustrating early morning pursuit of rationed goods.

Before coming to work that day, Chiyoko had spent over an hour in a queue at the rationing centre. Current rations had been posted on the local bulletin board and she wanted to get in before they ran short. There was another line in front of the shop where she got her rice ration. Sometimes there would be such a shortage of goods that the sign would be put out: 'Open, but not for business.' Sometimes people would line up without knowing what was being sold.

The rice Chiyoko got that day was brown, unhulled. She could pound it in a bottle with a bamboo stick to make white rice, but the result was a smaller amount. The rice had been mixed with barley. Worse was on the way. It was expected that with the generally cool summer of that year there was a poor rice harvest coming. Imports from China and Manchuria had practically ceased.

People talked about food, not politics or the war. Street conversations were about the failure of the rationing system and the difficulty of getting food. Anything more specifically critical of the government was risky. People who overheard critical comment were required to report it to the *kempeitei* (military police). Such talk was confined to guarded conversations out of earshot of eavesdroppers.

On her way back with her meagre provisions, Chiyoko passed another line, but this one was not for food. There were now often queues for cinemas, even though they showed only old Japanese movies because of the government's prohibition of Western entertainment. The line consisted mostly of idle workers from factories that were waiting for materials to come so they could resume production.

Because of her early morning jousting with the rationing system, Chiyoko arrived at the Shiroyama school in the mid-morning. Her day was spent with a group planting out a patch of *senposai*, a Japanese green similar to spinach. They turned the soil over, dug in fertiliser and, in the afternoon, sowed seeds in a square grid. Rapid-growing *senposai* could be picked in five or six weeks. By evening, the new vegetable patch was completed. Chiyoko Egashira went home a satisfied gardener.

◆   ◆   ◆

Koichi Wada, the tram-driving student, had a day off work after nine days in a row. So did Nishimura, a conductor with the Nagasaki tram company, who had come into Nagasaki from the mountainous region of Shimabara looking for work. The two friends caught the morning train to Isahaya, and changed to a local train that took them to Nishimura's home town a short distance further on.

They had lunch with Nishimura's family, whose harvest of short-grained rice was not only self-sufficient, but produced a surplus for sale, barter or giving away. Bright and white, this rice was fluffier than Koichi had seen for a long time. The farming family was determined to show how hospitable they could be to their son's new city friend in such difficult times. Three bowls, cooked to a soft, sticky texture, then a fourth was served. The visitor's stomach was as full as he could ever remember. He thought he wouldn't need to eat again for a week, but that would prove fanciful.

This was much less risky than robbing market gardens to take the edge off his hunger. A couple of weeks before, Koichi had spent his free day with workmates from a fishing village on the coast around from Nagasaki. It was a centre for sardines where big catches of large fish were still common. The friends visited the families of the local boys, returning to the city with hand-baskets of sardines they had bought. Police routinely patrolled the railway stations looking for people coming back from black market sites with rice and vegetables, but fish wasn't confiscated like the rationed staples. Seeing the youths with baskets, the police bailed them up for inspection, but found the baskets held only sardines. They waved them on.

There had been no problem getting sardines through the police check, but rice was a rationed staple and so an altogether different matter. When Wada and Nishimura returned from Shimabara, they each had a small bag of rice and local vegetables. They knew police, who wouldn't be interested in the distinction between black market and gifts, would be stopping people at Urakami and Nagasaki stations. The produce was supposed to go into the ration system and the police would confiscate it.

As the train approached Urakami station, the young men flung their bags out the window at a spot by Ohashi Bridge where there weren't people walking about. They noted a landmark, a tree with two distinctive flattened layers of foliage, to guide them back to where the bags lay near the tracks. Getting off the train at Urakami, the boys pushed through disembarking and boarding passengers on the station, past police mingling in the crowd peering intently at any packages they carried.

As soon as Koichi and his friend were clear of the station, they raced back to where they had thrown their bags. Not a minute was to be wasted. The longer they delayed, the greater the chance that someone would come across the bags and take them. When the friends got to the landmark tree, they poked around in a small clump of bushes beside the railway line. To their relief, the bags were still there, partly obscured by bushes. They waited until twilight dimmed to night before making their way to their respective homes, taking circuitous routes to avoid police *kuban* (booths) placed on many of the street corners.

Unlike the stolen vegetables, this generous gift from the Nishimuras could be shared with Koichi's own family. His grandparents might have objected to robbing a market gardener of his livelihood, having known many in their working days, but they had no compunction about skirting around the ration system to their benefit.

First, the rice was used to make the thin rice porridge, *okayu*, that they ate each morning. Koichi's younger sister took some of the new rice for her contribution to the meals ahead. Chiyoko made *zosui*, the rice gruel cooked up with whatever vegetables were available and boiled with *miso*, soy sauce or some other stock. She added daikon radish to the *zosui*. Enough was made for the Wadas to alternate *zosui* and the remaining sardine-flavoured dumplings for the next few days. It was something they could look forward to with unaccustomed relish.

The variety was a blessed relief from the discouragingly shrunken sameness of Koichi Wada's meals. On this Tuesday evening, he settled for a small serve, since he had lunched so well. By the following evening, the family would start to keep the meals small to ensure there was enough to spread across the ration timetable. The following evening, Koichi would discover he was hungry once again. In the absence of any end that could be seen to their austerity, he returned to the subject that consumed his thinking most days: how could he fill his empty stomach?

Chapter 7

Nagasaki, Tuesday 7 August 1945

Marquis Koichi Kido, Lord Keeper of the Privy Seal, walked briskly through Fukiage Gardens on his way to meet with Emperor Hirohito. It was one thirty in the afternoon on 7 August. Since the May firebombing, Hirohito had moved his residence into the Imperial Library with its construction of reinforced concrete. The emperor had learnt about Hiroshima from a military aide the day before. He was a worried man with many questions to ask his closest adviser. Kido told him of the Truman statement, picked up by Domei's monitors, and of the claim that it was an atomic bomb.

The emperor asked, 'Has all this been confirmed?' and was told there was no doubt about the damage, but the army had doubts about whether it was an atomic bomb. Hirohito looked away in silence, lost in thought.

Kido wrote some years later that the emperor concluded by saying, 'If things have come to this, there is no other way. I don't care what happens to me personally, but we should lose no time ending the war so we don't have another tragedy like this.' Hirohito's resolve in response to the bomb might be overstated here—there is no mention of the statement in Kido's diary of the time—but it reflects his general view of the state of the war at that time. The diary of the emperor's aide-de-camp notes that Hirohito continued to ask questions about Hiroshima after Kido had left.

About the same time, Foreign Minister Togo spoke to his cabinet colleagues, War Minister Anami and Army Chief of Staff Umezu. Leading voices in the faction arguing for Japan to fight on, the two military men claimed the bomb did not seem to be an atomic bomb, but an extremely powerful conventional bomb. Togo responded that the army should conduct an urgent investigation to resolve this.

While America gave the Japanese leadership a short time to ponder the implications of the Hiroshima bomb, there was to be no let-up in the program of firebombing Japan's cities and installations. On 7 August an attack by 124 B-29s on a naval ammunition plant in Toyokawa resulted in 1408 killed, many of them high school girls working in the factory.

◆ ◆ ◆

General 'Hap' Arnold cabled Guam with instructions to rush an airdrop of leaflets on Japan and to step up radio broadcasts on Japanese domestic frequencies. While on Tinian bomb parts were being checked before being installed in Fat Man's metal casing, on the neighbouring island of Saipan the US Office of War Information started designing leaflets calling on the Japanese people to petition their emperor to end the war. Printing presses had been captured from the Japanese when the American marines landed on the Pacific island. It was planned to airdrop sixteen million of the leaflets on forty-seven Japanese cities over the next nine days.

Earlier attempts at propaganda had not been very effective. Using archaic or inept phrases in Japanese, they showed men wearing kimonos like women, and chopsticks placed like a knife and fork. The Japanese had reacted to them in much the same way Westerners respond today to fractured English ('Chinglish') on Asian T-shirts. The initial mistakes had since been rectified and the message was now strong, with the Japanese more convincing. It said (in translation):

TO THE JAPANESE PEOPLE:
America asks that you take immediate heed of what we say on this leaflet.

We are in possession of the most destructive explosive ever devised by man. A single one of our newly developed atomic bombs is actually the equivalent in explosive power to what 2000 of our giant B-29's can carry on a single mission. This awful fact is one for you to ponder and we solemnly assure you it is grimly accurate.

We have just begun to use this weapon against your homeland. If you still have any doubt, make inquiry as to what happened to Hiroshima when just one atomic bomb fell on that city.

Before using this bomb to destroy every resource of the military by which they are prolonging this useless war, we ask that you now petition the Emperor to end the war. Our President has outlined for you the thirteen consequences of an honorable surrender. We urge that you accept these consequences and begin the work of building a new, better, and peace-loving Japan.

You should take steps now to cease military resistance. Otherwise, we shall resolutely employ this bomb and all our other superior weapons to promptly and forcefully end the war.
EVACUATE YOUR CITIES.

Three Japanese prisoners helped with translation of the text. One of them suggested dropping a two-page, Japanese-language tabloid newspaper with the leaflets. They were designed and written with the prisoner's assistance, describing the Hiroshima strike and carrying a photo of the atomic cloud taken from *Enola Gay*. Half a million of them were printed.

In addition to the airdrop of leaflets and newspapers, the propaganda campaign included broadcast of news bulletins by shortwave radio from Saipan every fifteen minutes. Tokyo Rose had been turned around. Another plan was to broadcast propaganda messages through loudspeakers on planes flying at low altitude over Japanese urban areas. This proposal never materialised. Someone pointed out that it's hard to hear a message over the engine roar of a low-flying aircraft.

◆   ◆   ◆

At the meeting of cabinet called by Prime Minister Suzuki for that after-noon, War Minister Anami and Home Minister Abe provided reports on the Hiroshima bombing, to the extent it was understood. Foreign Minister Togo informed the meeting that President Truman had announced that an atomic bomb had been used. Togo argued that the advent of a weapon of its power offered a reason for the military to terminate the war and that the military should consider doing so on the basis of the Potsdam Declaration. He suggested such a bomb enabled the military leaders to blame 'the backwardness of scientific research' for Japan's inability to continue the war.

This is somewhat unfair to Japan's scientists. In 1943, then-prime minister Tojo had urged development of a Japanese atomic bomb under Dr Yoshio Nishina, an internationally respected physicist. The project moved slowly, in part because of difficulty in obtaining the uranium ore, pitchblende. A 2-tonne shipment by submarine from Czechoslo-vakia was intercepted by the Allies and never reached Japan. Some ore arrived late in 1944, but the mines in Czechoslovakia and Saxony were bombed by the US before the advancing Red Army could get to them. April raids on Tokyo destroyed the main research facility, followed by the loss of Nishina Laboratories' centrifugal separator. The project had ground to a halt. Its lack of progress was as much to do with the mili-tary's inability to keep the enemy at bay as with any shortcomings of Japan's scientists.

Military members of cabinet—the chiefs of staff of the army and the navy, their deputies and War Minister Anami—argued at the meeting that the Hiroshima bomb might be no more than a huge conventional weapon with Truman's press statement calculated to deceive the Japanese into thinking it was more. 'The fact that President Truman announced it does not necessarily make it true,' Anami pointed out. The Americans might, for instance, have devised a proximity fuse to detonate a bomb in the air. It was known that a bomb blast in the air could do considerably more damage than one exploding on impact with the ground. In fact, the Japanese had developed such a device themselves, but had not yet had an opportunity to use it, so depleted was their capacity to fly.

One of the military men recalled an old Japanese legend about an army commander who mistook the fluttering of a flight of birds for the sound of the approaching enemy and fled. They insisted the Truman statement should be kept from the Japanese people until the army's investigation team, already under way, was able to report back.

Admiral Soemu Toyoda, the Chief of Navy General Staff, added a rider in case the investigation revealed it was in fact an atomic bomb. The United States, he said, could only have a few bombs at most and world opinion would intervene to stop another 'inhuman atrocity' before it could use even those. This prompted Togo to recommend to cabinet a further measure if the bomb was confirmed as atomic. In that eventuality, he proposed, the Japanese government should register a protest through the International Red Cross and the Swiss legation about a serious US violation of international law prohibiting use of poisonous gas in warfare. Cabinet agreed.

◆ ◆ ◆

The crush that jammed Koi railway station was the result of refugees trying to get out of Hiroshima. There was only one train and it was going to Nagasaki. Tsutomu Yamaguchi managed to find a seat on it. Feeling ill with high fever, he was vomiting frequently. Thirst tore at his throat. Through the window he saw water dripping from a pipe, but he didn't want to lose his seat. He also saw his friend Iwanaga in the urgently surging crowd, pushing his way towards a nearby carriage. Iwanaga and Sato had reached the station and muscled their way through the crowds pressing to get on the Nagasaki train. They were separated in the crush and got into different cars. The three shipyard co-workers from Nagasaki waited silently in their three separate carriages for the start of the journey that would take them home.

When the train finally pulled out of Koi station, a railway employee handed out boiled rice. It was Yamaguchi's first food for two days. Up the other end of the train, Sato sat opposite a young man clasping on his knees a large bundle wrapped untidily in cloth. The bundle smelt badly, but with every lurch of the moving carriage the man tightened his grip on it. Sato asked him what it was. 'I married a month ago, but my wife died yesterday. I want to take her home to her parents,' he said and lifted the cloth. Even after all he'd already seen Sato felt a wave of revulsion. In an upturned helmet lay the severed head of the young man's wife.

◆   ◆   ◆

Lieutenant-General Seizo Arisue boarded one of two military DC-3s standing in a camouflaged bunker at an air base west of Tokyo. Arisue, the chief of the Army Intelligence Bureau, led a twenty-man investigation team, a mix of army personnel and civilians, to find out what they could about the Hiroshima bomb. In the group was the physicist Dr Nishina, head of the research team that had been developing an atomic bomb for Japan. As the men boarded the aircraft, an air-raid siren sounded. American bombers had been sighted approaching Osaka. Arisue decided the army staff would leave immediately, but the civilians would have to make their own decision about whether to take the risk. They decided they would and took off soon after in the second plane.

The army group arrived at the Hiroshima airfield as dusk was approaching. The plane circled above a lifeless wasteland a few times, landing on a grass strip near the harbour. Pieces of planes and collapsed buildings were scattered around the airfield. Arisue stepped out into a landscape so disconcertingly unfamiliar it could have been the moon. Every blade of grass had turned brown. Each was bent in the direction of the sea. 'I looked towards the town and found nothing obstructing my view,' Arisue later recalled, 'except a solitary tree scorched totally black. Nobody came to meet us. We waited until a man came tottering out of a nearby shelter. It turned out to be the commander of the airport defence unit.'

Half the face of the saluting lieutenant-colonel, the left half, was red and inflamed. The other side was untouched. Bizarrely, the officer was excited about a conclusion he had drawn: everything exposed gets burned, but anything covered escapes the burns, suggesting possible countermeasures against future attacks.

The military men waited in the dark for the second plane to arrive, but eventually gave it away. They were taken by motor launch to the army shipping depot at Ujina, from where the early reports of Hiroshima had come. They were met there by a friend of Arisue from the military academy. General Hideo Baba had lost his daughter that day, killed on the way to school by the bomb. It wasn't a time to swap memories of training days together. The visitors were told there was no water or electricity in Hiroshima. They sat gloomily at long tables lit by candles, but no-one had much to say. They had no idea what had become of the civilian members of their investigation team, but their plane couldn't land anyway in the pitch dark of night. In fact, the civilians' aircraft had developed engine trouble and returned to the air base.

Later that night, in a preliminary report to Tokyo written by candle-light, the intelligence chief recommended that both soldiers and civilians wear white clothing to protect themselves against flash burns. The sugges-tion of the officer with the half-burned face had found its mark.

Unknown to Arisue or his superiors in Tokyo, the Imperial Japanese Navy was conducting its own investigation of the destruction of Hiro-shima. With intense rivalry running between the two services, the army and the navy would sometimes work cooperatively but just as often would be in competition or even at cross-purposes.

Captain Mitsuo Fuchida had been an observer at an army planning conference at Hiroshima, but was called away on 5 August to attend to some issues in central Honshu. A navy chief phoned Fuchida there, told him what he knew about Hiroshima—which wasn't much—and sent him to investigate the blast site with some navy engineers flying in from Tokyo. Fuchida was to meet the group at Field Marshal Hata's headquar-ters on the slopes of Mount Futaba. Reports had come in from Kure naval base nearby that a second object had been dropped over Hiroshima from one of the B-29s. It could be an unexploded bomb.

By the time Fuchida was flying over Okayama, he could see smoke drifting up from Hiroshima ahead. He tried to contact the army airfield but got no reply. Flying over the eastern side of the city he saw through the smoke that fires were still burning, but the city was no longer there.

Fuchida landed at the airport, its control tower demolished, and got out of his plane. There was no transport about and nobody to ask about it. He walked into the city in his clean naval uniform, past bleeding, staggering people. Some were naked; some had blisters like bubbles on skin burnt dark purple. Fuchida, who led the attack on Pearl Harbor in 1941, was speechless. He'd never seen anything like it.

Eventually he shouted, 'What happened?' Most seemed not to hear him. A few shrugged. Some spoke, but had little to say as if they didn't really understand the question. Walking on, Fuchida talked to rescue workers and soldiers, beginning to piece together a picture of what had happened to Hiroshima.

Fuchida got to Hata's shelter as darkness fell, meeting up with Captain Yasukado Yasui and his party of navy engineers from Tokyo. Huddled underground with local survivors, they were told of an unexploded bomb that had come down by parachute. That night there were two investigation teams in Hiroshima, one from the army on the harbourside and one from the navy in the north of the city, but neither knew of the presence of the other.

◆　◆　◆

Dutch POWs had left Nagasaki's Camp 14 at five thirty that morning for the 3.5 kilometre march to Mitsubishi's shipyards. There was little building of ships taking place. Their day was spent clearing debris left behind by the previous week's air attack.

The Australian, Allan Chick, had been escorted to the foundry next door to the camp at eight that morning for his daily shift. Only a handful were working at the furnace because of Mitsubishi's reduced output. Chick's job on this day, as it was the day before, was to knock the spurs off metal castings after they came out of their mould, the molten leaks where the halves of the mould were joined. The parts currently being cast were hawse-holes, oval rings with thickened bases through which a ship's anchor is fed. Having worked as a fisherman himself at one time, Chick recognised what he was making on this occasion, although often he didn't know and didn't really care.

It wasn't that Chick was antagonistic to his captors. The slightly built, shy farm boy from St Helens, Tasmania, kept to himself. Not the talkative

type, he didn't smoke or drink, although the latter was of no conse-
quence here. To him, this place 'could have been an Australian camp' for
all that he went through. Camp 14 seldom had the frustrated brutality
characteristic of most of Japan's other POW camps.

At five, Chick was marched the short distance back to camp with
the other POWs working in the foundry. The Dutch returned from the
shipyard at six. Peter McGrath-Kerr too was brought back to Camp 14
at the end of his shift in the motor workshop of the Mitsubishi foundry.
He'd spent the day dismantling and repairing motor tricycles and fash-
ioning ad hoc spanners from truck springs. Tomorrow, he'd been told,
he would be working on the damaged bridge over a small service canal
nearby. A sergeant in the Intelligence section of 2/40th AIF (Australian
Imperial Force), McGrath-Kerr had been captured in Timor waiting for
reinforcements from Darwin. A quiet, thoughtful man, the Tasmanian
took life as it came, good, bad or indifferent. Getting belligerent with his
captors made no sense to him. Much better to keep a low profile. Life
in the prison camp could then at least be tolerable and the possibility of
emerging from it alive significantly better.

While the guards' actions in Camp 14 might have fallen short of
atrocities, they did include moments of institutional bullying. If prisoners
couldn't remember words they were expected to know in Japanese, they
got a slap (*binta*) on the face. Sometimes they were made to slap each
other as punishment and, if they didn't slap hard enough, guards would
step in and slap them both. If a prisoner was too tall, he was made to
kneel so the guard could administer the *binta*.

In the wartime conditions, illness was rampant. Many POWs brought
dysentery and beri-beri with them from the tropics, but the biggest killer
was pneumonia during the harsh winters. Bodies of dead prisoners were
placed in coffins and carried under guard to the crematorium across the
river. Ashes in a box, labelled with name, age and date of death, were
placed in the foreigners' graveyard at Sakamoto.

With poor sanitation, fleas and lice were endemic throughout POW
camps in Japan, especially in summer. The unwelcome residents lurked
between floorboards, and in the straw matting and thin blankets of camps.

The men would routinely kill all fleas they could find in their blankets before going to bed. That way, they'd get some sleep before the fleas came back.

As he wandered up the corridor in his barracks, McGrath-Kerr observed his pale work trousers accumulating dark specks. By the time he got to the other end, he was black to the knees with fleas. He brushed and shook them off and walked slowly back. The result was the same. It was the sort of activity POWs used to while away the time: a study for no particular purpose to establish something already known.

Dormitory rooms contained twenty double bunks, each with an open drawer at the head. There was a table and chair between bunks. The men slept on *tatami* mats, with a hard blanket, an unbleached calico sheet and a small canvas pillow filled with sawdust. A bare 15-watt light bulb hung from the ceiling. It was required to be left on all night.

Having left at an early hour, the men who had been working on the new air-raid shelter had already returned and were hanging around waiting for the evening meal, such as it was. They were on the morning shift. In the rush to get the shelter completed before the next air attack, two shifts were digging the tunnel. At the end of the shift, the men were preserving what little strength their malnutrition allowed, sitting around smoking or just lying on their bunks. McGrath-Kerr told his roommates he'd been ordered to join the next day's shelter construction gang to work on the bridge.

Rice and other ingredients were provided for POWs to prepare meals in Camp 14. Food was as scarce as it was for the general populace. A typical meal was a bowl of rice—often extended with a little barley and kaffir corn—with a cup of *miso* soup and some pickles. A small piece of meat was provided from time to time, but as the war continued the meat became more and more infrequent, eventually disappearing. In earlier days, before the survivors of the *Tamahoko Maru* joined the camp, Iwanaga the cook would go regularly to the fish co-op with five of the Dutch POWs to get provisions. Shortages and rationing had put an end to that.

A horse had died after bringing a cartload of scrap to the foundry. That night the camp residents had their first fresh meat stew for some time. It was the exception that highlights the rule, and the rule was a desperate scarcity of food. Hunger and illness were critical problems, even if conditions at Fukuoka Camp 14 were milder than at other camps. The original commandant is said to have been reported for lenient treatment of the prisoners and replaced.

◆　◆　◆

In the warmth of the late afternoon sun, Sumiteru Taniguchi the postman made his way home by ferry across Nagasaki Bay and up to his grand-mother's house underneath Mount Inasa. He'd left his red bicycle behind at the main post office. Often he worked a night shift and when he finished after the last ferry he was allowed to ride home on the post office bicycle.

When he'd got back to base that afternoon, his supervisor was waiting to tick him off. Sometimes Sumiteru would ride down sets of steps where they weren't too steep. It was a bit of boyish derring-do for the teenager, showing off his riding skills. Some unknown person with a strong sense of civic duty had apparently spotted him and reported it. The supervisor was not pleased.

'This will damage post office property,' he said.

Sumiteru assured him he wouldn't do it again, but he knew he would.

By the time he got home he'd already forgotten about the repri-mand. It was no big deal. His grandmother and sister were working in the vegetable garden so he gave them a hand. Oba-chan grew enough crops in patches around the house—soybeans, maize, potatoes, tomatoes, cucumbers—for the family to be self-sufficient. She also kept chickens and rabbits, and silk worms on mulberry bushes. The animals provided fertiliser for the gardens, but human fertiliser was far more productive.

As dusk approached, Oba-chan (her real name was Sakataro) did her regular round of the neighbourhood, collecting human manure for her crops. She was paid to collect the toilet waste and this supplemen-ted the irregular earnings of Ji-san and the money Sumiteru brought in from his postman's pay. Oba-chan had married again after her first

husband, Sumiteru's grandfather, had died. Ji-san didn't work much, occasionally providing labour to builders, carpenters and plasterers around
the district when the work was available. With the trickle of income
and two extra mouths to feed, the family wasn't wealthy, but Oba-chan's
crops and animals kept them going. By 1945, there wasn't much they
could buy anyway with the little money they had.

◆　◆　◆

With no head of the family present, the Takigawas were finishing their
modest dinner when the air-raid siren howled. Sakue and Ryoko put
down their meal and grabbed their padded air-raid hoods, little Tamashii's mother strapping him to Sakue's back. In the evening gloom, the
two young girls ran along the levee path alongside the river. As there was
no railing and with the baby in their care, they had to tread carefully to
ensure they didn't stumble off the edge of the path. In twenty minutes,
Sakue, Ryoko and Tamashii reached the shelter, dug into a hill above a
park.

The girls had wanted their mother to come with them—they always
did—but she had other responsibilities. Mother and older daughter were
required to stand by for fire-fighting at a nearby concrete tank filled with
water. The girls ran to the shelter without their mother and waited for
the all-clear to sound.

For some time, neither Sakue nor Ryoko had any idea that the adults
they called 'Mum' and 'Dad', Miwa and Maseru Takigawa, were not in
fact their parents. This couple was actually their aunt and uncle, the two
girls being the children of Mrs Takigawa's younger brother, Tomosaku
Kawasaki, and his wife.

Kawasaki had migrated to Japan's colony in Manchuria, renamed
Manchukuo. He worked with Manchurian Railways and married an
expatriate Japanese woman. They had two small children. Sakue, born in
1935, was named after the hero's family in a popular story, *Human Bullets:
Three Brave Warriors*. In that tale, the warriors held bombs to themselves
and ran at the enemy. Two years later, Ryoko was born and named after
a major railway junction not far from the Manchurian capital. Ostensi-

bly there to contribute to Japan's development of this backward region, Kawasaki was able to send considerable wealth back to his family in Kyushu, Mrs Takigawa's family.

Much of the native population of Manchuria viewed the Japanese who had settled there as invaders, the civilian arm of Japan's Kwantung Army. Hatred consumed some Manchurians. In 1938, when Sakue was three and Ryoko one, their father was kidnapped from alongside the railway line, with five senior officials of the railway company.

At knife-point, Kawasaki and his fellow captives dug a hole in the ground. When it was large enough, they were tied up and pushed in. The bandits (or insurgents, depending on your point of view) dumped soil on top of them, stamping it down with their feet. Forced to dig their own grave, the six Japanese had been buried alive.

Kawasaki's older sister, Miwa, happened to be in Manchuria at the time, visiting other members of the family. Mrs Takigawa took her nieces home to Nagasaki and she and her husband treated the little girls from that point on as if they were their own children. They were still called Kawasaki and, too young to understand, had never questioned the different surname until they went to school. Asked why her family name was different, Sakue in turn asked her mother and was told the story of her real father and mother.

The girls' natural mother stayed on in Manchuria, but didn't keep in contact with her dead husband's family or with her daughters in their care. It was said she had remarried and started a new life in the colony.

◆　◆　◆

In the evening, Togo and Anami met at the latter's temporary residence near the Imperial Palace in Tokyo. As leading spokesman for the army, the war minister was arguably the most powerful man in the Japanese government even if he lacked the drive and charisma of some of his predecessors. Keeping himself in good shape with archery and fencing, he presented to the younger officers as a dependable paternal figure. He did nothing to dissuade them of that impression. Their belief that, unquestioning, he would continue the war Japan had undertaken ensured their support. As with the military's two chiefs of staff, however, Anami was the captive of the firebrands of Japan's armed forces.

Togo and Anami were the dominant figures in the two opposing groups, the 'peace' and 'war' factions, competing to guide the country's destiny. They talked informally for over two hours but resolved little. Anami agreed with Togo's opinion that defeat was only a matter of time, but he argued that continuing the war could put Japan in a better position to extract concessions when the time came. In any case Anami, unlike Togo, had a constituency of hotheads to keep happy.

Anami's diary entry for 7 August concedes that Hiroshima was attacked by an atomic bomb. That day, he wrote, he had privately consulted some of Japan's physicists about the implications. He was keeping a delicate balance between his growing suspicions and the demands of the military's hard-liners in his pursuit of the best option in his nation's surrender scenarios.

◆　◆　◆

By the end of the afternoon, the assembly team at Tinian had completed the tense operation of carefully setting the internal mechanism into Fat Boy's casing. Two spherical halves were ready to be bolted together. In the haste to complete assembly within the shortened schedule, many of the safety-check procedures were skipped. The shed had become so crowded that project chief Deak Parsons had to order non-essential personnel out. In the heightened atmosphere, surrounded by double fencing and armed sentries, some of those leaving thought they saw a Japanese boat with frogman saboteurs. The suspected operation was never reported and the supposed saboteurs never revealed themselves.

The air force is a military service that runs to a considerable degree on swagger. The US force is no exception to this generalisation, but Chuck Sweeney didn't sit clearly inside the mould. He wasn't a complex man. He read a bit and thought a bit, thought about 'things'. Sweeney was no radical. Stolidly Roman Catholic, he was conventionally middle class about what was 'right and proper'. He was flattered by the responsibility given to him in the next mission, but something was niggling and it had to be put to rest. He wanted to be persuaded.

In the Tinian dusk, the Irish-American airman borrowed a jeep, drove over to a neighbouring group of 313th Bombardment Wing and hunted down their priest. He could have met with Captain Downey, the Lutheran minister assigned to the 509th, he explains in his memoirs, but as a devout Catholic he wanted to talk with a priest. He doesn't mention that the 509th had a Catholic chaplain as well, in Father George Zabelka. Later Zabelka spoke out, critical of his own silence at the time about the moral issues implicit in the bombing missions. It might be that Sweeney didn't take a shine to Zabelka or that it was actually Zabelka he met. By the time he wrote his memoir, Sweeney might have wanted to avoid being caught up in the controversy Zabelka was creating for himself. Chuck Sweeney shunned controversy and disliked conflict.

Sweeney was looking for someone to work through the issues that were troubling him. As he tells it, he and the priest walked over to the open-air theatre where Sunday services were held. Sweeney was asked if he wanted to confess, but no, he just wanted to talk. He had 'things' on his mind that he needed to get clear. Sweeney wanted to know if war and the brutal actions in it could sometimes be 'justified'. The discussion ranged over the 'sneak attack' on Pearl Harbor, the '300,000 unarmed civilians' slaughtered in the Rape of Nanking, the conquering and 'enslavement' of Asia by Japan—all the points one side might drag out in a debate they weren't having about US policy and the dropping of the atomic bomb. They talked about medieval theologian and philosopher Saint Thomas Aquinas and concluded that some situations render a war just.

Sweeney took the discussion to the next stage. Could weapons that cause widespread destruction be justified, he wondered without mentioning either Hiroshima or the second atomic bomb that was now due to be dropped in two days' time. The priest put it like this: war is mass destruction; the death of one person is no less tragic than the death of ten thousand, but you must be certain of the cause for which it is done and of your intentions.

By this point of the discussion, the two men were sitting in darkness by the restless swell of the Pacific Ocean. Sweeney lapsed into thoughtful silence, satisfied with the answers, running through them again in his mind.

◆ ◆ ◆

At ten that evening, a report was sent to Tokyo from an air base south-west of Hiroshima. It summarised the intelligence it had accumulated to that point, mostly through eyewitness accounts. The bomb, the report said, had been dropped by a formation of between one and four planes. Some said it was attached to a parachute. It exploded a short distance above the ground with a 'blinding flash and a violent blast' that people were calling *pika-don* (flash-boom). Over the centre of the city, the two were almost simultaneous, but on the outskirts the blast came two or three seconds later, followed by a mass of white smoke billowing up into the sky.

'The flash was instantaneous, burning objects in the immediate vicinity, burning the exposed parts of people's bodies as far as three kilometres away, and setting fire to their thin clothing.'

The report went on to describe the damage and injuries sustained, noting particularly injury by burns from the flash and by objects shat-tered by the blast. Among the countermeasures suggested were to keep a strict watch even for a small number of planes. By the end of the day after the bomb was dropped on Hiroshima, the Japanese military was starting to get a good fix on the new weapon and what it could do. The Japanese people, however, were not much the wiser.

Chapter 8

Nagasaki, Wednesday 8 August 1945

In Moscow on the afternoon of 7 August, seven hours behind Tokyo, the Soviet–Chinese negotiations resumed after being suspended for the Potsdam Conference. Premier TV Soong and the new Foreign Minister Wang Shih-chieh flew to Moscow from Chungking. They were met at the airport by Molotov and US Ambassador to the USSR, Averell Harriman. While the two were waiting, the American asked Molotov what he imagined the Japanese would be thinking of the atomic bomb. 'I haven't heard yet,' said Molotov and then added, 'You Americans can keep a secret when you want to.' He knew, but Harriman didn't, that the Americans had done no such thing.

Molotov later told the Chinese delegation that Japan was on the verge of collapse. The parties should try to conclude their negotiations before that happened rather than risk having things unresolved when hostilities ceased.

The Japanese also wanted a meeting with Molotov, having heard the previous day that he and Stalin had returned to Moscow. Togo had sent an urgent cable instructing Sato to see Molotov immediately and demand an early reply. The diplomat had contacted deputy foreign affairs minister Lozovsky again to get an answer from Molotov on the proposed Konoye mission. He got no reply. Now, with the extent of Hiroshima's destruction clearer, Togo was getting desperate. Another cable was sent:

7 August 1945   1540 hours
From: Togo
To: Sato
No. 993

Regarding your No. 1519. The situation is becoming so acute that we must have a clarification of the Soviet attitude as soon as possible. Please make further efforts to obtain a reply immediately.

Sato received his foreign minister's cable in the late morning. A couple of hours later, his patience just about exhausted, he once again contacted Lozovsky and requested a meeting with the Soviet foreign minister. The request came as a bolt from the blue to Lozovsky. It was as unexpected to him as it would be when he passed it on to Molotov and Stalin. This was not the request of a country preparing to surrender, but of one that intended to press on regardless. Lozovsky had to do some fast thinking. He said that Molotov had just left for the airport, but that he would get back to Sato when he returned later in the afternoon. Sato had heard it all before. This exercise continued to go nowhere, as he always thought it would.

When Stalin heard of the Japanese request, he sprang into action. His assumption that the Far East had slipped from his grasp was incorrect. Japan had not surrendered and was not considering it. The imperial forces were going to fight on, no matter how futile this might seem to the outsider. This presented an opportunity for the USSR to play itself back into the Far East game. Stalin's despondent mood turned to elation.

At four thirty that afternoon, Stalin and General Antonov signed an order for the Red Army to invade Manchuria. It was to move into action as soon as it could. Although negotiations with the Chinese hadn't reached agreement, Stalin would wait no longer. If agreement was reached in that evening's talks, well and good; if not, the drive into

Manchuria would go ahead anyway. The Soviet leader issued the order for his Supreme Commander in the Far East, Marshal Vasilevsky, to begin the Manchurian operation at midnight on 9 August. Vasilevsky ordered the three fronts on the Manchurian border and the Pacific Fleet, already standing by in the Sea of Japan, to begin operations at twelve o'clock local (Trans-Baikal) time in Manchuria.

Late that afternoon, Lozovsky told Ambassador Sato that a meeting with Molotov was scheduled for 8 p.m. on 8 August—the next day. Sato was surprised, gratified and more than a little relieved. Whether it would achieve anything remained to be seen, but at least it was progress after the weeks of frustration. Soon after, Lozovsky rang again and changed the time of the meeting to 5 p.m. He didn't offer an explanation, but clearly someone had done the arithmetic with time zones, as would later become apparent. Sato sent a telegram to Togo advising him of the turn of events:

7 August 1945   1950 hours, Moscow
8 August 1945   1200 hours, Ministry of Foreign Office, Tokyo
From: Sato
To: Togo
No. 1530 (urgent, ambassador's code)

Regarding my No. 1519. As soon as Molotov returned to Moscow, I requested a meeting. I also asked Lozovsky to help arrange it. On the seventh, Molotov notified me that he would see me at 1700 tomorrow, the eighth.

With such a dramatic turn of events, Stalin's evening was filled with meetings. On either side of the negotiation session with the Chinese, he met with Molotov and with the defence minister. Diplomatic and military preparations for the coming war against Japan were commenced.

Between these meetings, from 10.10 p.m., Stalin met with Chinese Premier Soong and his delegation for an hour and a half. The Soviet Union wanted to lease the port of Dairen and its connecting railway as a bulwark against any future Japanese threat. Chiang Kai-shek was prepared to agree to Port Arthur being in the Soviet military zone in return for USSR support for the Nationalists as the legitimate government in China. Soong, coached by the US Ambassador Harriman, refused to include Dairen. It should be a free port administered by the Chinese, he argued, and Dairen hadn't been part of the Yalta agreement anyway. The 7 August negotiations failed to reach agreement.

◆   ◆   ◆

Some of the scientific staff at Tinian had met with Deak Parsons. In the rush to push through assembly of Fat Man in two days less than originally planned, they warned him, they were getting 'dog-tired'. There was a risk that key checks might be compromised. But Parsons was under pressure from his military masters with their concern about approaching bad weather. The scientists' warning was to no avail, but he made the gesture of clearing extraneous people from the shed. When everyone went to dinner on the night of 7 August with bomb assembly near completion, time away from the workroom provided another circuit-breaker for the growing tension.

A little before midnight, one of the assembly team returned with a technician for a final check of Fat Man's working parts before they were encased in two pieces of hemispherical armour. Barney O'Keefe had to connect a firing unit on the front of the implosion sphere to four radar units in the tail by plugging in a cable threaded around the sphere inside. To his surprise and horror, the cable wouldn't fit into its plug. Both firing set and cable had female plugs. He checked the other end of the cable and found two male plugs. In the rush, someone had installed the cable backwards.

O'Keefe was in a quandary. Removing and reversing the cable would involve partly disassembling the implosion sphere. The best part of a day had been spent assembling it. The project couldn't remain on schedule if Fat Man was now pulled apart to turn the cable around, so O'Keefe bent the rules. With no-one else in the shed other than the technician, he figured he could get away with it. Generating heat in the assembly room was strictly forbidden, but he decided the only practical course was to unsolder the connectors from the two ends of the cable, swap them over and resolder them.

The navy scientist ran an extension lead for his soldering iron from the electronics lab next door. He had to prop the door open, which was also against regulations. O'Keefe removed the connector backs, unsoldered the wires and resoldered the plugs onto the other ends of the cable, all the time keeping soldering iron and detonators as far apart as circumstances allowed. The nerve-racking operation was completed without incident and without the knowledge of anyone in authority. The plugs plugged in O'Keefe and the technician left for the night.

In the morning, the boxy tail fin assembly was moved onto the bomb casing and jiggered into place before moving to the loading pit. A technician found that an upper hole on the tail didn't register on its counterpart on the casing. The alignment was out by only a few millimetres. It might have been a mechanic's error or the product of the heat and humidity of Tinian, but it was enough to prevent a bolt going through the two holes to attach the tail to the casing. The technician had to use a rat-tail file and brute force to finish assembly of the already-armed weapon. The tension of the assembly process had not abated.

Assembly was completed by the middle of the day on 8 August. Fat Man was armed and ready to be transferred to the loading pit for securing into the forward bomb bay of *Bockscar*. There were still test drops to be done for the bomb's firing mechanisms that day, but they would have to be carried out from *The Great Artiste*. With its primed cargo standing by to be loaded, *Bockscar* was going nowhere but Kokura. It had been the back-up target on the first bombing mission.

◆ ◆ ◆

The USS *Augusta* finally docked at Newport News on the Virginia coast in the late afternoon (6 a.m. Tokyo time) with President Truman on board and journalists flocking to the wharf. The voyage from Britain had taken five days. Truman's party immediately boarded a special train to Washington. While the rest of the Potsdam group went home in their different directions from Union Station, Truman arrived at the White House to be greeted by a group from his cabinet. The president invited them and the three press secretaries present into his study on the residence floor for a drink. He sat down at the piano, played a few bars, and then phoned his wife in Independence, Missouri.

Truman told the assembled courtiers that he thought Stalin was a man of his word, whether you liked what he said or not. Stalin and Molotov might be rough men but they knew common courtesies. The new president hadn't been able to form an opinion yet of Clement Attlee, the newly elected British prime minister, but Ernest Bevin, his foreign secretary, was crude and uncouth. He was 'a boor'.

At a quarter to twelve, one of the guests signalled to the assembled group that it was time to leave. The president needed rest. Truman seemed to want to party on, lingering at the door with one of the press secretaries. As this last guest was leaving, the President of the United States confided in him that he was glad to have left Europe and never wanted to go back. His first foray into international politics had been a draining experience.

◆　◆　◆

After a long and uncomfortable journey from Hiroshima, punctuated by frequent stops for air raids, the three returning marine draftsmen reached the outskirts of Nagasaki. Yamaguchi knew Iwanaga was on the train because he'd seen him from inside his carriage, heading for another carriage. Iwanaga was confident Sato was on board. They'd arrived at Koi station together but had been separated in the crowd on the platform. There was no reason to suppose Sato would not have managed to get on the train, but Yamaguchi would not have known this. The publisher Takejiro Nishioka was also aboard, but the three men from Mitsubishi didn't know him even though the four now shared a defining experience.

It was morning on 8 August, two days after the American B-29 Superfortress had dropped the world's first atomic bomb on Hiroshima and obliterated 80 per cent of the city. The morning newspapers reprinted the imperial rescript (a policy statement) issued on 8 December 1941, as it had done on the eighth of every month since the beginning of the Pacific war. 'We, by the Grace of Heaven, Emperor of Japan, seated on the throne of a line unbroken for ages eternal . . .' it began.

Akira Iwanaga left the train at Isahaya, 25 kilometres before Nagasaki city. His parents lived there. He wasn't feeling well and had decided to spend the day with them, stopping overnight before continuing to Nagasaki the next morning. Kuniyoshi Sato went on to Nagasaki. Expecting further bombs like the one he'd experienced in Hiroshima, he removed glass from the windows in his house. As it was summer, he could continue for the time being without them.

Tsutomu Yamaguchi arrived at Urakami during an air-raid alert. The streets were deserted. With the burning sensation still in his arm and face and its accompanying painful swelling, he made his way to the Mitsubishi company hospital and waited for medical staff to return from the shelters. He was treated by the company doctor, who carefully cut off hanging shreds of his skin with surgical scissors. The flesh beneath was raw red, 'like whale meat'. Three times the procedure had to be suspended while they responded to air-raid alarms and waited in a company shelter. Eventually Dr Sato applied lotion to the tender exposed flesh and re-dressed the wounded areas. The draftsman was ready to join his family in the new house he had not yet seen.

Yamaguchi's wife, Hisako, and one-year-old Katsutoshi had been staying with his parents while he was in Hiroshima. He got there to find the house empty, its residents away at an air-raid shelter. Yamaguchi took off his shoes in the stone-paved *genkan* (front porch) and waited for them there, sitting cross-legged on woven grass matting on a raised floor.

Ghosts in Japanese folk mythology don't have feet. Yamaguchi's mother was the first to return and saw him in the vestibule, head and one arm swathed in white bandages and feet hidden from sight. He had sent a telegram to say he was returning on 7 August, but the family had heard rumours about the Hiroshima bomb. When Tsutomu didn't arrive as planned, they feared the worst. Wanting to go to Hiroshima to recover her son's ashes, his mother had been talked out of that by Yamaguchi's father pointing out she wouldn't know where to look. Her first reaction now was that she was confronted with her son's ghost, ashen and feetless.

'Have you got feet?' she asked, refusing to enter the *genkan* until the matter was cleared up. Yamaguchi stood up. Satisfied and relieved, his mother came into her house and greeted her returned son. His father followed with Hisako and their son.

◆　◆　◆

Tsutomu Yamaguchi had returned to his home town with an experience he could barely begin to describe. The remainder of the citizens of Nagasaki knew little or nothing of the extraordinary happenings in Hiroshima two days earlier. They went about the drudgery and duty of their daily grind on this Wednesday morning much as they had for weeks, if not months. Sometimes people operated in a state of semi-numbness, asking themselves no questions; sometimes they wondered when it was going to end. Sometimes they believed, as they were assured the emperor believed, that somehow the Japanese military would engineer a remarkable victory out of what looked suspiciously like certain defeat. Such fortune had driven the Mongol invaders back centuries before. If then, why not now?

Foreman Torahachi Tagawa was one such citizen, arriving at work at seven as he did every day to lead warm-up exercises at the munitions factory. Another, the deputy director of the same Ohashi works, arrived later from the home of an elderly doctor, where he'd been staying since his wife was evacuated to the north. He dreaded the outcome of the assurance he'd been given that a consignment of coal would arrive that day, sufficient to lift the factory's output. Yoshiro Fukuda's stomach ulcer was already telling him he'd be let down . . . and it would prove to be right.

And so it continued at all levels in the city of Nagasaki. At seven thirty, about 150 prisoners marched down Route 206 from Urakami Prison to the Mitsubishi steelworks. Under the watchful eyes of a dozen guards and Warden Minami, their green work clothes and peaked caps made clear to passers-by who they were. Since it was a daily occurrence, nobody was greatly concerned—or even interested. A few small boys ran alongside them for a short distance then darted off. Escape wasn't highly likely with these men even if it were possible. The repercussions far outweighed the benefits and, in any case, the culture of discipline and regimentation that kept the Japanese people in check seemed also largely to be accepted by the convicts. Generally the same prisoners volunteered for the daily change of scenery and the same ones elected not to leave the prison. The inmates who might have considered escape were not given that option.

At nine o'clock, Tsuneo Tomita, the third-year pharmacy student at Nagasaki Medical School, began his day's work, as he had for the last three weeks, digging the new air-raid shelter at the university. The only good thing about the wartime routine was that he was still able to pass the time with his mates in the evening.

◆ ◆ ◆

Although they were supposedly on vacation, pupils at Yoshiro and Tatsuro Yamawaki's school were still required to attend school on speci-fied dates of national importance. On the eighth day of each month since December 1941, people gathered at workplaces and schools for *taisho-hotai-bi*, a morning ceremony to mark the start of the war with the Western colonial powers. It generally involved reading some national policy document or an informational talk about some aspect of the war.

Their father and brother had already gone to work when, on this eighth day of August, the twins caught the ferry across the bay to Ohata terminal and walked to their school. As they came through the school gates, the two boys paused and bowed deeply to the photograph of the emperor and empress in a display case at the entrance.

All students were herded into the school quadrangle and stood to attention. The children, ranging in age from five to eleven, had to stand still for about an hour without coughing or sniffling or making any sort of noise. The school's principal read the Imperial Rescript on Edu-cation to the gathering, rolling it out on a long scroll as he spoke. He wore white gloves to handle the document. It was read to the students on most occasions like this, a long pronouncement in very formal language with the emperor referring to himself in the plural, so that 'I' became 'we' and 'my' became 'our'.

On one wall of the quadrangle was the slogan, '*Hishigiri masen, katsu madewa,*' literally 'We will never say we want something until we win,' or, more simply, 'No luxury until victory.' The slogan had won a nationwide children's competition for wartime slogans. It was found everywhere around the walls of Nagasaki, among the myriad patriotic bugle calls stuck up on public walls.

The twins caught the late-morning ferry back, returning to an empty house. Their mother and younger brothers and sisters were already on a train to the greater safety of Saga prefecture.

◆ ◆ ◆

Dr Takashi Nagai woke on the morning of 8 August, alone in the house and feeling quite unwell. From time to time, the leukemia was making its presence felt. His wife, Midori, returned soon after from Koba, having installed the two Nagai children and their grandmother away from danger. She had barely returned when the air-raid siren sounded. Nagai was not well enough that morning, with a swollen spleen and shaky legs, to get to the shelter unaided. Midori supported him, gripping his arm over her shoulder as the couple made their way unsteadily to the shelter.

Takashi and Midori put their time in the shelter to good use, making plans for the Feast of Assumption, now only a week away. Midori said she would make the traditional bean-jam cakes, laughing at how their young boy had overeaten them the previous year. It would probably happen again. Neither of them had yet been to confession for Assumption, so timing for that had to be decided. Midori would go the next morning, Takashi would go in the afternoon.

When the all-clear sounded, the Nagais returned to their house and had breakfast. This time, Takashi seemed more confident on his legs. Midori wanted to walk with him to the college, but he said he felt better and could manage on his own. In the *genkan*, she helped him put on his white shoes. Smiling, she knelt on the *tatami* and dutifully bowed low. Takashi bowed in response and walked off, his stick providing support.

A short distance down the street, Nagai realised he had left his *bento* (lunch box) in the kitchen. As he approached the house, he saw Midori lying face-down in the *genkan*. She was sobbing quietly. Not sure what to do, Takashi drew back a little until she got up and went indoors. He followed shortly after. He was on air-raid duty that night, having refused to be left off the roster, and would not see his wife again until after work the next day. Taking his *bento*, Nagai resumed his laboured walk to Nagasaki Medical College.

With an extraordinary tale to tell that morning, the college dean Dr Tsuno addressed a gathering of faculty and students in one of the lecture rooms as part of *taisho-hotai-bi*. Returning from Tokyo the day before, his train had been unable to go beyond the outskirts of Hiroshima. Railway lines were buckled and broken from an enemy bomb dropped on the city the day before that, the sixth. Tsuno, like other passengers wanting to travel beyond Hiroshima, had to get off the train and make his own way across the city to the railway station at Koi on its western side. He described what he had seen in that journey, a scene that defied belief even in an audience fearfully aware of the intensive firebombing of Japan's cities in the last four or five months. This was a once bustling metropolis reduced to burnt wasteland, people wandering in a daze, some with horrific injuries. Corpses—dogs, horses, humans, the weapon made no distinction—littered streets no longer defined by buildings. Dean Tsuno was concerned that one of these new bombs, whatever they were, might be dropped on Nagasaki. He urged the audience to prepare for the worst, but they had difficulty grasping the full enormity of his story.

Dr Akizuki of the Urakami Dai-ichi Hospital had been down at the college that morning and, hearing about the dean's lecture, joined the audience. By the time he was returning the kilometre and a half to his hospital on Motohara Hill, the morning had built into a typically hot August day. Pleased to be back in the cool of the corridors in the hospital, he was tracked down by a medical student who was boarding at the theological college. The student had heard that something had happened at Hiroshima and that Dr Akizuki had been at the dean's talk at the medical school. Akizuki told him what he could remember. The general picture he passed on was probably fairly accurate, but he was still coming to terms with the more specific detail Dr Tsuno had related.

The reason for the student's interest soon became clear. His girlfriend's family lived in Hiroshima and she was there visiting them. Akizuki said it was too dangerous to go to Hiroshima, judging by the sea of fire and stench of dead bodies he had heard described. But the impetuosity of youth was not to be swayed by mature advice. Love overrode all. The young man left Nagasaki that afternoon for Hiroshima.

◆ ◆ ◆

Having made little progress the evening before, two military investigation teams set out independently in the morning of the eighth to scrutinise Hiroshima and find clues to identify the bomb that caused such devastation. The navy captains, Fuchida and Yasui, were taken by truck up a mountain road north of the city to where a sheet of white silk had been sighted billowing in the wind. They stopped a short distance from the fluttering material and climbed out of the truck. This was the object reported the previous evening as a possible unexploded bomb.

Cautiously following parachute cords, the investigators came to a metal cylinder about a metre in length. They tugged at metal rings—it didn't look like a bomb—and dislodged the container's contents. Out came instruments connected by electrical wires, a thermometer, a radio transmitter. There was no explosion, nothing left in the capsule that could possibly be a bomb. They loaded their find on the truck and drove back to Hiroshima.

General Arisue of army intelligence travelled around the flattened city in another truck. He saw endless misery and horror, but nothing to pinpoint its cause. His investigation team found two more calibration cylinders attached to parachutes. One carried 'a sort of barometer . . . fitted with an electric wave transmitter'. Its function was presumed to be recording 'the changes in atmospheric pressure caused by the explosion'. That might explain the cylinder, but it didn't identify the bomb.

In the afternoon, Dr Nishina's plane finally arrived at Hiroshima, further delayed by a morning attack near Tokyo. While it circled over the city, the physicist concluded that only an atomic bomb could have caused damage of that kind and on such a large scale. On landing, he observed melted roof tiles, further evidence of the bomb's power. To examine American claims that uranium fission was involved, Nishina asked the escort driving him around Hiroshima, 'Can you find a corpse without external injuries?'

The body of a soldier was brought to a laboratory outside the blast area. Nishina opened the dead man's abdomen with a scalpel. Pointing to the liver inflamed by radiation, he exclaimed, 'There's absolutely no doubt about it now. This was caused by an atomic bomb.'

Dr Nishina advised General Arisue that in his opinion the Americans had used a uranium bomb similar to the one he was developing. Nishina asked if he should continue its development. He got no response.

◆ ◆ ◆

After consulting with Prime Minister Suzuki that morning, Foreign Minister Togo had an audience with Emperor Hirohito in the underground shelter of the Imperial Palace. Initially held up by the alert for the morning air attack, Togo went through large steel doors and down a flight of stairs into a hillside in the palace grounds. At the end of a narrow corridor, he entered the concrete-walled conference room. Traditionally, an imperial audience began with an exchange of courtly conversation. Togo had neither the patience nor the humility on this occasion for the procrastination in this protocol. The pleasantries were put aside and the minister presented an unembellished report.

Togo outlined the Truman statement about Hiroshima and showed the emperor preliminary reports that had come in from the devastated city. He argued that Japan must accept the terms of the Potsdam Declaration as soon as possible. Hirohito considered the new weapon made it 'less and less possible to continue the war'. He urged Togo to do his utmost to bring it to a conclusion. The prime minister should be advised of the emperor's view.

Withdrawing, Togo went back to Suzuki and asked him to call an emergency meeting of the Supreme War Council, the 'Big Six'. Suzuki did so, but it had to be held over till the next morning because one of the six was 'unavoidably delayed by more pressing business elsewhere'.

Hiroshima had created no sense of urgency in at least some parts of Japan's leadership. With others, news was filtering through to add to the pervading sense of increasing hopelessness. In a climate of pessimism about the lack of response from the Soviet Union—the telegram from Ambassador Sato had not yet arrived—Navy Minister Yonai of the 'peace' faction complained to his principal adviser about Suzuki's shifting views. The prime minister had argued in cabinet that talking about ending the war would encourage frontline soldiers to mutiny, but he seemed to have no idea what was happening at home.

◆ ◆ ◆

On the morning of 8 August, Chuck Sweeney and his crew flew *The Great Artiste* out from Tinian and over the Pacific Ocean. A dummy bomb (called a 'pumpkin') was dropped, with all the components of Fat Man except the plutonium core. *The Great Artiste* was Sweeney's regular plane, named in honour of his bombardier, Kermit Beahan, who was considered to be an artiste both with his precision placement of bombs and with women. Beahan had a rakish, pencil-thin moustache that gave him an Errol Flynn look. Sweeney would not be piloting his usual plane on the upcoming mission to Kokura. Instead, he would fly Fred Bock's plane, *Bockscar*, already standing by to move to the bomb loading pit.

An aerial drop test of Fat Man with non-nuclear high explosive had been conducted over Wendover Field in Utah on 4 August. Before that, detonation unit tests had been done at Wendover. None of the results of these tests were forwarded to Tinian. The tests had to be duplicated to obtain the same data. Detonation units didn't arrive until the end of July and were first tested on Tinian on 1 August. Premature detonation under the plane belly had also occurred in the Wendover tests, unknown to the scientists at Tinian. A detonation unit loaded on a B-29 had to be unloaded and modified. The corrected unit was tested again two days later. This time it worked.

In the 8 August test drop, all components—switches, fuses, detonators—were being tested perilously close to the mission date. Sweeney took *The Great Artiste* to 10,000 metres and dropped the concrete-filled pumpkin offshore, with a fuse set to detonate a puff of smoke at 1890 feet (600 metres). The crew went through the full procedure for a bomb run, Beahan activating the tone signal fifteen seconds before bomb release. He yelled, 'Bomb away,' when the tone stopped and the pumpkin fell away. The plane turned sharply at 155 degrees, the bomb fell and a puff of smoke on detonation was measured to be at 1890 feet by scientists on the shore. The pumpkin splashed harmlessly into the ocean. All the switches, fuses and detonators had worked admirably. Commander Ashworth, who would be weaponeer on the coming mission, was on board. Fortune was favouring them. He was delighted.

♦ ♦ ♦

Mitsue Tabata sat in the *genkan* of her home with her baby daughter and eight-months-pregnant belly and watched a small group of prisoners of war being taken down to Mifune Canal. She'd often seen larger work gangs of the captured foreigners on their regular short march to the foundry under the watchful eyes of Japanese soldiers bellowing instructions—or just bellowing, it often seemed to her—and carrying rifles with bayonets attached. They always sounded much more belligerent than she felt they needed to be. Ironically the guards' chest-puffing behaviour disturbed the expectant mother more than it disturbed their charges. To the prisoners this came with the territory and they were able, for the most part, to put up with it or ignore it.

Since that terrifying morning of the 1 August raid, she hadn't seen prisoners going to the foundry at all. The only groups she'd seen were being taken to work on the new air-raid shelter by the canal. Small groups were still taken to the factory as well—Allan Chick and others casting hawse-holes, Peter McGrath-Kerr tinkering with engines in the workshop—but their hours had become more erratic and she hadn't been looking out at the time they passed by.

Mrs Tabata lived with her husband and eighteen-month-old daughter across the tramway and the train line from Mitsubishi's factory complex and the prison camp next to it. The steelworks and shipyard had been particularly targeted in the previous week's air attack. Her young son and other daughter had been evacuated a year before, along with her husband's parents, to a small house they had rented north of Nagasaki. Mitsue's husband was exempted from the military draft because he worked at the Nagasaki Shipyard, an essential war industry even if the Japanese navy now barely existed and merchant shipping was paralysed by the Allied blockade.

A primary school teacher, Mitsue Tabata had resigned when she became pregnant for the fourth time. She knew there were mutterings that this was an act of disloyalty at a time of national crisis, but she was embarrassed at being pregnant again in a little over five years of teaching at the school. She had spent the last three months at home, providing for the needs of a busy husband, preparing for childbirth in difficult times and watching the regular passing of POW work gangs.

◆   ◆   ◆

The newspaper publisher, Takejiro Nishioka, had left the overnight train from Hiroshima at Urakami station. Going to his home across the river, he found his wife and two daughters had joined the evacuation from the city. As he had proposed before going to Tokyo, they were now at a resort on Shimabara Peninsula, two hours from Nagasaki.

Nishioka went on to the official residence of local governor Waka-matsu Nagano. A member of the prefectural assembly, the respectable businessman barged with flustered urgency into the governor's office, behaviour quite out of character. Something was amiss.

Nagano had seen only a few lines in the newspaper about the Hiro-shima attack and the new bomb that was used. Nishioka tried to fill the gaps in the governor's scant knowledge. He'd just come from Hiroshima, he said breathlessly, where a new type of bomb had been dropped. Im-mediately after, he'd seen the havoc created. It was beyond imagining. The state of the city was extremely bad. Nishioka ran through the powerful effects of the blast. Large trees had been felled. Stone temple lanterns had been blown off their pedestals. Steel-reinforced buildings and other structures were flattened. The bomb had ignited wooden sleepers under railway tracks. The whole city of Hiroshima was a sea of flames, he told

A streetcar in Nakajima valley. City Hall is in the background.

Urakami Valley. Shiroyama is in the foreground and Nagasaki Commercial College is right centre. This is where Ukichi Egashira was a teacher and Koichi Wada a student before they were mobilised.

Urakami Cathedral.

A street in the Hamano-machi shopping precinct, Nakajima valley.

A wartime neighbourhood meeting in the middle of the Nakajima valley.

Members of the Student Patriotic Volunteer Corps. Mitsue Takeno is first left in the front row.

Dr Tatsuichiro Akizuki

Sugako Murai

Dr Takashi Nagai

Mitsue Takeno (right) with her friend
Setsuko Nakamura, 'N-san'.

Sergeant Peter McGrath-Kerr.

Private Allan Chick.

Robert Oppenheimer and General Leslie R Groves at the Trinity Test site, New Mexico, July 1945.

Colonel Paul Tibbets
receives a DSC from
General Spaatz.

The *Enola Gay* crew debriefing after the Hiroshima mission. Around the table from centre
foreground are: Hazen Payette (intelligence officer), 'Dutch' Van Kirk (navigator), Paul Tibbets
(pilot), Admiral Purnell, General Twining, General Farrell, General Spaatz, 'Deak' Parsons
(weaponeer), Maurice Jeppson (weapon test officer), Bob Lewis (co-pilot), Tom Ferebee
(bombardier), George Caron (tail gunner).

'Fat Man' armed and readied for transport to the loading pit. Note the message scribbled on the tail.

Pilot Chuck Sweeney checks *Bockscar*'s undercarriage.

Bockscar's crew for the second atomic bombing mission. Top row: 'Kermit' Beahan (bombardier), Jim Van Pelt (navigator), Don Albury (co-pilot), Fred Olivi (third pilot), Chuck Sweeney (pilot). Bottom row: Ed Buckley (radar operator), John Kuharek (flight engineer), Ray Gallagher (assistant flight engineer), 'Pappy' Dehart (tail gunner), Abe Spitzer (radio operator).

Navigator Jim Van Pelt, pilot Chuck Sweeney and third pilot Fred Olivi confer before boarding for the second atomic mission.

The Nagasaki bomb from the ground.

Survivors on Route 206 leaving the Urakami valley.

The destruction 300 metres south of the hypocentre on 10 August 1945. Chinzei Middle School is on the right beyond the tramlines poles. Smoke stacks of Nagasaki Steelworks are on the left.

Survivors in the aftermath.

Emperor Hirohito records his surrender speech.

A Shinto shrine demolished by the bomb.

Relief workers in the Urakami valley the day after the bomb.

The dormitory of Mitsubishi Armoury (400 metres south of the hypocentre). The remains of the fire-prevention wall are still standing.

The steel girders of a factory bent over by the blast wave.

The aftermath of the bomb on Urakami. A few concrete building and tree stumps remain standing in an otherwise flattened landscape.

A few buttresses and the entrance are all the remained of the Urakami Cathedral. Its two domes lie on rubble in the middle.

Shiroyama Primary School's main building where Chiyoko Egashira sheltered with her baby.

A view across Nagasaki ground zero towards the ruins of Urakami Cathedral.

A streetcar destroyed by the explosion near where Koichi Wada's tram might have been but for a derailment earlier that morning.

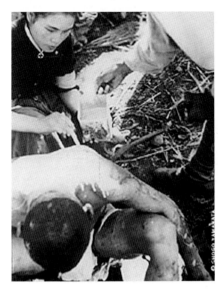

A bomb victim being treated for burns.

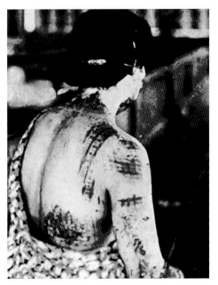

Thermal burns showing the darker pattern of clothing burnt through.

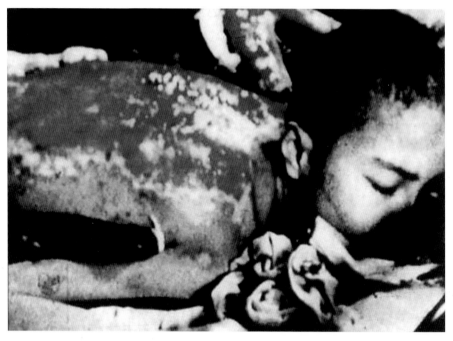

The postman Sumiteru Taniguchi photographed a couple of weeks after the bomb.

A makeshift hut built on the rubble left behind from the bomb. It was in a hut like this that Mr Taniguchi and his family lived on their return to Nagasaki.

Nagano. People's bodies had been incinerated. Those who survived were running everywhere in panic.

Nagano found Nishioka's staccato description so graphic, so beyond his own experience that he wondered whether it had been embellished somewhere along the line. He asked the publisher if he was talking about something he'd actually seen with his own eyes or whether it was something he had heard from other people.

'Everybody saw it,' spluttered Nishioka, 'and they're telling everybody about it.'

Nagano had never before seen the urbane businessman so agitated. Nishioka urged the governor to set up urgent countermeasures. It was only a matter of time, he predicted, before Nagasaki was a target for the new American bomb.

Chapter 9

Nagasaki, Wednesday 8 August 1945

While the airdropped leaflet campaign began over Tokyo, the Japanese set out to block American propaganda broadcasts from Saipan, Manila and Okinawa. With army encouragement, newspapers and radio tried to nullify the message in the leaflets. An editorial in the Tokyo daily *Asahi Shimbun* ran the headline, 'Strength in the Citadel of the Spirit'. Regardless of the intensity of the bombing and the number of cities destroyed, it said, 'the foremost factor to decide the war is the will of the people to fight and how well they are united to fight ... now we have to strengthen the citadel of the mind'. Ingratiating itself with its readership, it added, 'The people in Tokyo can stand these difficulties better than the people in the provinces.'

At the same time, the government of Japan filed a formal protest through the Embassy of Switzerland in Tokyo against the government of the United States for its use of the new inhumane weapon. It was described as 'a new crime against the whole of humanity and civilisation'. Arguably the worst manifestation of the new weapon was only just becoming apparent.

Radiation had only been a marginal concern during the development phase of the atomic bomb. If the safety of the Manhattan Project's scientists and servicemen was not a high consideration, it was unlikely that much thought would be given to the effect of radioactivity on the Japanese populace in target cities. This proved to be the case, to the point perhaps of constructive indifference.

Norman Ramsey, head of the Los Alamos team on Tinian, was surprised to hear that Tokyo Rose, the English language voice of Japan's propaganda broadcasts, was claiming large numbers were sick and dying after Hiroshima. They were reported as suffering from some unknown disease, not the effects of burns from the bomb's blast. The claims were easy to dismiss as propaganda, but a little thought might have raised the question of how the broadcaster managed to invent so accurately a potential outcome when they knew so little about the weapon. As it was, Ramsey had assumed—or had been led to believe—that the 100 per cent kill area was larger than the radiation-affected area. In other words, anyone who might have been close enough to be affected by radioactivity was too close to survive the blast.

Reports of radiation sickness were already appearing in the American press. Oppenheimer told the *Washington Post* on 8 August there would be little radiation on the ground at Hiroshima and it would decay rapidly. He continued to hold this view long after the war despite all evidence to the contrary. General Groves heard the reports and contacted Oppenheimer for reassurance. Groves' diary entry that day suggests he got it: 'Oppie said "this is of course lunacy" . . . Oppie said further that based on the test in New Mexico there would be no appreciable [radiation] activity on the ground and what little there was would decay very rapidly.'

The Manhattan Project's official assessment summed it up:

No lingering toxic effects are expected in the area over which the bomb has been used. The bomb is detonated in combat at such a height above the ground as to give the maximum blast effect against structures and to disseminate the radioactive products as a cloud. On account of the height of the explosion, practically all of the radioactive products are carried upward as a column of hot air and dispersed harmlessly over a wide area . . . In the very unlikely and unanticipated case that these radioactive particles should be suddenly precipitated to the ground, the amount of radiation could be very high but would remain so for only a short period of time.

The report doesn't nominate what it considers a 'short period of time'. Two seconds? Two weeks? We're not told. The uncertainty is consistent with the recollection of Stimson's undersecretary of war, John J McCloy, that 'when the bomb was used, before it was used and at the time it was used, we had no basic concept of the damage it would do'.

The apparent cavalier attitude to lingering radiation seems on the surface to have had one exception. Pilots of the bomb-carrier aircraft, and presumably their support aircraft, were instructed to get at least 4 kilometres (2½ miles) from the hypocentre by the time the bomb detonated. Post-bombing reconnaissance planes were likewise instructed not to fly through the cloud generated by the explosion. This might have been because of the expectation that what radiation there was would be carried upward rather than concern limited to their pilots. The proposition that the atomic bomb should be followed with an incendiary raid was rejected, not for safety reasons but so the effects of the atomic bomb could be studied undisturbed by other bombing.

◆　◆　◆

About eight that morning, Sugako Murai had come down from her room on an upper floor of Urakami Dai-ichi Hospital. The cook had found her daily journey from home in the southern hills of Nagasaki too tiring. In June, the hospital had given her one of the empty rooms in the old college dormitory that was not being used by patients. Some of the nurses slept there as well if they didn't live locally.

Until lunchtime, the doctors dealt with out-patients who came up from the city. In the afternoon, they did house calls in the neighbourhood. While they were away, staff worked in the hospital's vegetable gardens, digging, planting, harvesting, to maintain a steady food supply and reduce reliance on the ration system. That Wednesday, Sugako was out in the garden, digging up sweet potatoes ready for eating. Some of the people who lived around the hospital helped out. Even the nurses, when they had finished with in-patients, would help weed vegetable patches. The heavier work of turning over the soil for a new crop was mostly done by the monks, who also looked after the hospital's cows. Brother Iwanaga— Joseph was the saint's name he'd adopted—did the milking every day in the late afternoon.

Busy days of manual work—cooking and gardening—belied Sugako Murai's background. Her mother had died when she was a young girl and she had been brought up from that point in her maternal grandmother's large household. Sugako's uncle, her mother's younger brother, lived with them also and was like an older brother to her. He had married and the family grew as they produced nine children. Indicative of the family's comfortable financial position, they hired two nannies. Sugako's father remarried and, although she kept in contact with him, she continued to live with her grandmother.

The family could afford to send her to Kwassui Women's College, an expensive Methodist school near the city centre, then to the four-year course at the prestigious St Luke's College of Nursing in Tokyo. When she graduated from St Luke's, she was qualified as both nurse and health-care teacher.

Sugako Murai was something of a dreamer, capable of applying herself tenaciously, capable of getting discouraged and allowing her life to drift. During her nursing training, she spent a month as a sanitarium intern in a hot springs town near Nagano in central Japan. Enchanted by the alpine beauty of the surrounds and inspired by the potential for recovery from tuberculosis in the clear mountain air, she resolved to return to the town as a qualified nurse. She didn't get there. Persuaded by the principal of St Luke's to assist his friend, the mayor of Kumamoto, she agreed to spend the year in 1941 training nurses at a new school in the central Kyushu city. The principal had approached Sugako on his friend's behalf because she was a Kyushu girl.

She intended to apply to the sanitarium at the end of the year, but by then Japan was at war and her beloved grandmother was ill. Persuaded now by her family, she came home to Nagasaki to look after her grandmother and help look after her uncle's children, their nannies having been drafted by the military. She stayed there until 1945, out of obligation as much as choice.

Young women were expected to contribute to Japan's war effort. The military were not going to allow Sugako to stay home as a lady of leisure. She received a call-up notice which would send her to Manchuria, a dangerous posting in a war Japan seemed destined to lose. Her family sought the help of their doctor, Dr Takahara, owner of the mid-city hospital. Since Sugako had suffered lymphadenitis and lung damage as a child, Takahara suggested presenting someone else's lung X-ray to the military with her own medical history. The ruse worked and the military told Sugako to come back when she was better.

Takahara warned that the military would soon be back, suggesting she look for work at a hospital he knew to be short of nurses. It was the Urakami Dai-ichi Hospital. Applying with a letter of recommendation from the respected doctor, she was surprised to be turned down. Sugako was told she was too highly qualified for their medical needs. Ironically they were similar to those of the sanitarium she had long dreamt of joining. An irritated Dr Takahara spoke to the hospital. She didn't need a nurse's job, he said, and would be happy to work in any capacity. In April, she was hired as cook.

By now, Sugako Murai had developed a routine as cook and garden hand. In the mid-afternoon, she returned to the kitchen to finish preparing the evening meal. Vegetables, fresh from the hospital gardens, were peeled and chopped. Steamed rice, grey-brown from the barley mixed with it, was simmered with the vegetables into a soup in large metal pots sufficient to feed up to a hundred patients, staff and volunteer helpers. At four when the patients filed in, the soup was ready. Hospital staff followed in dribs and drabs. Sugako and the volunteers cleaned up and another day in the kitchen was completed. The working day went smoothly because Murai was an efficient and capable worker, but she was getting itchy feet. Yearning for the profession for which she had been trained but never worked in, she had raised the issue with her dormitory friend, Tsuyako Fukahori, who was also the head nurse. Fukahori said she would look into it.

◆ ◆ ◆

After air-raid warnings early in the morning of 8 August, the schoolteacher Ukichi Egashira was able eventually to get to his wartime workplace at the Ohashi weapons factory. He'd missed foreman Tagawa's warm-up exercises, but so had many of the workers at the factory that day. They'd been rescheduled for later in the morning after the all-clear had sounded. After bowing towards the emperor and praying for his guidance, Egashira commenced the monotony of a day supervising mobilised students of the Patriotic Corps on the production line.

Ukichi's wife, Chiyoko, had a more interesting day mapped out for her. Shiroyama Primary School had agreed to provide its staff to weed the rice paddies that had been established at a village school on the outskirts of the city. After the all-clear was sounded, the staff gathered at Shiroyama school and marched as a deputation. By then everyone in Japan acted as if they were in the military even when they weren't. People moved briskly in groups as if in formation. Most men wore a uniform of some sort. Women wore the loose-fitting *monpe* which while not being military still gave them a uniformity suited to the times.

Arriving with the confidence of a fix-it team, the working party from Shiroyama was surprised at the extent of the job. It was bigger than they had been led to believe. Because there were few at this small school to maintain them, the paddies had become badly overgrown with weeds. There was much to do, but the visitors attacked the task diligently with all the thoroughness they could muster. As they picked their way down their allotted rows, it seemed the weeds spread through those paddies endlessly, but working as a team made bearable and productive what would otherwise have been a tedious chore. They took advantage of the challenge to cement the group's *esprit de corps* at a time when anything that could divert them from the ongoing grimness of life was to be welcomed.

Because of the late start and the extent of the weeds, the Shiroyama working bee didn't finish clearing the paddies until well after the usual hour for a meal-break. They had a late lunch together of *zosui* with squash and potatoes. Chiyoko and her colleagues were pleased to finish what had seemed such a daunting task when they arrived. They rejoiced in a good job well done, so chuffed that the group chattered through the remainder of the afternoon. There was no point at that late stage in going back to Shiroyama to start on anything. In any case, they had earned a break to enjoy the company of colleagues and friends.

The party broke up as the evening dark crept in. They hadn't noticed the time pass. Shiroyama's principal told the workers that their task that day had gone so well they could start the next day an hour later than usual. For Chiyoko Egashira the world felt so good in the warmth of friends and the twilight of a Japanese summer that it was hard to imagine anything capable of breaking the spell.

◆ ◆ ◆

Back in Tinian after the test drop from *The Great Artiste*, the crew of *Bockscar* was told its mission was confirmed for the next day. It would be a pre-dawn start. Weather reports continued to predict unsettled conditions over Japan for the following five days. Major Charles Sweeney would be the command pilot for Special Bombing Mission No. 16, even though he wasn't the highest ranking of the three pilots. A little unsure of his ability to carry the necessary authority that came with that role, he went across to the hardstand to chat to the crew checking systems on *Bockscar*. The command pilot wanted to be seen as a hands-on leader.

At two, Sweeney, along with bombardier Kermit Beahan, co-pilot Don Albury and navigator Jimmy Van Pelt, attended a briefing session inside a guarded Quonset hut. They pored over maps and reconnaissance photos of the two targets. These were the same two targets they had scrutinised, along with Hiroshima, three days earlier. This time, however, they were dropping a bomb on an aiming point, not canisters in the vicinity.

The intelligence officer, Hazen Payette, ran through the latest information they had about Japanese ground defences: anti-aircraft positions, intensity of fire and fighter capability around each target. Kokura had a ring of anti-aircraft batteries around it and significant intercept fighter protection. On the other hand, Nagasaki, the secondary target, had less concentrated defence. The latest weather report had a front moving to Japan from the east, from out over the Pacific.

After the session, Sweeney returned to his room for a short nap but he couldn't get to sleep. The heat and nervous anticipation were conspiring against him. In the enlisted men's quarters, five sergeants who would be on *Bockscar* waited, tense with expectation and uncertainty. There was little conversation. Thinking about what he'd seen at Hiroshima, assistant engineer Ray Gallagher tried to write home but couldn't concentrate. Abe Spitzer, the radio operator, noticed his silence and thought he looked depressed. Radar operator Ed Buckley and tail gunner 'Pappy' Dehart were silent also, brooding about what had been and what was to come.

◆ ◆ ◆

Following his productive day with his friend from the country, Koichi Wada was back in the driver's seat of a Nagasaki streetcar. Twice during the day as he ran his route, he caught sight of the older Noguchi girl. Once she was struggling with a dangling rope to swap the tram's pole across to the adjacent overhead wire. The other time he glimpsed her between standing passengers on a car passing in the opposite direction. Neither time could he see the younger Noguchi. He wondered if she was still sobbing behind the toilet block in Ohashi.

In the afternoon, the air-raid siren screeched as Koichi's tram moved down the valley. He continued for a short distance, stopping near where he knew there was an air-raid shelter. Regulations required he ask his passengers to go to the shelter. If there wasn't a dugout nearby, you were supposed to find a trench. Koichi had done that a couple of times and found the trenches dirty. Now he didn't go anywhere, even if there was a shelter handy. While his passengers sheltered, he stayed in the tramcar.

Koichi Wada had been issued with an iron helmet which he was supposed to carry at all times tied to his back. That was a nuisance and, in any case, he thought it looked like a saucepan. He had no intention of putting a cooking pot on his head, so the helmet always sat on a ledge near the driver's seat. He had never worn it.

Koichi was a fatalist. 'If a bomb hits, it hits,' was one of his mantras. Another was: 'I can't do anything about anything that happens.' *Que sera sera.* While he waited for the all-clear to sound and his passengers to return, Koichi thought about a garbled report he'd heard during the day. The previous afternoon, the newspaper had said a new bomb had been dropped on Hiroshima causing enormous damage, but didn't say what 'enormous damage' amounted to. The radio at home had reported the bombing of Hiroshima too, but with the poor reception they had with no antenna Koichi had heard no detail. It hadn't sounded as if any was offered.

The week before, he had watched from the Hotarujaya terminal as American B-24s appeared over Mount Hiko to the south, passed over the tram sheds and flew on to Dejima and Urakami. In impotent fascination, he saw the bomb-bay doors open, saw black lumps fall out, spread and tumble down toward the shipyards. He heard the new bomb was ten or twenty times bigger than those bombs. How could a plane carry such a big bomb? It was all beyond his understanding so he thought no further about it.

◆ ◆ ◆

Mrs Takigawa's girls, Sakue and Ryoko, had spent much of the morning in the shelter. Waiting underground, they were hungry because they were always hungry. There was enough food those days to stay alive, but never enough to drive away the pangs of youthful hunger. When the all-clear was given, they ran home along with everyone else who had been sheltering. Lunch was *okayu*, rice porridge, that the older women garnished with wild grasses they picked up, goosefoot and mugwort.

Masuichi, the girls' older brother, returned from medical school in the early afternoon. The family rarely saw him these days. Medical students were being used at the college hospital to replace doctors who'd been conscripted. When Masuichi wasn't at medical school, he was at the squadron. Someone suggested they should celebrate the whole family being home . . . apart from Mr Takigawa at work in Isahaya. Mrs Takigawa gathered up one of her remaining kimonos, a few small items and some money and went out looking for the black market.

Masuichi had been at Dr Tsuno's talk at the college that morning. He told the two young girls and his older sister what the dean had related. A new type of bomb had been dropped on Hiroshima, he said, causing unimaginable destruction. It had happened after the all-clear had sounded. The explanation of that was unclear, but Masuichi impressed on his little sisters that they should not leave the shelter as soon as the all-clear rang out.

Mrs Takigawa returned with a small amount of special white rice, *shiroikome*, for the evening meal. The family wardrobe, kimono and obi, was gradually disappearing, but it was frowned on to wear such elegant clothing at that time anyway. Since the quantity of rice bought was small, the family expected to eat all of it that night, but their pragmatic mother pointed out they would be hungry again tomorrow. She saved some of it in a small urn, leaving it under the sink in the corner of the kitchen.

Instead of the anticipated bowlful of fluffy white rice, it was bulked up with shredded daikon, but the Takigawa family was still glad they could be together for a modest feast, even when their father could not join them. They would have to wait for a happier future for that. Sadako said she wished they could have had *shiruko* as well, the sweet porridge of red beans eaten with rice-flour dumplings, but the days when *shiruko* could be on the menu had long since gone. Masuichi repeated his story of the bombing of Hiroshima for his mother's benefit and repeated his warning to the girls to stay in the shelter after the all-clear.

'There are people in some areas having a very hard time of it,' sighed Mrs Takigawa.

◆　◆　◆

At the end of his shift at Ohashi, Ukichi Egashira packed up his things and walked dejectedly down to the tram stop. Another tedious day had ended. The mobilised students he supervised were good kids by and large. He knew that from having taught many of them, but their enthusiasm for factory work ran hot and cold. The only thing that seemed to sustain them was that they were with their friends. It all seemed quite futile, but there was a war on. Was that futile too? You were not allowed to entertain such thoughts.

Egashira got on the tram, packed as always at this time of the afternoon, and glanced at the uniformed driver. It was young Wada, a student from Nagasaki Commercial School where he taught before he was transferred to duties at the arms works. The teacher pushed his way through to his former pupil. Patting the young man gently on the shoulder, he asked him how it was going. 'It's okay,' said Koichi, as non-committal as Egashira had found young males always to be. 'I know the work is tough,' the teacher said, 'but try your best.'

Egashira got off at the stop nearest to where he lived over the river at Shiroyama. He felt good for having spoken to the boy, unaware of the positive impact he'd had on Wada by doing so. Koichi's heart was filled with cheer. Mr Egashira had seen him in his uniform and taken the time to offer a few words of encouragement. For a short while, he forgot he was hungry. For a short while, he forgot about the Noguchi sisters.

◆　◆　◆

Junji Sato, the Domei reporter, returned home after a day at work in which none of his fears about the enemy's weapons were put to rest. It was developing momentum in a direction Sato didn't like. An Imperial HQ notification had arrived in the early afternoon, passed on by Nagasaki Fortress Command without the usual directive attached. It reported a new type of parachuted enemy bomb that exploded with a blinding light 500 metres above the ground. The skin of people exposed to the blast became ulcerated, although burns were slight for those wearing white clothes, whatever that might signify. Wooden buildings were knocked flat. The journalist noted that no report had come from the Domei bureau in Hiroshima where the new bomb had already been used, suggesting damage was extensive.

Later in the afternoon, he'd been notified by the chief of prefectural air defence of a press conference scheduled for eleven o'clock the next morning. The chief would be talking about the new bomb for 'reader information'. Reader information was code for prescribing the news. It was a sure sign that there was a worrying reality to this new weapon.

Sato was relieved to get home after such a day. His younger sister, Teruko, was making a *monpe*, already home from the arms factory where she was a leader of the Student Patriotic Corps. Their mother was away, visiting a relative. Junji tried to unwind by telling his sister all he knew and all he suspected about the new bomb, but she had no real idea what he was talking about.

◆　◆　◆

As evening approached, prisoners of war at the end of labour shifts were brought back to Fukuoka Camp 14 the short distance from Mitsubishi's iron foundry. Allan Chick was in that group. Others, including fellow Tasmanian Peter McGrath-Kerr, had been working on the bridge over Mifune Canal and the new dugout on the other side. There was little more to be done on the bridge but they were trying to stretch the work out as long as possible. They too came back under guard, past the solitary watching figure of the very pregnant Mrs Tabata waiting for her husband to return from the shipyards.

◆　◆　◆

Tsuneo Tomita, the third-year pharmacy student, had also been at Dr Tsuno's talk that morning. It hadn't had a lasting impact. Life was still good . . . within the constraints of a nation at war. With dusk creeping in, Tomita and his fellow students sprawled near Urakami Cathedral on a patch of grass that had not yet been dug up and turned into a vegetable garden. The cathedral bell was ringing, as it had been on and off all day, this time for Angelus, reminding the faithful that it was time for evening prayer.

Earlier, it had announced confession in preparation for Assumption. The cathedral's two remaining priests had been busy once more during the day hearing confession by the townspeople. Fathers Nishida and Tamaya were holding two well-attended sessions of confession daily at this time of the ecclesiastical calendar, one in the morning at ten, the other in the afternoon. Scheduled between these were other pastoral duties of the day and, increasingly it seemed, funerals. The visiting priest had spent the middle period of the day with children of the *kirishitan* and the late afternoon officiating at a funeral with its long procession and women in white silken veils.

On their grassy knoll, the students watched the sun set over Mount Inasa on the western side of the Urakami valley. The bells didn't toll for them, although they had just watched the funeral procession from their safe distance. They chattered on about the things that occupied young Japanese males at that time: hunger and how you might supplement your food supply. Later, Tomita went with two of his mates to a third friend's house to talk more and drink *sake*. Afterwards, they all slept in the college buildings, on platforms set up in classrooms.

◆ ◆ ◆

In the afternoon, Takejiro Nishioka joined four of his fellow newspaper executives and editors. They met with the chief of Nagasaki police and one of his unit heads. The group inspected possible sites in the south of the city for an underground shelter where they could publish their emergency newspaper. There was no place suitable to dig a tunnel and cavern into the hill and install presses. They tentatively decided instead on a site west of Urakami River, near the shelter where Mrs Takigawa's adopted daughters now spent much of their day. One of the newspaper group had already looked at the site and was confident it could serve their purposes. They arranged to meet there at eleven o'clock the next morning, 9 August. On top of the hill sat the Gokoku Shrine, dedicated to the military dead. It was felt to be a good omen.

Nishioka went to his home, now empty with his family evacuated to Unzen on the Shimabara Peninsula. By evening he had developed a fever. Blue spots were appearing under the skin on his lower legs. Contacting his colleagues, he explained he was feeling unwell and asked if they could postpone the morning meeting. It was agreed to meet in the afternoon instead if by midday he was feeling better.

The newspaper proprietor was beginning to feel so feverish he decided to join his family in Unzen in the morning. He checked into a hotel near his newspaper office, one he frequently used when he needed to oversee an important issue of the paper. It was also near Nagasaki Railway Station. By staying there, he would be well positioned for an early start to Unzen.

At 11.30 p.m. Nishioka woke, feeling extremely nauseous and anxious. In his fevered state, he resolved to start his morning journey immediately. A hotel maid was called to recover his personal ivory chopsticks that were kept in the hotel in an elegant wooden box. He went to the newspaper office and took out of his desk drawer some letters he would need for the meeting if he went to it. His mind was in such a state he wasn't even sure he would do that. His only certainty was his need to join his family. Nishioka found a small truck on the premises. It had a little petrol in its tank and, since none was available, had been unused for some time. It would be enough to start him on the way to Unzen.

By the time he approached Okusa on the railway line out of Nagasaki, the truck's tank was near to empty. Rather than risk going on, the fevered Nishioka decided to stop, abandon the truck and continue his journey on the morning train. Driving into Okusa, he stayed in a shabby Japanese-style inn on the beach.

◆ ◆ ◆

That day, P-51 Mustang fighter-bombers from Iwo Jima bombed and strafed industrial targets in Osaka. An assault plane was brought down by ground fire, leaving the pilot, Lieutenant Marcus McDilda, floundering in the bay in an inflatable dinghy. He was picked up from the water, brought ashore and marched blindfolded through the streets where bystanders pressed in on him, punching him. The bleeding airman was taken for interrogation to the headquarters in Osaka of the military police, the *kempeitei*. For several hours, McDilda's evasive answers drew a succession of beatings. He lied about his single-seater plane and was beaten. Shown to be exaggerating the number of planes on Iwo Jima, he was beaten again. He was asked what he knew about the atomic bomb and said he knew nothing, but his interrogators kept returning to the subject.

After dark, a general arrived and questioned McDilda about the bomb. Unsatisfied with the American's reply, he drew his sword and jabbed at McDilda's already swollen lip. Blood ran down his chin and onto his flying suit.

'If you don't tell me about the bomb, I'll personally cut off your head,' screamed the general and left the room.

McDilda was convinced the threat wasn't bluff, but he knew no more about the atomic bomb than what he'd heard in the president's statement. To keep himself alive, he talked about splitting the atom and producing lots of pluses and minuses. In a huge container, thirty-six feet by twenty-four, they were kept apart by a lead shield which melted when the box was dropped from a B-29. The resulting explosion pushed back the atmosphere, knocking out everything with a 'tremendous thunderclap'. The explosion atomised six square miles. Due to a technical flaw, the bomb could not be dropped at night or when rain was falling. He buried the barely plausible story in an overcooked Florida drawl, forcing the interpreter to pad the story with guesses at what McDilda was saying.

Asked what the next target was, the captured man said, 'I believe Kyoto and Tokyo. Tokyo is supposed to be bombed in the next few days.'

A report of the interrogation was sent by telegraph from Osaka to Tokyo. It was intercepted by Ultra radio decryption in Manila.

◆   ◆   ◆

In the evening, Dr Akizuki was joined at the Catholic hospital by two doctors who had come up from the city. One visitor told Akizuki about another talk given by Dr Tsuno in Nagasaki that afternoon. Both medicos were concerned about the ramifications of this apparently new bomb. Did the Americans have a store of them? Where would the next target be? It was too early to have any inkling of the dangers posed by radiation. Neither knew, and nor did Tsuno, that he'd been dangerously exposed to the radioactivity while walking through Hiroshima the day before.

The other doctor had transferred to the Urakami hospital after his wife's operation for acute appendicitis. He'd also come because it was a safer place to be if there was a firebomb attack on the city. Nagasaki had so far come under limited attack, but its turn couldn't be far away.

Akizuki was pleased to have two more doctors at the hospital. He was its only resident doctor that night for the seventy tubercular patients. Tomorrow a group of patients requiring pneumo-thoracic treatment were coming from Takahara Hospital in the downtown area. They would be accompanied by Dr Yoshioka and two nurses. While this would add to the number of patients, it would also increase the medical staff, easing the pressure Dr Akizuki felt himself under. He was a skilled doctor, but he didn't handle pressure well.

◆ ◆ ◆

Chuck Sweeney had supper at Dogpatch Inn, the Tinian mess named after the hillbilly village in the comic strip *Li'l Abner*. Afterwards, he walked to the top of a hillock that overlooked the runways. Watching the steady flow of B-29s taking off in the dark, he lit a cigar. Over two hundred bombers were leaving Tinian to firebomb Yawata, an industrial city adjacent to Kokura. One plane struggled to get airborne with a full load of fuel and bombs. Sweeney watched numbly as it crashed, sending plumes of flame and smoke into the night sky. The sound of explosions filled the air . . . and the thoughts of a man who in a few short hours would himself be rolling down that runway. Inside his plane's belly would be a bomb with the explosive capacity to annihilate a city.

Two physicists working at Tinian, Luis Alvarez and Robert Serber, decided to send a letter to a prewar colleague at the University of California in Berkeley. Riyokichi Sagane was now a professor of physics at Tokyo University. The letter appealed to him to tell the Japanese government about the dangers involved with nuclear weapons. Alvarez drafted the letter, Serber and another colleague edited it. Alvarez wrote out the final version with two copies.

The message said:

Headquarters
Atomic Bomb Command
August 9, 1945
To: Prof. R Sagane

From: Three of your former scientific colleagues during your stay in the United States.

We are sending this as a personal message to urge that you use your influence as a reputable nuclear scientist to convince the Japanese General Staff of the terrible consequences which will be suffered by your people if you continue this war.

You have known for several years that an atomic bomb could be built if a nation were willing to pay the enormous cost of preparing the necessary material. Now that you have seen we have constructed the production plants, there can be no doubt in your mind, all the output of these factories working 24 hours a day will be exploded on your homeland.

Within the space of three weeks we have proof fired one bomb in the American desert, exploded one in Hiroshima and fired the third this morning.

We implore you to confirm these facts to your leaders and to do your utmost to stop the destruction and waste of life which can only result in the total annihilation of all your cities if continued. As scientists we deplore the use to which a beautiful discovery has been put, but we can assure you that unless Japan surrenders at once, this rain of atomic bombs will increase manyfold in fury.

Copies of the unsigned letter were placed in three envelopes addressed to Professor Sagane and taped to the outside of the instrument cylinders to be parachuted from *The Great Artiste* as the bomb fell from *Bockscar*.

◆　◆　◆

The US Secretary of War, Henry Stimson, would turn seventy-eight in a month. After landing in a thunderstorm when flying into Washington from Long Island the previous afternoon, he suffered a 'rather sharp little attack' in the early hours of 8 August (Washington time). His doctors saw him in both the morning and the afternoon, offering positive predictions for his health. Stimson can't have been too reassured. The page of his diary for that day is headed, 'Heart attack'.

Later in the morning, Stimson told Truman his doctors had advised he take a complete rest. Truman said to take a month off and come back when he could. At that meeting, Stimson argued that the US should 'proceed with Japan in a way which would produce her surrender as quickly as possible'. He was concerned that too many people influencing American strategic decisions—or trying to—didn't have any real insight into the culture or people of Japan, and certainly not his experience or understanding of the Japanese. He complained that those seeking unconditional surrender didn't recognise the fundamental difference between the Japanese and the Germans.

The demand for unconditional surrender had surfaced in a Roosevelt press conference after the 1943 Casablanca meeting of the Allied leaders, although it hadn't been part of the Casablanca communiqué. 'What Truman inherited from Roosevelt,' concludes historian Ronald Takaki, 'was a slogan not a policy.' It was proving a dead weight on Japan's fumbling attempts to find a way out of the war.

'When you punish your dog,' Stimson explained to Harry Truman, the president with little experience of foreign policy, 'you don't keep souring on him all day after punishment is over if you want to keep his affection. Punishment takes care of itself.' Stimson paused to let the message sink in. 'It's the same way with Japan,' he concluded. A strange choice of allusion, but not out of character for a man long given to paternalism. Presumably the Germans were dogs whose affection didn't need to be kept.

Mixed with his patronising of non-European cultures was a contemptuous scorn for those who didn't have his insights. Two days later, Stimson would write in his diary about 'uninformed agitation against the Emperor in this country, mostly by people who knew no more about Japan than has been given them by Gilbert and Sullivan's *Mikado*'.

◆　◆　◆

On the island of Tinian, the hook of an overhead crane was slipped carefully into a metal loop on top of Fat Man's bulbous body. The fully armed weapon was winched gingerly and carried sideways like an abattoir carcass out through the large open doors of the shed. It was lowered onto a waiting transport dolly, sitting close to the ground on large rubber tyres. Technicians covered Fat Man with a tarpaulin. A prime mover pulled it across the asphalt, escorted by armed MPs, a couple of photographers and the technicians. Travelling slowly but smoothly for over a kilometre, the cortege arrived at a floodlit loading pit. The dolly was wheeled on tracks over a 3-metre pit. A hydraulic lift came up and raised the bomb and its detachable cradle, so the crew could wheel the dolly away. The tracks were removed and the bomb was rotated 90 degrees and lowered into the pit. It was getting towards ten o'clock at night.

Bockscar was towed alongside the loading pit. With its pitside landing gear run on to a turntable, the B-29 was positioned over the pit, its forward bomb doors open. The hydraulic system again whined into action and Fat Man rose to a point just below the open doors. A plumb-bob hung from inside so the bomb's metal loop could be lined up accurately. With little clearance from the plane's catwalks, this was a delicate operation. With a shackle locked onto the bomb, the live weapon was cautiously winched upwards, a large white and orange beast disappearing into the B-29's belly. Only a single shackle held the bomb and the adjustable sway braces bearing on it. *Bockscar* was approaching 'mission-ready' status.

At eleven, the crew members of Mission No. 16 dropped their wallets on the beds of men not flying that night and crossed to the briefing room. The pre-flight briefing was for all crew of the three primary planes. Two British observers, who would fly in the photographics plane, were also present. William Penney was a physicist who, assigned to the Manhattan Project, had become one of its core scientists. Group Captain Leonard Cheshire, a highly decorated RAF pilot, was the official British observer. Both Penney and Cheshire had been scheduled on the Hiroshima mission, but at the last minute US authorities had held them over to the third plane of the follow-up mission.

Colonel Tibbets, commander of 509th Composite Group and

command pilot on the Hiroshima mission, opened proceedings with a few general remarks. Fat Man was a different bomb from the one used on Hiroshima, he told the men. More powerful and able to be mass produced, it would make Little Boy obsolete after only one outing. Tibbets wished the crews good luck and handed over to the intelligence officer.

Hazen Payette outlined the mission. Major Sweeney would carry the bomb in *Bockscar*. Captain Bock would fly Sweeney's plane, still fitted out with the instruments installed for Hiroshima. They would record data transmitted by capsules Bock's plane would drop as soon as the bomb was released. Lieutenant-Colonel Jim Hopkins would fly *The Big Stink* with movie cameras, scientific personnel and the official UK observer. Sweeney had asked for Bock to be on the mission, but was surprised that Hopkins would pilot the third aircraft. Having joined the 509th as group operations officer, the third pilot had limited mission experience but a high belief in his own ability. Jim Hopkins had the swagger that opened doors in the air force. Chuck Sweeney, a more humble personality, did not. But whether Hopkins had the skills to match the swagger remained to be seen.

The communications officer reported that the weather was expected to be rough. Two weather planes would report on current conditions at the targets just before the mission's arrival. Already it was looking inclement. A typhoon was gathering over Iwo Jima. The mission would involve flying some five hours through turbulent weather in complete radio silence and carrying an armed atomic bomb. It was an unsettling prospect.

Payette conceded the Japanese might recognise the purpose of three unescorted B-29s and that they didn't know what the Japanese fighter strength in Kyushu was. To mitigate this, the altitude at which they were to fly towards Japan was raised from the normal 3000 metres—the altitude for the Hiroshima mission—to nearly 6000 metres. The price of flying at the higher altitude would be greater fuel consumption.

The rendezvous point for Hiroshima had been Iwo Jima, but that was no longer practical with the prevailing weather. They would rise to 10,000 metres at Yakushima off the south coast of Kyushu. From that small island, they would proceed in formation towards Kokura.

The mission's operations officer was Jim Hopkins, pilot of its third plane. He notified key scheduled timings: take-off was to be at 0345 hours Tinian time, an hour after the weather planes had left, and rendezvous at Yakushima at 0915 hours (8.15 a.m. in Japan). Hopkins also outlined the air-sea rescue plan in place, a network of submarines, ships and special aircraft. In an emergency, four B-29s were standing by to guide any stricken aircraft to submarines, which would pick up ditched personnel. They would carry survival equipment to drop to crash-landed crews.

Tibbets finished the briefing by stressing two important directives for the mission. One was that the planes should wait no more than fifteen minutes at the rendezvous point before proceeding to Kokura. The other was that Fat Man should be dropped visually. They must be able to see the aiming point to minimise the chances of a wasted drop. The unstated other reason was to allow the effect of the bomb to be photographed. The meeting closed with a short prayer by Chaplain Downey and the crews went to their mess hall for a late night pre-flight snack.

As the crews shuffled out, Sweeney took Jim Hopkins to one side to a map on the wall. He pointed to one corner of the island of Yakushima and suggested they should cross that point for rendezvous. Circling the island risked not seeing each other. Hopkins said he knew how to rendezvous and walked away. The high-handed lieutenant-colonel did not want to be tutored by a mere major. Sweeney was gobsmacked, but there was little he could do about it. He put the same suggestion to Fred Bock, who agreed.

After the briefing, Chuck Sweeney walked pensively around aircraft No. 77 on the hardstand. The name 'Bockscar' was not yet painted on it. That would be done years later when it was installed in a museum.

Sweeney and Bock were different personalities from Paul Tibbets who, conscious of the media coverage planned, had his mother's name painted on a plane that wasn't his on the afternoon before the Hiroshima mission. Bob Lewis, who was co-pilot on that mission, was the pilot normally assigned to aircraft No. 82. Tibbets, as 509th commander, didn't have an assigned aircraft. It's not known whether Lewis had a name for his plane but it's unlikely he would have named it after Tibbets' mother.

When Lewis had come across a serviceman painting 'Enola Gay' on the side of his plane, he had exploded. The painter, who had been pulled from a softball game to do the job, explained he was acting on the colonel's orders. Lewis, already miffed he had been reduced to co-pilot for this important mission, protested to Tibbets, to be told he hadn't thought Lewis would mind. Tibbets had spoken to Sweeney and Marquardt, the pilot of No. 91, about it and they had raised no objection. But why would they?

With the second mission rapidly approaching, Sweeney circled the plane on which no-one saw the need to paint a name. He checked the aircraft's surface and looked for telltale fluid on the tarmac below it. The bomb-bay doors were open and he looked inside. Fat Man was waiting there silently, as if taking the nap that Sweeney had not managed to grab. Painted white with rough orange circles around it, the bomb's boxy tail had rude messages to Emperor Hirohito scribbled on it in crayon.

As Sweeney backed out from the fuselage his heart jumped. An admiral was there standing alongside him, watching silently.

'Son, do you know how much that bomb cost?' the admiral asked.

'No, sir.'

The admiral paused for dramatic effect. 'Two billion dollars,' he eventually informed the command pilot.

'That's a lot of money, Admiral.'

'Do you know how much your airplane costs?'

'Slightly over half a million dollars, sir,' Sweeney replied.

'I'd suggest you keep those relative values in mind for this mission.'

Sweeney had no idea who this senior naval officer was. In fact, it was Admiral Purnell, one of the Tinian Joint Chiefs. So far, Purnell hadn't made much impact on the mission personnel.

Chapter 10

Nagasaki, Thursday 9 August 1945, morning

Naotake Sato arrived promptly at five at the People's Commissariat of Foreign Affairs in Moscow, accompanied by the embassy secretary. The ambassador was cautious in his optimism that this meeting could generate the momentum needed to end the war. While the secretary waited outside, Sato was ushered into Molotov's office where the foreign minister was standing alongside his formidable desk. Ever the diplomat conscious of the conventions of diplomacy, Sato began congratulating Molotov in Russian on his safe return from Potsdam, but the foreign minister cut him off with a wave of the hand.

'I have here an important document to read in the name of the government of the Soviet Union,' he said. He picked up a paper from his desk and sat at the head of a long table, motioning Sato to sit at the other end.

Molotov read the document aloud:

After the defeat and capitulation of Hitlerite Germany, Japan remained the only great power which still stands for the continuation of the war. The demand of the three powers, the United States, Great Britain and China, of July 26 for the unconditional surrender of the Japanese armed forces was rejected by Japan. Thus the proposal made by the Japanese Government to the Soviet Union for mediation in the Far East has lost all foundation. Taking into account the refusal of Japan to capitulate, the Allies approached the Soviet Government with a proposal to join the war against Japanese aggression and thus shorten the duration of the war, reduce the number of casualties and contribute toward the most speedy restoration of peace. True to its obligations as an Ally, the Soviet Government has accepted the proposal of the Allies and has joined in the declaration of the Allied powers of July 26. The Soviet Government considers that this policy is the only means able to bring peace nearer, to free the people from further sacrifice and suffering and to give the Japanese people the opportunity of avoiding the danger of destruction suffered by Germany after her refusal to accept unconditional surrender. In view of the above, the Soviet Government declares that from tomorrow, that is from August 9, the Soviet Union will consider herself in a state of war against Japan.

He handed a copy of the pronouncement to Sato, who asked him if he could read it again. Molotov did so. He told Sato that Ambassador Malik was at that very time making the same declaration to the Japanese government in Tokyo. Sato expressed regret that the Soviet Union had decided to break its non-aggression pact with Japan almost a year before it expired. 'I don't understand how Soviet entry into the war would save the Japanese people from further destruction when Japan was asking the Soviet Union for help in ending the war,' he commented.

Sato asked if he could send a coded telegram to Tokyo before midnight about the declaration and his conversation with Molotov. He was assuming the declaration referred to Moscow time. The Russian said he could send any cables he wished and in code.

Concluding the meeting, Molotov said he personally regretted what had happened, but he was pleased the two of them had managed to maintain good relations despite the difficulties.

'It's a sad thing that we shall have to part as enemies,' replied Sato, 'but that cannot be helped.' They shook hands.

On the way back to the Japanese embassy, Sato said to the secretary, 'The inevitable has now arrived.' The pursuit of the Soviet Union as an intermediary for peace had become the lost cause he had always feared it would be. Japan's position in the war now seemed even more hopeless than ever. Sato would soon be returning home. He still had no idea whether Molotov was a genuine friend or just feigning friendship.

Soon after the meeting with Molotov, the telephones at the Japanese embassy were disconnected and its radio equipment confiscated. Sato had written a message in plain Japanese text and sent it to the cable office. It never reached Tokyo. Nor did Ambassador Malik read the Soviet declaration of war to the Japanese government that day.

◆　◆　◆

The crews for the second atomic bomb mission sat on the edge of their bunks, waiting for trucks to take them to their respective aircraft. When they arrived at the planes at 2 a.m., the airfield was dark with only their own landing lights and a few runway lights left on. It was 1 a.m. in Tokyo. The two weather reconnaissance planes had just taken off, one bound for Kokura, the other for Nagasaki.

A handful of airmen from other crews and well-wishers were standing around, along with a couple of photographers and the PR officer, Major Moynahan. Photos were taken of the crew, the plane, some scientists and a few high-ranking hangers-on. It was all very low key compared with the Hollywood production of the first mission's departure. The PR man noted that the plane's number, 77, was the same as the number star halfback Red Grange used to wear in gridiron. It was probably a lucky number, suggested Moynahan.

'It's a nice thought,' was Major Sweeney's comment, 'but we don't need it. We've got the best damned crew in the Air Force.'

Sweeney walked around *Bockscar* with flight engineer Kuharek, co-pilot Albury and the chief of the ground crew. Sweeney circled planes in the same way a potential car buyer kicks the tyres. Everything looked fine, so the mission leader gave a short pep talk to his assembled crew. He wanted this mission to go as smoothly as the Hiroshima mission. 'We will get the bomb to the target,' he said. 'I don't care if I have to dive the airplane into the target, we're going to deliver it.'

There's no record of how much comfort his men took from this statement, but they could not have missed his determination. His group commander, Colonel Tibbets, stood silently to one side puffing his pipe.

While the crew climbed on board, Sweeney went over maps spread out on the bonnet of a Jeep with navigator Van Pelt and bombardier Beahan. He bid farewell to his pipe-puffing commander and climbed aboard after the others. Chuck Sweeney strapped himself into his leather seat and went through the checklist with Don Albury.

◆   ◆   ◆

As soon as Soviet army engineers had laid the first pontoon bridges across the Argun River, a spearhead of tanks crossed into western Manchuria. There was no artillery or air barrage to soften up the defenders because there were no Japanese defenders there. Foreign Minister Molotov had told the Japanese ambassador that the USSR would be at war the next day and they were. It was ten minutes past midnight, local (Trans-Baikal) time—ten past one in Tokyo, ten past two on Tinian, still only seven in the evening in Moscow. Advance units rolled across the flat, arid waste-land of the north-eastern corner of the Gobi Desert.

Marshal Malinovsky had positioned his Trans-Baikal Front to penetrate along three stretches of Manchuria's western border. West of the spear-head there was no river to cross. Tanks just drove across a nominal border and onto the Gobi Desert. To the north, infantry units were carried over the rain-swollen Argun in assault boats and makeshift rafts to provide cover for engineers building pontoon bridges across the river. Japanese outposts on the opposite bank were first peppered with a ten-minute artillery barrage in darkness and dense river fog. This was the only resist-ance encountered by the Trans-Baikal Front as it entered Manchuria. Convinced the terrain was impassable and failing to detect over 600,000 Russian troops amassing on their western border, the Kwantung Army, the one-time elite Japanese force occupying and defending Manchuria, had only placed token defenders in the area.

Marshal Vasilevsky's strategic planners had laid out a three-pronged attack to subdue the Japanese. A classic pincer movement, simultaneously attacking both flanks, was designed to encircle and defeat the Kwantung Army. The Trans-Baikal force moved in from the west. At the same time, the First Far Eastern Front would drive from the east. The smaller Second Far Eastern Front would attack from the north to prevent reinforcement from there of the Japanese central defences.

Under General Otozo Yamada, a thin, solemn career soldier who had previously been Japan's chief of military training, the Japanese in Manchuria were woefully underprepared for an invasion on this or any scale. The Kwantung Army had been asset-stripped. After the fall of Iwo Jima in March, Tokyo had withdrawn all Manchuria's elite divisions and its only tank division to defend the homeland against the expected US offensive. Half of General Yamada's twenty-one divisions existed only on paper.

The Kwantung Army had called up reservists and new recruits to create a semblance of a formidable fighting force, but more than a quarter of the combat force of 710,000 had been mobilised only ten days before the Soviet attack. One newly formed infantry division had no artillery pieces. Some soldiers were armed with sharpened bamboo sticks. Half the Kwantung Army's ammunition stocks had been ordered to be returned for defence of the homeland. Only seven or eight divisions were rated as combat effective.

Japan's defensive plan was to build fortified areas along a thousand kilometres of border in the north and east and leave the uncrossable western approaches undefended. A delaying action along the border would be followed by withdrawal to prepared lines and then to a stronghold at Tunghua in south-eastern Manchuria for a final defensive action. The terrain, long distances and determined resistance would combine to weaken the attacking forces so effectively that by the time they reached the final defensive positions they could be driven back. Only a third of the Kwantung Army was stationed near the border. The rest was deployed in depth in central and southern Manchuria.

The Kwantung Army's leadership was caught on a bad day by the Soviet drive. On the evening of 8 August, the commanders were at Fifth Army Headquarters in Changchun for a tabletop strategy exercise. Those present were made aware of the plan to withdraw troops to Tunghua, but junior commanders in the field and the 300,000 Japanese civilians and 'agricultural pioneers' in Manchuria had not been told. As well as being ignorant of the Soviet build-up along their western border, they had seriously underestimated the numbers on the eastern side. The offensive was not expected before September. The Japanese in Manchuria were relocating their troops and building fortifications when the Russians attacked in the early hours of 9 August.

While the Trans-Baikal Front drove in from the west largely unopposed, nearly 590,000 troops of the First Far Eastern force were spread along a 700-kilometre front stretching up from the border near Vladivostok past Lake Khanka, which straddled the border line halfway up the eastern side. This frontier of the Japanese colony was heavily fortified with large reinforced concrete pillboxes along a defensive line some 80 kilometres inside the border. Small covering units patrolled the frontier edge.

Marshal Meretskov's First Far Eastern Front pushed across the border in several places. To minimise detection, tanks and rifle corps held back from their launching points for an attack on the southern border town of Tungning until half an hour before midnight. Light rain was starting to fall. As soon as the clock ticked past midnight into 9 August, Russian sappers cut through barbed wire strung along the border line. The rain intensified into torrential thunderstorms as assault forces moved through gaps in the wire. Although the inundation hindered the advance, Japanese defenders could hear little above the thunder and pounding downpour. The border watchers were caught by surprise in their posts and quickly subdued.

More to the north, other units of the First Far Eastern Front set out under cover of the stormy dark to cross marshland and forest around the large wetland of Lake Khanka. On one side of the lake was the heavily wooded and mountainous taiga the Japanese believed too difficult for a large-scale offensive. They were almost right. Engineers had to cut roads through the mossy-floored forest of pine and larch, made more arduous by the soaking rain. Progress was slow but unhindered by defenders.

On the other side of the lake, troops crossed the Ussuri and the Sungacha rivers on small, lightly armed boats. Within an hour they had eliminated outposts across the border. From there it got harder. The heavy rain and flooding made the marshy area farther on impassable. Engineers had to build makeshift corduroy roads—timber posts laid across the muddy track—over swampland before the advance could resume.

A third axis of the Soviet attack provided a supporting role from the north. The objective for the Second Far Eastern Front's 340,000 troops was the northern cities of Harbin and Tsitsihar to prevent the Japanese withdrawing their forces there to the south. A fleet of monitors—shallow-draft river warships with 130 mm guns—gunboats and armoured launches provided landing and fire support as troops, tanks and mortars were ferried across the Amur River. The Japanese had detected preparation on the western flank of this front and were alert for the force to advance. Unfortunately for them, this part of the front was held back until 11 August. Elsewhere, the front faced determined resistance along its advance lines and was held up at several river crossings, but Japanese troops holding up their advance were troops not available to come to the aid of their compatriots facing crushing defeat in the south.

◆　◆　◆

Chuck Sweeney was about to give the command, 'Start engines,' when an anxious John Kuharek leaned his head back and bent around from his nook of instrument panels. 'Major, we have a problem,' he said. 'The fuel in our reserve tank in the rear bomb-bay bladder unit isn't pumping.' Six hundred gallons of fuel were trapped in the auxiliary tank, inaccessible. The flight engineer's suspicion was that a solenoid needed replacing.

Climbing down the nosewheel well ladder, Sweeney advised the watching Tibbets of the problem. Time was not a luxury available to them. Replacing the pump could take a few hours. Transferring the bomb to another plane would be time-consuming and, now that the weapon was activated, risky. The weather was closing in and might take a few days to pass through. Delaying the mission was not an option they were prepared to consider. Tibbets puffed thoughtfully and told Sweeney he would leave the decision to him. They could refuel if necessary at Okinawa or Iwo Jima, although the weather had already precluded Iwo Jima as the rendezvous point it had served for the first bombing mission.

The crew sat in their places, unable to hear the two men and conscious that lying silent in their midst was the large metal form of an atomic weapon primed to detonate. A few could watch the conversation between Sweeney and Tibbets outside the plane as mime play, but it gave little away. After a few minutes, Sweeney climbed back into the plane and settled once more into the pilot's seat. 'Roger. All set,' he said.

At a quarter to four in the morning, *Bockscar* wheeled down a Tinian taxiway, making its way to the western end of Runway A on the base's North Field. With radio silence for the mission, there was no communication with the control tower. Major Sweeney ran the engines up in sequence, pushing the throttle to fully open with the brakes on. The plane stood on its spot, vibrating, alone at the end of its take-off path. *The Great Artiste*, with Fred Bock at the helm, had taxied out to another runway.

Co-pilot Albury lowered *Bockscar*'s flaps and told Sergeant Kuharek, the flight engineer, 'Ready for take-off.' The crew were instructed to stand by. Sweeney eased the throttle back, then opened it slowly, releasing the brakes at the same time. The bulky craft rolled forward, crawling at first but gathering speed. Over 75 tonnes were lumbering down the tarmac. Sweeney looked up and saw that the spotlight at the far end of the runway had not been switched on. In the darkness he couldn't see the end of the runway at the ocean's edge. The failed take-off he'd watched the night before crossed his mind.

The genial Irish-American pilot was all concentration. Holding the yoke down, he kept the plane on the ground as its speed increased, a calculated risk to get up enough momentum to ensure take-off. With the live Fat Man on board, he had to do it before they reached the end of the runway he couldn't yet see.

At 200 km/h, *Bockscar* was still touching the ground as it powered down the 3-kilometre-long runway. Its speed increased to 225 km/h.

B-29s had a history of engines overheating and bursting into flames, but there was little Sweeney could do about that except hope this wasn't going to be one of those occasions. At 260 km/h the craft slowly lifted as it ran out of runway. At the instant of take-off, the tarmac rushing below them disappeared and in its place the Pacific Ocean sped past underneath. *Bockscar* strained to rise, eventually lurching to 2500 metres.

Soon after, Captain Fred Bock's plane rose into the air from Runway B. On Runway C, Jim Hopkins took off in *The Big Stink* loaded with photographic equipment and observers, including the official British observer, Group Captain Cheshire.

The physicist Robert Serber had also been assigned to fly with Hopkins to operate photographic equipment. After he'd boarded the plane, Serber realised he'd forgotten his parachute. Hopkins became the pilot who was a stickler for the rules. He wouldn't allow violation of military regulations by a civilian and ordered Serber off the plane. The scientist was left standing on the taxiway in the pitch dark as *The Big Stink* continued to the head of Runway C. It took him an hour to walk back to the communications centre and report back to General Farrell. The Project Alberta chief was far from impressed with Hopkins flexing his authority, but it wasn't practical to break radio silence and call him back. Farrell, as well as Serber, just had to wear the circumstances as they unfolded.

Parachutes might have been superfluous on this mission anyway. On the Hiroshima mission, Colonel Tibbets had secretly carried a pack of twelve cyanide capsules to distribute to the crew if they were shot down over Japan. He thought of the prospect of torture by Japanese with apprehension although he had little useful information he could give up to any interrogators. Most of the others had even less, with the exception of the weaponeer, Deak Parsons. Unaware of Tibbets' poison capsules, he'd borrowed a revolver from a military policeman just before boarding *Enola Gay*. He hadn't had to use it. There's no record of Chuck Sweeney taking suicide tablets with him on the second mission or even that he was aware Tibbets had them for the first.

◆ ◆ ◆

Two hours after his meeting with Sato and as the Red Army launched its invasion, Molotov met with the American and British ambassadors, Averell Harriman and Clerk Kerr. He told them he had just delivered to Sato a declaration of war on Japan. While once the Soviet Union had thought it would not be able to move onto a war footing with Japan until mid-August, it was now able to keep to its Yalta undertakings. The announcement of Russia's entry into the Far East war would go to the press and radio at 8.30 p.m. (2.30 a.m. in Tokyo, 1.30 p.m. in Washington). Molotov told Kerr that he regretted the necessary treatment of Sato in this development. Sato was a 'kind-hearted man' with whom Molotov said he'd always had good relations.

Immediately after the meeting with Molotov, Harriman met with the Soviet leader. In the exchange of diplomatic pleasantries, each explored what the other knew—and what the other knew of what they knew. The American expressed his nation's gratitude at Russia's entry into the war.

'The United States and the Soviet Union are now allies again,' he said.

Stalin told Harriman of the advances into Manchuria by each front of the Red Army there . . . in advance of the events. Harriman asked how Stalin thought the atomic bomb would affect the Japanese. Neither would have been aware that at that time *Bockscar* was on its way to Japan. Stalin replied that the Japanese were looking for a pretext to replace their present government with one committed to undertake surrender.

'The bomb gives them that pretext,' he said.

The reality, however, was that Stalin knew that Japan was not contemplating surrender at that time. The Americans must have known it also, from their intercepts of Sato's coded cables, but that information may not have reached Harriman.

The ambassador said it was good that the US and not Germany had invented the atomic bomb, innocently echoing a diary comment by Truman without including the Soviet Union. Stalin commented that Soviet scientists had found harnessing atomic power a difficult challenge. The British had got nowhere too, he said, although they had excellent physicists. However, German laboratories working on the project had now been seized by the Russians. A breakthrough might come out of that, was the implication.

Harriman told him that the United Kingdom had pooled its knowledge with the US since 1941 under an arrangement through Churchill, something the Russian already knew from his spies.

'It must have been expensive,' Joseph Stalin said.

'It cost two billion US dollars,' was the reply. Money was no object to the US was the subtext.

On returning to the embassy, Harriman sent a cable to Truman and Byrnes advising them of the evening's developments. An hour later, NV Novikov of the Soviet embassy in Washington called on the US State Department and formally advised what the Secretary of State already knew.

At three o'clock, Truman held an impromptu press conference in the Oval Office. Byrnes was seated on his left; Truman's Chief of Staff, Admiral Leahy, came in and sat on his right. Each held a sheet of pink paper headed 'TOP SECRET' in red ink.

The president read a statement: 'I have only a simple announcement to make. I can't hold a regular press conference today, but this announcement is so important I thought I would call you in. Russia has declared war on Japan. That's all.'

Truman was disappointed. He had wanted a Japanese surrender before the Soviet entry into the war, but that hadn't happened. Stalin had assured him the USSR would not join the war without agreement with China. That hadn't happened either despite American efforts to stonewall those talks. Truman was left with his thoughts while there was a rush for the doors by the assembled press.

Jim Byrnes made a statement to the press soon after. The Soviet declaration, he said, would shorten the war and save many lives.

◆ ◆ ◆

At one in the morning, the Kwantung Army's headquarters was told the Soviet Army had crossed the border into eastern Manchuria and that Mutanchiang was under air attack. Half an hour later, an air raid on the capital Changchun was further evidence something significant was afoot.

Ambassador Sato's cable to Tokyo advising of the Soviet declaration of war had never been sent, despite Molotov's promise, but it wasn't long before the news got through anyway. At 2.30 a.m., Domei News Agency picked up a TASS broadcast from Moscow announcing the Soviet Union's declaration of war on Japan. It was an hour and a half since the Russians had moved into Manchuria.

An hour later, Domei's foreign news editor Hasegawa rang cabinet secretary Sakomizu, who happened to be an old school acquaintance, to report what the Domei monitors had heard. Sakomizu in turn rang Suzuki, asleep in his private residence, and was told to come immediately. By the time the cabinet secretary got to Suzuki's home, the prime minister was in morning dress. Togo had just arrived. The radio room of the Foreign Ministry had also intercepted the Soviet broadcast and alerted its minister.

Suzuki rang Lieutenant-General Sumihisa Ikeda, the chief of army budget planning. Until three weeks before, Ikeda had been Vice Chief of Staff in the Kwantung Army. If anyone knew Japan's capacity to resist attack in Manchuria, he should.

'Is the Kwantung Army capable of repulsing a Russian advance?' the prime minister asked.

'The Kwantung Army is hopeless. Within two weeks, the Russians will occupy Changchun.'

'If the Kwantung Army is that weak,' said Suzuki, 'then there can be no doubt the game is up.'

Togo told Suzuki the war had to be brought to a speedy finish, criticising him for not calling a meeting of the Supreme War Council, the 'Big Six', the previous day. The council must meet immediately, Togo said, and Suzuki agreed. He instructed Sakomizu to call the meeting for ten thirty that morning.

Suzuki said to the cabinet secretary, 'Let our present cabinet take responsibility for seeing the country through termination of the war.' Normally, cabinet would resign for the government's failure to enlist the USSR as mediator, but the times were not normal.

◆ ◆ ◆

In the pre-dawn darkness of Manchuria, the Russian offensive continued along a number of axes, most of them unchallenged by Japanese
defenders. Two wide columns of Soviet and American-made tanks, 80
kilometres apart, sped across the Gobi's Barga Plateau. Occasional buttes
and dry streambeds were circumvented without much difficulty. On each
tank, a group of Russian soldiers clung to the turret as keen as adventure tourists. With few natural obstacles, the tanks roared over steppe
grass and patches of dense brush, leaving in their wake a cloud of sandy
dust hanging in the cold night air and highlighted by the headlamps
of following vehicles. It might have been an impressive spectacle had
anyone been there to see it. But there wasn't.

The Kwantung Army had fortified along the river running through
the centre of the Barga Plateau. The Chinese Eastern Railway line and
the only major road ran alongside. The Trans-Baikal force used instead
the numerous hardened tracks crisscrossing the plateau. The same thing
happened with Japanese defences along the railway line to Solun. The
Russians simply moved through the Grand Khingan Mountains running
up western Manchuria, the terrain thought by Japan's strategists to be
impassable, and isolated Solun's fortified defenders.

On the storm-soaked eastern side of Manchuria, the Soviet advance
pressed on, leaving isolated Japanese units behind to be dealt with by the
forces following. Along with the tanks were self-propelled guns, lightly
armoured artillery pieces on motorised chassis. These tended to stand
back and bombard a target, whereas the tanks drove into and over it,
crushing anything or anyone in their path.

Progress was slow through the forests and across the marshland around
Lake Khanka, in some places no more than twelve kilometres by dawn,
but they were still moving forward. To the south, advance units were
pushing west in the inundated darkness along the valley to the target
town of Tungning. By six in the morning, the downpour was starting
to ease, but by then it had served its purpose of cover for an attack by
stealth.

At the far north of the First Far Eastern Front's line an assault had been launched on the border town of Hutou. While the town was subjected to artillery bombardment, the assault units had crossed the Ussuri River then waited while Soviet bombers pounded the area for two hours before the sun rose. The townsfolk of Hutou were among the first to taste the awful power that had been unleashed on this hapless spoil of Japan's now-disappearing military might.

◆ ◆ ◆

Bockscar cruised at nearly 6000 metres, trying to stay above the sky's turbulence. Sweeney didn't want to take any risks with a live bomb, but neither did he want to use up any more fuel than necessary. The higher the altitude, the greater the rate of fuel consumption.

Once they were in the air, there was a burst of repartee between Spitzer the radioman and some of the others, but that soon faded away. The atmosphere became subdued as those with immediate tasks went about them. For others, their time to contribute would come later. Don Albury took the controls while Chuck Sweeney, third pilot Fred Olivi, and bombardier Kermit Beahan catnapped. Jimmy Van Pelt worked over his charts, keeping tabs on the course to Yakushima, the rendezvous point, and occasionally checking radar with Ed Buckley. John Kuharek kept a close watch on the fuel gauges, knowing how important fuel consumption might become later in the mission. Abe Spitzer, having run out of conversationalists, read a *Reader's Digest* condensed book.

At four thirty, Olivi took control of *Bockscar*, and an hour later Sweeney was back at the wheel. He had tried to steer around the storm clouds but eventually found himself trapped in the middle. A storm broke, sheets of pouring rain lashed the aircraft's windows, lightning flashed all around. All the while, in their midst the fully armed Fat Man was poised to carry out its two-billion-dollar function. Little was said. The plane bobbed up and down, buffeted by the weather, as Sweeney tried to get either above or below the storm without success. The whirling giant propellers had become luminous blue discs. Then, without warning, *Bockscar* flew out of the storm and into the vestiges of a clear, starry night. It was as magical as the instant relief all on board felt. The few stars slowly washed away as the sun spread its glow over the horizon.

As the dawn came, *Bockscar* started the climb to the rendezvous altitude of 10,000 metres. Commander Fred Ashworth, the project officer and weaponeer for this mission, watched while his assistant, Lieutenant Phil Barnes, checked the electrical units that monitored the workings of Fat Man. In the course of this precaution, Barnes found a red light flashing irregularly on the bomb's fuse monitor. Properly installed, this would indicate the firing circuits were closed and some fuses were activated. What it indicated in this instance neither could be sure. Ashworth quietly advised Sweeney of their discovery. If a time fuse was activated or the plane dropped below the pre-set detonation height of 600 metres, they could be in serious trouble.

Barnes removed the cover of the black box and started a prescribed emergency examination. A check of the four key points revealed nothing. Referring to a circuit diagram, his fingertips traced along wire, switches and coils, checking every wiring sequence, looking for any abnormality in the circuitry, a spaghetti bowl of wires. After several tense minutes, his fingertips found the problem. Someone had placed two rotary switches in the wrong positions. The result was a malfunction in the monitor's circuits. The firing circuits weren't closed; the fuses weren't activated. Phil Barnes flipped the two switches back to their proper positions and the light commenced its regular flashing. Ashworth reported to Sweeney that all was well. His assistant resumed monitoring.

A cable in backwards. Two switches in the wrong position. The mission might yet pay a heavy price for the haste with which it was obliged to prepare a weapon never before used in active service. The weather had dictated the shortening of mission preparation, but no-one had asked: why don't we let the weather pass through, then drop the second bomb? The invasion of the Japanese home islands wasn't scheduled till November.

◆　◆　◆

On his way back to the Foreign Ministry after meeting with the prime minister, Shigenori Togo called in at the Navy Ministry to let Admiral

Yonai know what had eventuated. Not surprisingly, the navy minister agreed that the Japanese government should pursue a peace settlement with the Allies as quickly as possible. For some time, he had been a consistent advocate for peace in the Supreme War Council.

While there, Togo ran into Prince Takamatsu, a strong voice in the ear of his brother, the emperor. He too was in agreement with Togo's view.

Also present at the ministry was Morisada Hosokawa, an adviser to former prime minister Konoye, with a plan, the first of a day of intrigues within Japan's ruling cliques as various players tried to point the foundering ship of government in their favoured direction. Hosokawa proposed Takamatsu assume premiership of a new cabinet and negotiate directly with the US and Britain. Takamatsu deflected the suggestion, saying, 'Let Konoye take over.'

With that in mind, Hosokawa went in the prince's car to Konoye's home and told him of the Soviet invasion. 'This might be God's gift to control the army,' was the elder statesman's response. Nothing ever came of the Hosokawa plan.

About that time, the deputy to Army Chief of Staff Umezu was woken and told of the Soviet declaration and reports that were coming in from Manchuria. Torashiro Kawabe was more shocked by this news than he was by the Hiroshima bomb. Japan had been enduring devastating bombardment of its cities all year, but the entry of the Soviets into the fight tipped the scales dangerously.

Kawabe devised a recipe for his embattled country: proclaim martial law and dismiss cabinet; then abandon Manchuria and defend southern Korea only. He presented his martial law plan to his chief, but Umezu's response was lukewarm at best. Kawabe got a more enthusiastic response from the war minister, whom he collared as he was leaving for the Supreme War Council meeting. Anami said he understood Kawabe's view was shared by most of General Staff and it should be looked at. He told Kawabe he would defend the war faction's position at the morning's council meeting at the risk of his life, although it was probably at more risk if he didn't.

Anami stood up, smiled and said while leaving, 'If my view is not accepted, I'll resign as minister and request assignment to a unit in China.'

Such a move would trigger the collapse of cabinet if the military refused to nominate a replacement. The threat could derail any peace initiatives. Anami never acted on this resolve, nor possibly had any intention of doing so.

The prime minister had his own strategies to engineer. He wanted to chart a course around the chronic deadlock in the Japanese leadership regarding ending the war. Suzuki met with Hirohito at 7.30 a.m. and advised him of the Soviet declaration. We must now accept the Potsdam demands, he said, and the emperor agreed. Suzuki had serious doubts about his ability to secure unanimous agreements in the Supreme War Council and cabinet. He spoke in veiled language.

'Though I know such drastic action is against all custom and usage, I beg you grant to me, please, your special help.'

'I'll give you my assistance,' said the emperor. 'Of course.'

◆ ◆ ◆

In a spacious room in the large house high on the slopes of Junin, Mitsue Takeno, her landlady, Mrs Hirai, and the landlady's daughter, Chifusa, all slept in *monpe* on futons laid side by side. That month, the frequent air-raid warnings were regularly interrupting the sultry nights. By sleeping in their workpants, the three were able to go quickly, any time the shrill sirens sounded, to a shelter in the basement of the building next door.

On the night of 8 August, the Hirais and their boarder went to the shelter during the night and returned soon after when the all-clear sounded. Back on her futon, Mitsue lay awake, worrying about where the world—and Japan—was heading. While still a child in many ways, she was obliged to take a role in an adult world she didn't comprehend. Mitsue longed to be with her family in the simple rural life of the small offshore islands. Always hungry here, she felt as a boarder she couldn't say anything about it. In any case, Mrs Hirai and Chi-chan were always very kind to her. How could she say something that might be construed as criticism? Mitsue finally managed to fall asleep just before dawn.

When she woke unrefreshed, sunlight was flooding the room. Mitsue got up, went over to the front window and looked out at the Nagasaki summer morning, so bright when she felt so drained. Mrs Hirai, a devout Buddhist, chanted a sutra in another room as she did every morning and evening. The city spread far below like a scrupulously detailed model. With a vista of such splendor, Mitsue forgot what it was that worried her much of the night.

Mrs Hirai already had two lunch boxes prepared for the girls, each with gleaming white rice balls. By then, most brown rice was mixed with barley, which dulled the whiteness of the rice when it was polished. Mitsue asked the landlady where she got the unmixed rice, but her reply was an enigmatic smile. She wouldn't say.

After a spartan breakfast, the two girls made their way down hillside lanes to the tram stop, Mitsue wearing a soft rayon blouse, serge *monpe* and volunteer's armband. Her air-raid hood and first-aid pouch were, as usual, strapped diagonally across her chest. Before the Urakami tram arrived, Chi-chan decided she wasn't going to work that day and, without explanation, turned back. Puzzled, Mitsue watched her go.

◆　◆　◆

Sumiteru Taniguchi was asleep on a *tatami* mat when his grandmother arrived at the post office. She woke him to give him two *bento* boxes she'd brought across the bay. One was for breakfast, the other for lunch. Sumiteru thanked Oba-chan and urged her to hurry home. There had been raids overnight on the northern Kyushu industrial city of Yawata. Nagasaki might be a target at any time and he didn't want his grandmother caught in it.

Sumiteru had been on night duty, helping to move important documents in the post office records to a safer place. He also took his turn at fire-watch duty during the night. By the time he finished it was too late to go home, so he slept at the office until Oba-chan gently shook him awake.

He was on afternoon shift that day, delivering telegrams, but one of the older workers had asked if he would swap shifts. Morning shift involved sorting letters and delivering them. As Sumiteru wouldn't now be back until late afternoon, he ate both the meals and left the post office before nine to do his rounds.

The young postman rode up the Urakami valley with a workmate, in the warm, cloudless morning. Eventually they parted ways, Sumiteru heading for the top of the valley, his friend delivering to suburbs across the river.

◆ ◆ ◆

Dr Akizuki's day began at six thirty with his usual routine. He rose, washed and had breakfast. Walking to work, cicadas shrilling all around, he noticed clouds gathering in what had been a clear blue sky. Another sweltering day is coming, he thought.

At the main entrance of Urakami Hospital, Dr Akizuki was button-holed by Brother Iwanaga. Four new X-ray machines had arrived overnight and had been put in the basement. Akizuki thanked him. Brother Joseph was a strong, young country boy of simple faith and with a willingness to work. His faith was neither here nor there to the non-Catholic doctor, but he was extremely useful in a time of labour shortage. Why Iwanaga hadn't been drafted into military service, Akizuki had no idea. It was not his concern, but he was glad of it. However, the doctor didn't want to get caught up in conversation with the chatterbox monk. He excused himself and hurried off.

On an upper floor, Sugako Murai had already been approached in the corridor by the head nurse as she emerged from her room. Looking pale and drained, nurse Fukahori said she felt ill and would spend the day in her room. She asked Sugako if she could assist Dr Akizuki. The cook was glad to help. Behind the polite mask, she bubbled with excitement. This, she thought, is going to be a great day. Anticipating the response, the senior nurse had already sent a message to Akizuki and organised for someone to take charge of the kitchen for the day. Her staffing problem solved, she retreated to her room.

When Akizuki got to his office, his temporary nurse was already waiting for him. Before they'd even finished exchanging greetings, the first siren sounded. It wasn't yet eight o'clock. Forty minutes later, they returned to Dr Akizuki's room and began treating out-patients. By ten, nearly thirty people were sitting in the clinic's ante-room. Among the patients was the group from Takahara Hospital requiring artificial pneumo-thorax treatment, a controlled temporary collapse of the lung. They had come earlier that morning with Dr Yoshioka and two nurses. Unusually for the times, Dr Yoshioka was a female doctor. Akizuki guessed she was in her thirties.

The day was already moving apace. Akizuki's older sister had rung that morning with something on her mind about a younger sister's marriage proposal. She needed to talk to her brother about it and would come to the hospital at lunchtime. As the older of only two boys of nine siblings, Akizuki felt obliged to listen, but it wasn't something that greatly occupied his thoughts.

One of Dr Akizuki's visitors that morning was a research engineer at Mitsubishi's ordnance factory. He'd come to ask about his daughter, who'd been in the hospital for three weeks with mild tuberculosis. The gloomy engineer was not the sort of company Akizuki would have preferred if he had the choice. He talked about the destiny of Japan and what he'd heard about the Hiroshima bomb. The damage was too great for a chemical reaction, the engineer said. He guessed the explosion might have been produced by atomic fission.

That bleak assessment was interrupted by the long continuous wail of the air-raid siren. Instructions to hospital staff were to ensure patients went down to the basement shelter and to stay there with them. Almost inevitably there was no threat. The enemy planes, if there were any, always seemed to be going somewhere else. Akizuki didn't always bother with evacuation these days. Since the patients were waiting for breakfast, they remained on the second and third floors instead of being taken down to the shelter. Dr Akizuki went outside to assess the threat from above. It had become hot, as he had predicted, but had clouded over. He could neither see nor hear a bomber formation.

◆ ◆ ◆

Early in the morning of 9 August, Masuichi Takigawa left home to attend classes at Nagasaki Medical College, a kilometre's walk. Ten-year-old Sakue had slept in her *monpe* with her air-raid hood lying alongside her on the bed. She was shaken awake with the air-raid warning siren wailing, rubbed her eyes, gathered her thoughts as she gathered her hood and picked up a backpack. All week she had stayed overnight in the air-raid shelter, but last night she had slept at home after the modest celebratory dinner. It was still early morning.

Sakue wanted to stay with her mother—or, at least, the person she once believed to be her mother—and deliberately lingered in the house, but Mrs Takigawa was alert to the ruse and shepherded her out the door after Ryoko. Sakue's older sister asked her if she would take the baby and strapped him on her back. In those days of large families it wasn't unusual to see a baby strapped on an older sibling's back.

The two younger sisters ran with the baby in a growing neighbourhood group to the shelter across the river. They followed the levee path, up a side creek and up the hill where the shelter had been built. When they got there, they took their hoods off and sat on *tatami* mats reserved for their respective school classes. People didn't move around in the shelter, staying in their designated positions and waiting, mostly without conversation. Five or six boys and seven or eight girls were already there. Their classes had been depleted by evacuation to the country.

The girls were hungry. They hadn't had their morning meal, usually *omoyu*, the watery porridge little more than rice broth. Sakue looked in her backpack of first-aid and emergency items and found some dry biscuits. Small voices piped, 'I'm hungry!' She dipped the biscuits one by one in water so they expanded. Soggy pieces of biscuit were shared with her classmates while they waited for the all-clear to sound.

◆ ◆ ◆

The morning of 9 August began for the Egashira family much as any other day at this stage of the war. Ukichi and Chiyoko Egashira had breakfast with their five children amidst the usual exchange of everyday chat. Ukichi's mother, who lived with them, had already eaten. Their eldest and only son suggested they go fishing on Sunday. His sisters were too busy gossiping with each other to agree or disagree with his plan.

When that morning's air-raid warning rang out, Ukichi took the five children and his mother to the dugout. Father and son returned as soon as the all-clear sounded. Takashi put on the leggings of his civil defence uniform. His father put on the whole uniform and cap and the pair left for work, father to the weapons factory at Ohashi across the river, son to Nippon Express as a mobilised student.

Having been told that she could start work an hour later than usual, Chiyoko was in no hurry to leave for school. As she was leaving, her mother-in-law returned with the four daughters. Naomi, the youngest, was crying because the shelter had got too hot in the humidity that had built up under the overcast sky. Chiyoko decided to take her to school with the intention of putting her down to sleep in a quiet corner of a classroom. She left her mother-in-law and the three older girls at home in Shiroyama and walked to the school with Naomi on her back.

◆　◆　◆

At Nagasaki Medical College, Dr Nagai had been on air-raid duty overnight along with other members of staff on the roster. One of them had agreed to temporarily oversee the pharmacy students digging the shelter behind their department building. He headed off to make good his promise to Professor Seiki. Nagai's leukemia symptoms had abated.

Nagasaki's medical school was still running a reduced program of lectures, with lecturers and students arriving in air-raid dress with first-aid kits at the side. The start of the day's classes was interrupted by the air-raid warning responding to the lone American B-29. Unknown to the defenders of Nagasaki, it was the weather scout reporting conditions over the back-up target for the second atomic bomb mission.

With the siren wailing in continual bursts, patients were carried to a shelter near the hospital entrance. Those who could got there under their own steam. Medical students with duties as stretcher-bearers stood to attention in front of the shelter. Students working on the new shelter stood by at its entrance. Others wore steel helmets and tightly bound black gaiters. Students and nurses in uniform lined the wide hospital corridor. A couple had binoculars strung around their necks.

Dr Nagai was the leader of the local civil defence body, the Eleventh Medical Corps. He inspected air-raid equipment in the corridor: picks, fire-hooks and shovels. Outside, buckets filled with water, hoses laid out on the ground, all beside members of the student defence corps standing erect. Hand pumps were manned at the back gate. Cicadas kept up their unbroken screech in the camphor trees at nearby Sanno Shrine as the sirens faded into limp silence.

◆   ◆   ◆

As *Bockscar* approached the southernmost of Japan's home islands, Sweeney warned Spitzer to be on the alert for radio transmission from the two weather planes. The Japanese were still jamming frequencies, so picking up radio signals could be difficult. On the other hand, the weather reports seemed a foregone conclusion. The sun was shining and everything looked peaceful and serene. It seemed they had left the stormy weather behind and would have to find something else to worry about. Pappy Dehart, the tail gunner, reported an unidentified plane in the distance. Pulses quickened but it was identified as a B-29. In fact it was their usual plane, *The Great Artiste*, temporarily under command of Captain Fred Bock.

A radio signal started coming in, faint at first through the static and jamming. It was repeated twice and the third time came through clearly, in code from over Kokura. Weather was good, was the report, morning haze expected to clear. The primary target was recommended for bombing. A minute later, the second weather report came in. Nagasaki was also hazy, with 20 per cent cloud cover and clearing. Sweeney announced over the *Bockscar* intercom, 'Kokura it is, men.'

The mission command plane arrived at Yakushima at 8.10 a.m. Some scattered cloud had moved in, but the rendezvous island was still visible through breaks in the cloud. *Bockscar* had lost sight of *The Great Artiste*. After circling Yakushima for ten minutes it was spotted again. Bock moved into formation position off Sweeney's right wing, but there was no sign of Hopkins with the third plane. As they were under strict radio silence there was no opportunity to find out from Hopkins what the hold-up was. Sweeney's orders were to wait no longer than fifteen minutes, but a couple of distant planes were sighted and it took some time to identify them. They were other American planes on the prowl, not *The Big Stink*. At the same time, Sweeney worried about fuel consumption at their rendezvous altitude of 10,000 metres. After forty minutes, he'd had enough. With the weather beginning to deteriorate, he wiggled his wings to indicate to Bock they were proceeding to Kokura without the camera plane.

As it turned out, Hopkins had made a number of errors stemming from his refusal to discuss a rendezvous plan with Sweeney at the Tinian briefing. He took a huge circle around several of the islands, keeping wide of the other two planes all the time. However, his greatest mistake was probably to invite the experienced English fighter pilot, Leonard Cheshire, into the cockpit and then lecture him about breaching regulations in removing his parachute to get through the connecting tunnel. Jim Hopkins had a bee in his bonnet about parachute regulations.

Hopkins managed to get right up Cheshire's nose. Years later, the Englishman revealed that Hopkins had flown at 13,000 metres over Yakushima, not the 10,000 metres of his brief. He also took a different path to the brief, but Cheshire felt that, as a guest, it wasn't his place to comment. Hopkins, it would seem, was flying higher and wider than the planes with which he was trying to make contact.

Hopkins broke radio silence and sent a message to Tinian: 'Has Sweeney aborted?' The first word was lost in transmission. When General Farrell returned from lunch at the base, he was given the truncated message and thought the mission had been abandoned for some unknown reason. He felt sick in the pit of his stomach. The air–sea rescue operation, standing by for the mission, was cancelled in the belief the mission was already on its way back home.

◆ ◆ ◆

A small group of POWs was taken down to the foundry, past the *genkan* where Mitsue Tabata sat cross-legged with her baby daughter draped across her pregnant belly. Watching the foreign soldiers march by in their grubby, threadbare clothing had become a meaningful ritual for her, but it wasn't reciprocated. For Allan Chick, she was just one of the many Japanese faces, sometimes mildly hostile, that stared impassively as they passed by. He hadn't noticed the young schoolteacher, even though he had marched past her most days. Sometimes he looked a little longer at a local face and wondered what thoughts occupied it behind the mask, but Mitsue Tabata had not been one of these.

The working party had only just arrived at the casting furnace when the air-raid siren went. They were all immediately bundled off to a shelter attached to the foundry. Before long the all-clear sounded and the men were returned to their work area but no sooner had they got back to the furnace than the air-raid siren started its long and plaintive wail again. Once more the civilian guards had to move all the POWs into the foundry shelter. By the time the all-clear sounded again, these guards were heartily sick of continually moving their charges into and out of the shelter. They sent the working party back to the camp next door. Let the prison guards deal with the shuffling back and forth!

◆　◆　◆

With the all-clear ringing out, students at Nagasaki Medical College loosened their helmet straps. Those who had classes went back to them. Dr Nagai went to his room in the department. Down the corridor he could hear the voice of Dr Tsuno starting a lecture in clinical studies.

Dr Nagai's wife, Midori, had gone to their local shelter when the alarm sounded. With the all-clear, she returned home with two relatives who had been with her. Tatsue and grandmother Urata chatted on the verandah with Midori while she dried a bag of beans in the sun for her Feast of Assumption bean-jam cakes. Asked about family, Midori confessed she was worried about her husband. 'Anyone as sick as he is couldn't work as he does and not get worse,' she said. 'He was on air-raid duty last night. I haven't seen him since breakfast yesterday.'

A young cousin came by, full of good cheer, and suggested a walk to Topposui Mill. She'd managed to get some wheat, which she needed to grind. Tatsue said she'd love a walk in the countryside, but Midori had things to do. She had to take her husband's lunch to him at the hospital as he hadn't been home since the morning before. Midori too had wheat to grind, but she would leave that till later and do it on the way to see their two children, evacuated to nearby Koba.

The two younger women said their farewells and headed off to enjoy a country ramble, although the day was clouding over. Midori Nagai postponed that pleasure until the afternoon.

◆　◆　◆

While the Kokura bombing mission was held up at its rendezvous point over Yakushima, the wind had shifted direction. A front was blowing in over eastern Japan from the China Sea. Smoke from the overnight bombing of neighbouring Yawata to the west was now drifting across Kokura. The sky was still hazy with broken clouds. Because of the wind change it hadn't cleared as the weather plane had predicted. Some landmarks were visible. Others were hidden below patches of cloud.

Bockscar and *The Great Artiste* arrived at Kokura at 9.20 a.m. without *The Big Stink*. On board *Bockscar*, radarman Ed Buckley and navigator Jimmy Van Pelt used the radar scope to line up the target, the armaments factory in the middle of the city. Standing orders were that it had to be sighted by eye.

Van Pelt called to Sweeney, 'Two degrees right. One degree left.'

'That's the target,' said Buckley. 'I have it in range. What's our true altitude?'

'Give me one degree left, Chuck. Fine. We are right on course,' continued the navigator.

'Roger,' said Sweeney. 'All you men make damned sure you have your goggles on.'

The crew put on their purple protective goggles. Grey clouds were scattered below. The ground was obscured by dark smoke from Yawata's burning steelworks.

'Twenty miles out now, captain,' said Buckley. 'Mark it!'

Van Pelt continued his commentary, 'Roger. Give me two degrees left, Chuck.'

'You got it, boy!'

The pneumatic bomb-bay doors opened with a humming sound. Beahan, in front of and below pilot and co-pilot, watched a live re-run of the map he'd studied in the Tinian briefing. From inside *Bockscar's* Plexiglass nose, the bombardier saw Kokura unfurl 10,000 metres below. He noted the railway yard a kilometre from the armaments factory, but features were covered after that. With his eye glued to the Norden bomb-sight, Beahan could find nothing apart from smoke and cloud to fix the crosshairs on.

'I can't see it. I can't see the target.'

Sweeney called into the intercom, 'No drop. Repeat, no drop.' He banked the plane sharply to the left and swung around for a return approach.

The bomb doors closed. This time the aircraft would pass over heavily fortified Yawata, well-armed with ack-ack defence. They had brought down four B-29s in the overnight raid. Flak started bursting around.

Dehart yelled, 'Flak! Wide, but altitude is good.'

'Roger that, Pappy,' replied the pilot. 'Keep your eyes open.' He climbed a few hundred metres more.

'This damned flak is right on our tail and getting closer.'

'Forget it, Pappy. We're on a bomb run.'

Bockscar rolled in again over Kokura with the noise of the bomb door mechanism opening and the rush of air outside. Through his rubber eyepiece, Beahan saw the stadium, then the cathedral, then the river near the arsenal, then . . . the same impervious screen and no munitions factory. 'No drop! No drop!' he cried out in frustration.

'Sit tight, boys. We're going around again.' Sweeney wheeled into another turn.

'Major, Jap Zeros coming up. Looks like about ten.' It was the radar operator, Ed Buckley, this time.

Jake Beser on electronic countermeasures detected activity on Japanese fighter circuits. As the plane came in for its third run, the crew were getting anxious and edgy. Van Pelt pointed out the stadium was near the arsenal. Beahan responded that the stadium was not the aiming point.

Kuharek voiced concern about fuel remaining. By his calculation, there was no longer enough to get to Iwo Jima to refuel.

Through the Norden, Beahan saw streets and the river, but once again the munitions factory was shrouded. Again, he reported no drop.

The tension released a rush of comments: 'Fighters below, coming up' (Dehart); 'Fuel getting very low' (Kuharek); 'Let's get the hell out of here!' (Gallagher); 'What about Nagasaki?' (Spitzer).

'Cut the chatter,' said Sweeney.

Abe Spitzer's comment, meant as a rhetorical question to himself, made sense. Fuel was getting dangerously low and the hornet's nest of defence they'd stirred up below was an unacceptable risk for a plane carrying so destructive a weapon. Sweeney conferred by intercom with Ashworth and Beahan. They decided to leave Kokura and head for Nagasaki, 160 kilometres to the south. The weather there didn't look any more promising than Kokura but the only other approved target, Niigata in northern Honshu, was too far away for their remaining fuel.

Sweeney waggled his wings at Bock and turned away so sharply he lost sight of the other plane now on his left side. He accidentally knocked the radio switch with his elbow when asking over the intercom, 'Where's Bock?'

Hopkins' voice immediately cut in out of nowhere. 'Chuck? Is that you, Chuck? Where the hell are you?'

A stunned silence, then Sweeney flipped back to intercom, gathered his composure and asked the navigator, 'Jim, give me the heading for Nagasaki.' It was as if Hopkins' interruption had never happened.

Van Pelt gave a direction and pointed out it would take them over the Kyushu fighter plane fields.

'I can't avoid it, Jim,' said Sweeney. Fuel was too critical to swing over water away from the Zero bases. What's more, they were an hour and a half behind schedule and Fat Man was still live in the bomb bay. *Bockscar* turned south for Nagasaki with a Zero following for a short distance before giving it away.

Sweeney said to Albury, 'Can any other goddamned thing go wrong?'

◆ ◆ ◆

On the ground at Kokura, the all-clear had sounded before the Americans' aborted bombing runs began. Many people came out of the shelters and were getting about their business when they heard the aircraft engines high above them. However, this wasn't the massed formations they associated with firebombing missions. They assumed it was a reconnaissance mission. Some noted the two planes made three passes over the city, their engines' drone fading and returning each time. Then the planes disappeared, never to return. Kokurans got on with their lives, the struggle to stay afloat in a war-ravaged country.

Japanese today have an expression, 'Kokura's luck'. It means avoiding a catastrophic event you didn't even know was threatened.

Chapter 11

Nagasaki, Thursday 9 August 1945, morning

Bockscar headed across the north of Kyushu towards Nagasaki with *The Great Artiste* trailing off its right wing. There had been no opposition from Japanese fighter planes. A check of fuel reserves by flight engineer Kuharek confirmed not enough to get to Iwo Jima and maybe not enough even to get to Okinawa—particularly if they were still carrying a heavyweight bomb. Major Sweeney asked Commander Ashworth to join him in the pilot's area. Sweeney was officer in charge of the plane, Ashworth officer in charge of the bomb. Major decisions had to be made jointly.

Sweeney said, 'Here's the situation, Dick. We have just enough fuel to make one pass over the target. If we don't drop on Nagasaki, we may have to let it go into the ocean. There's a very slim chance that we would be able to make Okinawa, but the odds are very slim. Would you accept a radar run if necessary and we can't see the target? I guarantee we'll come within five hundred feet of the target.'

'I don't know, Chuck.'

'It's better than dropping it in the ocean.'

'Are you sure of the accuracy?'

'I'll take full responsibility for this.'

'Let me think it over, Chuck.'

After a few moments of thought, Ashworth told Sweeney he'd decided to risk returning to Okinawa with the bomb. He could not agree to the radar drop.

No-one in the plane said anything. Ashworth looked perplexed. Even though he'd ostensibly made his decision, he was still torn between three unwelcome alternatives: disregard orders to target visually; return to Okinawa and risk the lives of the crew; or dump the billion-dollar bomb into the ocean to ensure the lives of the crew.

For some minutes, torment and doubt prevailed in Ashworth's mind until he spoke again to tell Sweeney he had reversed his decision. He now agreed they should drop on Nagasaki, whether by radar or visually. The crew cheered.

With fuel so critical, Sweeney told Spitzer to radio the air-sea rescue team off the south of Kyushu and alert them to the possibility of *Bockscar* having to ditch later. Spitzer did as instructed, but got no answer.

◆   ◆   ◆

Junji Sato woke and made his own breakfast. His younger sister had already gone to the munitions factory and his mother had stopped overnight with a relative. As soon as Sato arrived at work at Domei's Nagasaki bureau in the mansion, his boss told him to go straight to the steelworks for a press release. Before the reporter could set off, a cable came through from Fukuoka office further north. The Soviet Union had entered the war, it said, invading Manchukuo that morning. Lines were broken at Hiroshima, so news of the Soviet entry couldn't get through to Tokyo. Yamanaka called off the steelworks release and sent Sato instead to the wireless station at Isahaya to pass the news on to Tokyo through there.

Sato went to Governor Nagano's office at local defence headquarters for transport authority to get to Isahaya, 25 kilometres away. Nagano was stunned by the reporter's news of the Soviet attack. He folded his hands on the table, lowered his head and wept. As governor of a prefecture, Wakamatsu Nagano's power was extremely parochial. At moments like these he realised there were forces swirling far above him over which he had no influence whatsoever.

With a car duly authorised, Sato waited at his office until it came. As he opened the car door, Yamanaka poked his head out an upstairs window and shouted that communications had been re-established with Tokyo. Sato no longer need go to Isahaya.

Further detail came in of the Hiroshima attack three days earlier. The army had been annihilated there. Thousands of homes were totally destroyed by the bomb blast or burned away by the subsequent fires. Over a hundred thousand were reported dead. Sato's gloomy train of thought digesting this information was interrupted by Yamanaka. His boss wanted him to try to get some *sake* through their connections of press privilege.

Sato walked down to the prefectural office with the necessary form for the *sake*, but the relevant officials were away from the office. The governor had called an important meeting. Sato decided on a different tack to get Yamanaka's *sake*, went back to the Domei office and found a bicycle. Cycling towards the taxation office, he heard an airplane high above the clouds. Momentarily he was able to spot through a small gap in the cover a lone American B-29.

Having heard about the new bomb's devastation of Hiroshima from the newspaper proprietor Nishioka, Governor Nagano had called a morning meeting of all involved in local air defence planning. He was having difficulty coping with events and was yet to digest Russian entry into the war. In an underground shelter overlooking the Nakajima valley, the governor was outlining the meeting's agenda and stressing its impor- tance when the mayor of Sasebo, up the Kyushu coast, burst in. He had something of great urgency to pass on and started to describe what had happened in Hiroshima, as related to him by the commander-in-chief of Sasebo's large naval base. The meeting was slipping out of Nagano's grasp, but he regained control by stating dogmatically that disseminating infor- mation, including that provided by the visiting mayor, was precisely the purpose of the meeting. He invited Mayor Koura to tell the assembled bureaucrats what he himself had already started to tell them.

◆   ◆   ◆

Koichi Wada had arrived at Hotarujaya terminal at six o'clock that morning. He was taking out an early tram, although not the first for the day. Having pressed his *inkan* on the work sheet and showed his name plate, he was given a brake handle and car number. He wandered across to the trams, greeted the conductor rostered to work with him and started out on their first run.

During the morning rush, the streetcar was crowded, the conductor pushing his way through the passengers, as it rolled down the line between Ohashi and Shianbashi, near where Koichi lived. The morning had been shaping up as another hot summer day when he walked around from his home to work, but clouds were moving in. They had to pause twice along the route when sirens wailed.

Mid-morning, after the crowds had eased off, Koichi received word that one of the trams had been derailed, disrupting the morning schedule. His route was changed so that he would get back to Hotarujaya later than usual for his morning break. By the time he pulled into the shed just before eleven, Koichi was grumbling about the delayed break.

Inside the terminal building, a driver was being reprimanded by two of the managers. Apparently something he had done caused the morning accident. Koichi grabbed a bite to eat and sat down on a bench with his workmates. They talked about the biggest excitement of the morning so far, the derailment.

◆   ◆   ◆

After breakfasting at home, Yasuo Yamawaki had gone to work at the Mitsubishi Electric Corporation as usual that morning. Fourteen-year-old Toshihiro left for the munitions plant in the tunnel at Tomachi down near the entrance to Nagasaki Bay. The twins stayed at home, the rest of this large family now with their relatives in Saga.

Yoshiro and Tatsuro had the task of polishing rice the family had bought through the ration system. They wanted to get that chore out of the way early and were in the enclosed verandah of their substantial house, grinding the rice with a bamboo stick in an old *sake* bottle.

By mid-morning, the eleven-year-olds started to feel peckish from the exercise of grinding husks off rice. Although the Yamawakis were better off than most, the boys still seemed to be constantly hungry. They dug out some hard biscuits from the pantry and soaked them in water so they would swell and seem bigger. Sitting at a table in the back of the house, they nibbled at their soggy biscuits to make them last longer and discussed what they'd do when they'd finished grinding the rice.

◆ ◆ ◆

The leader of the army's Hiroshima investigation team sat in Marshal Hata's office, surrounded by the debris of fallen plaster and broken windows. Hata had been out of town when the atomic bomb was dropped, but had returned to take charge of nursing the stricken city back to life. General Arisue had brought him up to date with his team's findings including the assessment of the nuclear scientist, Dr Nishina.

Hata was optimistic Japan could defend itself against any future use of this bomb. Having white clothing and sheltering underground during the blast were key to his strategy against the initial blast. The conflagration that followed was a different matter. He didn't believe it was caused by the blast itself. His view was that many of the cooking fires operating at that time of the morning were tipped over by the blast, setting houses on fire.

Arisue had heard the news about the Russians on the radio and was anxious to return to Tokyo. Soviet entry into the war was a more serious concern to him than the new bomb. As far as he was concerned, Hata was welcome to his theories.

In the city that the intelligence chief was so keen to return to, the day's tactical manoeuvres in government continued. Just before the meeting of the Supreme War Council that Baron Suzuki had called for ten thirty, Sakomizu approached the two military chiefs of staff. The cabinet secretary asked both General Umezu and Admiral Toyoda if they would sign a petition for the prime minister to call an imperial conference, a gathering of the Supreme War Council with the emperor attending. Such a meeting required the written agreement of the two and the prime minister, although its purpose was ordinarily to inform the emperor of matters already decided.

'It's only a formality,' said Sakomizu breezily. 'If council makes a decision on the Russian invasion and cabinet ratifies it, we might want an urgent conference with the emperor.'

Both military men were hesitant to sign, suspicious of a possible ulterior motive in this simple request.

'I shall ask for your formal agreements, of course, before I present the petitions to His Majesty,' the cabinet secretary assured them. That could be done by phone since a signature would no longer be required.

The two signed with some reluctance, applying their handwritten seals.

◆ ◆ ◆

With the weather planes long gone and two other B-29s having flown past Nagasaki, the all-clear sounded. Up on the western slope of the Urakami valley, schoolboys in the shelter at Aburagi whooped with joy and ran outside to play. Some said they were going home. The girls relaxed on the *tatami* mats for a while, but Sakue got restless and went outside. Ryoko soon came out to remind her of their brother's instruction to stay in the shelter.

'Let's go back to Mum,' Sakue proposed, but her younger sister would have none of it, so both girls went back inside.

They had told the others of Masuichi's warning and eight of the girls sheltering with them stayed, along with the baby. The only adult who remained behind was a Korean lady from the neighbourhood. Her leg had been blown off in the aerial attack the week before.

Sometime later, the girls' older sister came to the shelter to give them their lunch boxes. She and her mother had packed them when they were released from fire-fighting standby. Sadako didn't wait around in the shelter. She checked that Tamashii was comfortable and left. It wasn't yet lunchtime, only about eleven o'clock, but Sakue opened her box to look for some small snack to tide her over.

◆ ◆ ◆

After leading morning exercises at the Ohashi arms works and present-ing the day's rollcall to the factory director, Torahachi Tagawa went back to his office. As he pulled out the reports he had been poring over the previous day, engineer Koga came in. Tagawa's boss wanted to know if a special part for the new rocket engine would be ready for delivery the next day, as had been promised. The workshop foreman went to look for Takemura to put the question to him. Before he got to the technician's workroom, the factory's air-raid siren rang out and Tagawa rushed to the shelter. The all-clear sounded half an hour later.

Takemura hadn't been in the shelter and he wasn't in his workroom either when Tagawa went there following the all-clear. Asking around, no-one could say what had become of him. The foreman's only option was to return to his own office where he found Koga smoking a cigarette, waiting for him, but Tagawa was not yet able to answer his question.

'I'll try again in a couple of hours,' he said, 'maybe about eleven.'

Koga thanked him. 'That information is important,' he said, 'but not the reason I'm here.'

He wanted to work through the next week's production schedule. Spreading papers across the foreman's desk, they started to map out a program for the following week. It was nine in the morning.

While foreman Tagawa and his boss worked their way through produc-tion plans for Mitsubishi's Ohashi arms factory, Yoshiro Fukuda arrived at his office there for the conference he had called the day before. The deputy director's ulcer was giving him hellish pain in the chest, flaring up in anticipation of another day of frustrating non-achievement.

At the meeting, the forge supervisor confirmed his advice of the previous afternoon that the shipment of coal had not arrived despite Supply's assurance that it would. An engineer reported that five of Supply's seven trucks were off the road, three in the last week. Perhaps there were no trucks to bring the coal, he suggested.

'This isn't getting us anywhere,' said Fukuda, reaching for the phone. With a couple of sharp stomach jabs to spur him on, the number two man at the works was going to ring his supply chief and find out exactly what the state of play was.

◆ ◆ ◆

Newspaper publisher Nishioka rose early after a fitful, feverish sleep in an unfamiliar and dilapidated room. He caught the six thirty train to Isahaya. After scouting around there for an hour trying to find a car that would take him to his family at Unzen, he went to see if the chief of the Isahaya bureau of *Minyu* could help. Nishioka's fever was starting to rise again, no doubt exacerbated by his frustration. He needed desperately to get to the resort town.

While Yonekura rang around to see what he could line up for his employer, he noticed through his window a taxi dropping a group of people at the station across the road. He called out and, with Nishioka puffing behind him, dashed across the street to catch the taxi-driver before he drove away. First to reach the car, Yonekura pressed the driver to take the businessman to Unzen. He was intending to return to Nagasaki, but after some persuasion agreed reluctantly to a detour.

The charcoal-burning car chugged over the hill to the hot springs resort of Obama. Nishioka was starting to feel quite queasy. His energy was sapping. They stopped for a few minutes by the bus station so he could get some fresh air in his lungs, away from the vehicle's smoking burner. A crowd was lined up nearby, waiting for a bus. While standing away from the car, Nishioka was spied by the resort town's branch manager of the government bus company. Business protocols required the local official to speak to this important passer-by from the city. The two struck up a conversation while the taxi-driver sat in his car.

◆ ◆ ◆

Tsutomu Yamaguchi was a conscientious employee, a model worker in a time of immense national difficulty. The day after he returned to Nagasaki, he reported to his workplace shipyard covered with bandages. He was still in some pain from the burns over much of his body, although that had eased a little. At the same time, reuniting with his family had eased his mental anguish. Nonetheless, recovery still seemed some distance away with only his eyes, lips and nose visible through the dressing around his head.

Mitsubishi had set up its Nagasaki shipbuilding works across the bay from the city, at the foot of Mount Inasa. In the sixth-floor offices where he worked, adjacent to the shipyards and not far from his new home, Yamaguchi told a group of horrified colleagues about his extraordinary Monday in Hiroshima. Extensive destruction of Japan's cities had become a fact of life in recent months but there were elements of the draftsman's story that strained belief.

The section chief joined the discussion in a cranky mood. When Yamaguchi explained that he'd come back on the same train as Iwanaga, but had lost contact with Sato in the devastation, his boss chipped him for abandoning his workmates. Neither Iwanaga nor Sato had reported for work that morning, but Sato by that time was actually on the Mitsubishi lot. He was in the shipyard, down by the quay, telling workmates his version of the Hiroshima bomb. They had heard rumours. This was the first chance they'd had to hear it first-hand.

At that time, Iwanaga was on his way on the train from Isahaya where he'd stayed with his parents. Too disturbed by what he'd seen and with a pain in his abdomen, he hadn't slept well that night. By morning he felt better and recovered some of his appetite. He decided to catch the train into Nagasaki and go to work, but once he got on the train he slumped in his seat and fell asleep. Iwanaga was still dozing as the train came into Nagayo on the city's outskirts.

Up in the drafting office, Yamaguchi's boss returned to the reported effects of the new bomb, a sceptical engineer who thought science and technology was already abreast of all that needed to be known about such matters.

'You're an engineer,' he said. 'Do the calculations. How could one bomb produce so much energy that it could destroy a whole city?'

He thought about it and added in a gesture of conciliation, 'You are injured, Yamaguchi-san. Your brain has been rattled.'

◆　◆　◆

Once more the pharmacy student, Tsuneo Tomita, had reported for his day's labour for the war effort, helping build the new air-raid shelter.

Digging with hoe and pick and carrying earth away in baskets, they were now deep inside the hollow that would be the shelter. With the day clouding over, it was not as hot working in the tunnel as previous days, but it was still tiring for young men not used to this amount of manual labour. The workers were given a break as it got towards eleven. Tomita remained in the tunnel, shovelling the last of a mound of earth into a basket, while his friends went out to get some water.

Professor Sugiura had supervised shelter construction while Professor Seiki gave his nine o'clock lecture. When Seiki returned at the end of his class, Sugiura went off to talk to a reporter from *Nishinippon Shimbun*. Seiki resumed his excavation, working on some entrenched rocks with the edge of his spade, crouching to get better leverage. A noise far above them somewhere caught his attention, the drone of an aeroplane or maybe two.

'Listen to that,' said the professor. Tomita, over near the entrance, had also heard the distant sound and was wondering whether he should attach any significance to it.

◆ ◆ ◆

At Shiroyama Primary School, Mrs Egashira, one of a group of teachers working in the school grounds, was weeding a newly established vege-table garden near the school's rear entrance. The rhythm of manual labour must have lulled the baby on her back to sleep.

Mrs Takahashi said, 'Naomi's fallen asleep. Why don't you put her down somewhere to sleep better?'

Chiyoko decided to put her in the first-aid room next to the princi-pal's office. She noticed that the principal was in his office and saw three of the school staff talking by the window in a room nearby. She could hear their voices drifting down the corridor.

In the dispensary, there were two beds by a wall. Futons had been piled up on one side by the women's civil defence unit. Chiyoko thought this would be a good place for Naomi to sleep, where the pile would provide some shade as well as a soft support to lie on. She lowered the child and began to untie the strings that had secured her to her back.

◆ ◆ ◆

With the Feast of Assumption Day rapidly approaching, Father Tamaya, the visiting priest at Urakami Cathedral, sat behind the heavy curtain of the confessional box. 'Father, forgive me for I have sinned . . .' said the anonymous voice, the drape and a grille between its owner and the priest. Tamaya recognised the voice, even from his short time in Nagasaki, on this occasion. It was someone he had known since he was a child growing up in the city.

Father Nishida was also hearing confession, occupying another box. It was a busy time in the church's calendar, but because the morning's duties had to be put on hold during air-raid warnings, the faithful arrived faster than the two priests could process them. By eleven o'clock, about twenty of Nagasaki's *kirishitan* were waiting patiently in line.

◆ ◆ ◆

At a bit before eleven, Torahachi Tagawa excused himself, leaving Koga at the table, and went down to the factory toilet. He was standing at the wooden urinal alongside another of the arms works foremen when he heard planes high above. The two foremen looked up, even though from deep inside the building they couldn't expect to see the aircraft.

Also above Tagawa, but much nearer than the aircraft, the deputy director was on the phone to his head of supply. He was told the coal warehouse chief had said there were no trucks available to deliver the coal. Perhaps in two or three days' time . . . Yoshiro Fukuda slammed the phone down in fury.

◆ ◆ ◆

The daily march of Urakami Prison's inmates down the main road of the valley had started promptly, as always, at seven thirty. The number of volunteers in their green dungerees and peaked caps was predictable. The hardened criminals remained at the prison, making uniforms. The family of Warden Kyobei Minami also remained in the prison grounds, kept well away from the workshop where uniforms were made.

As the prisoners arrived at the steelworks with Minami and the guards, the air-raid siren rang out its first warning of the morning. Steel workers and prisoners were shuffled into factory shelters. Half an hour later, the all-clear sounded and the prisoners were taken to their work stations. As they had been all week, they were put to making marine screws for coastal patrol vessels and torpedo boats.

Commander Kamizaki of the Fatherland Defence Corps came to Minami's room to talk about the quality of the prisoners' work. Both men knew it was unrealistic to expect either speed or craftsmanship from indentured labour, but Kamizaki felt his position required him to draw the warden's attention to the deficiencies, and Minami felt a responsibility to go through the motions of listening. Minami kept to himself his low regard for a civilian posturing as a military man. He assured Kamizaki he would instruct his men to get their charges to give greater attention to their work.

With an assurance he could duly record in his report, the overseer from the Fatherland Defence Corps returned to his office. Able to get back to his own paperwork, Minami thought, 'That was a waste of half an hour.' It was eleven o'clock and the morning was nearly gone.

◆ ◆ ◆

About a hundred metres from Sumiyoshi-cho post office, Sumiteru Taniguchi found his back tyre was flat. He looked in his saddlebag to find he'd forgotten to pack his puncture repair kit. Because he'd emptied his lunch box instead of taking it, he'd accidentally left the kit behind as well. The young postman pushed his red bicycle to the post office and left it standing against the wall. He took his mailbag and delivered on foot to nearby houses.

The sky had clouded over by the time Sumiteru came back to the post office. He borrowed a repair kit and set about mending the puncture. The air-raid siren howled but he ignored it, finishing the repair job a bit before eleven, as the all-clear sounded. He thought that odd because he could hear a distant plane.

Resuming his delivery round, the postman pushed open the front door of a house and dropped letters on the floor just inside. He shouted, 'Postman!' A voice from within replied '*Arigato* [thank you],' and Sumiteru rode on up the lane towards Sumiyoshi-jinja temple. He had mail for Mitsubishi's women workers' dormitory further on. Children in white shirts were playing in the lane. They were a familiar sight on the post-man's round so he waved at them and smiled. The plane was still up in the sky somewhere. It sounded much closer than before.

◆　◆　◆

Brought back to POW Camp 14, Allan Chick joined a work detail fire-proofing the camp storehouse, a low flat-roofed wooden structure partly set below ground level. Up on the roof, Chick and a Javanese prisoner spread soil brought in buckets by some of the other prisoners, Australian and Dutch. The Japanese overseers weren't worried about the new bomb that had been used on Hiroshima—they were only vaguely aware of it—but of an escalation of the Allied incendiary bombing.

Buckets were passed up to Chick and his companion on the roof. The soil was raked up to a long wooden paling that had been fixed around the roof's edge. The expectation was that Nagasaki, with its munitions factories and shipyards, wouldn't continue to be let off as lightly as it had up to this point.

Over on the other side of the camp was another group brought back early to base. Peter McGrath-Kerr had spent the morning in a work party of six Australians repairing the bridge over Mifune Canal. Bamboo and rope had been used to fix the handrails. Since it was in the open air and wasn't hard work, they had tried to drag the job out as long as they could. Their morning too had been interrupted by air-raid alerts. Either because of that or because they guessed the work was being stretched out, the guards brought the group back to Camp 14, only a few hundred metres away, just after ten.

Four of them went to the barracks room they shared. Murray Jobling and Les Prendergast killed time having a smoke until the guards returned to take them back to the canal bridge or to another job. McGrath-Kerr lay on his bunk and read a book. Bert Miller dozed off on his bunk.

Outside, on the storehouse roof, there was a short delay in the buckets of soil arriving. The reason wasn't obvious to the two men on the roof, but they waited and chatted, the Indonesian having a grasp of basic English. The conversation wasn't about anything significant. There wasn't anything significant the two had to share.

The men in the barracks, apart from the catnapping Miller, could hear the drone of a plane overhead somewhere. There was no air-raid alarm and the sound of planes flying around was not unusual. There was a flying school nearby. But something caught the ear of one of the Australians, a sudden change in the pitch of the unseen aircraft's engine.

'That's no Nip!' said Prendergast, getting up.

◆　◆　◆

When the all-clear sounded at Urakami Hospital, Dr Akizuki went back to the consulting room and found Dr Yoshioka giving pneumo-thorax injections. He told her it would be safer to pause during the air-raid warnings, but she said she had so many patients waiting she felt she couldn't afford the time. She looked tired. Akizuki suggested she have a break, saying he'd take over for a while. Dr Yoshioka went upstairs and Dr Akizuki began the next pneumo-thorax treatment with nurse Murai.

By late morning, the Franciscan hospital was a hive of activity. Brother Iwanaga was digging a new shelter with some farm workers he'd pressed into voluntary service. Noguchi, a young seminarian, was repairing wooden rigging over the well. Father Ishikawa, the Korean hospital chaplain, was hearing confession from some of the in-patients in the hospital chapel. Volunteer kitchen workers were providing a morning meal to other in-patients. Dr Akizuki and his temporary nurse had not yet eaten.

The doctor was in the process of inserting a pneumo-thorax needle into the side of a patient's chest when he heard a low drone that sounded like a distant plane engine. His new assistant went over to the window to check if it was a plane. Reacting instinctively, Dr Akizuki pulled the needle out of his patient's chest and threw himself beside the bed.

◆　◆　◆

At ten to eleven *Bockscar* and *The Great Artiste* arrived from the north-west, high above Nagasaki at 10,000 metres. The 20 per cent cloud cover of the eight thirty weather report had grown to 90 per cent as the front moving in from the China Sea blanketed the city, hanging at two or three thousand metres. Sweeney swung *Bockscar* over the bay and north towards the cloud-covered downtown area. Beyond that was the more westerly of the two valleys running up from the city centre, the Urakami. Cloud had broken a little on the outskirts, but was thick at the centre of the city. Sweeney instructed the crew to put on their goggles, although he left his off. He'd already experienced how little visibility they allowed. Navigator and radar operator coordinated the approach to the aiming point, Tokiwa Bridge on the Nakajima River in downtown Nagasaki. Beahan fed data into the bombsight.

'Right. One degree correction to the left. Good,' recited navigator Van Pelt.

Buckley on radar reported, 'We're coming in right on course. Five. Mark it.' They were two minutes away.

'I still can't see it,' muttered Beahan.

'Okay, Honeybee,' encouraged the skipper, 'but check all your switches and make damned sure everything is ready.' One minute to target and there were no dry runs. The bomb-bay doors opened and the plane shuddered as it caught the air stream. They would remain under radar control unless Beahan could see the target and lock on it.

'I'll take it,' came the bombardier's excited voice. 'I can see the target.' There was a substantial hole over the mid Urakami valley with some scattered low-lying cloud below. Through the gap Beahan, 'the great artiste', could see an athletics track. It looked nothing like Tokiwa Bridge, 4 kilometres away on the other side of the ridge separating the two river valleys. He put the Norden crosshairs on the oval track.

'You own it,' said Sweeney. The tone ran through the radio system indicating fifteen seconds to go. Beahan was silent, concentrating, the automatic bombsight locked on the stadium where sports events had long ceased to be held.

At 11.01 a.m., the shackle was released and Fat Man tumbled out, diving down. Wires snapped, the radio tone stopped abruptly. *Bockscar* lurched upward.

'Bombs away,' announced Beahan, and corrected himself. 'Bomb away.'

Sweeney turned sharply to port at a steep angle. In *The Great Artiste* the bombardier shouted, 'There she goes.' Fred Bock swung tightly to the opposite side as the cluster of three instrument capsules, each with its letter attached to Professor Sagane, fell under parachutes a short distance behind Fat Man, diving nose-first towards Urakami.

Chapter 12

The horizon burst into 'superbrilliant white with an intense flash', more intense than Hiroshima. From the air, a brownish cloud could be seen spreading horizontally across the city below. A vertical column sprang from the centre, coloured and boiling. A white, puffy mushroom cloud broke off at 4000 metres and sped upwards to 11,000 metres. Gallagher saw the cloud approaching and shouted. Sweeney pulled away and it shot above them, black and grey at the base, white and reddish above. Thick, dirty smoke filled the Urakami valley, with fires breaking out on the hills around the blast, but downtown Nagasaki appeared from the plane to be untouched.

As Sweeney circled back over the city for Beahan to verify the detonation point, Pappy Dehart filmed from the tail with a movie camera given to him by the scientist Alvarez. The plane was hit with five shock waves, one after the other. The experience was likened by weaponeer Ashworth to being inside a garbage bin when the lid was being thumped with a baseball bat. They had experienced only two shock waves at Hiroshima, but here the waves were reflecting off the steep hills around the valley.

Fat Man took 43 seconds to fall to its detonation point 500 metres above a tennis court at 170 Matsuyama-cho. From the ground, a huge

199

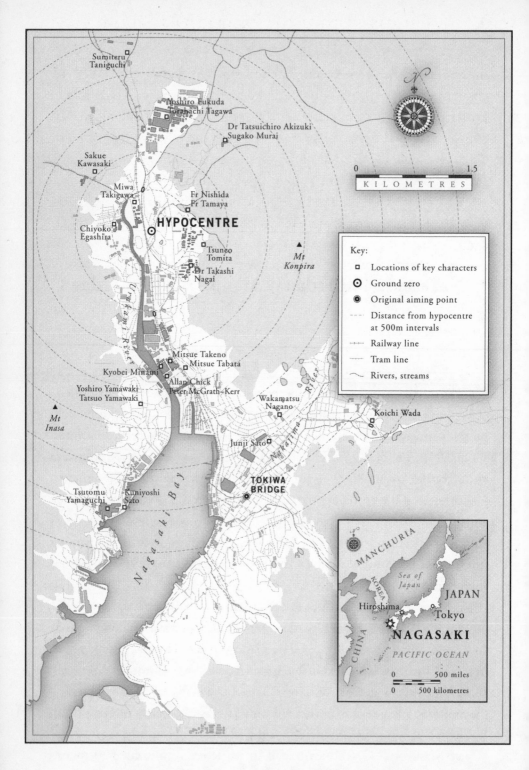

Sumiteru
Taniguchi

Yoshiro Fukuda
Torahachi Tagawa

Dr Tatsuichiro Akizuki
Sugako Murai

Sakue
Kawasaki

Miwa
Takigawa

Fr Nishida
Fr Tamaya

HYPOCENTRE

Chiyoko
Egashira

Tsuneo
Tomita

Dr Takashi
Nagai

Mt
Konpira

Urakami River

Mitsue Takeno
Mitsue Tabata

Kyobei Minami

Allan Chick
Peter McGrath~Kerr

Wakamatsu
Nagano

Koichi Wada

Nakajima River

Yoshiro Yamawaki
Tatsuo Yamawaki

Mt
Inasa

Junji Sato

**TOKIWA
BRIDGE**

Tsutomu
Yamaguchi

Kuniyoshi
Sato

Nagasaki Bay

Key:

□   Locations of key characters

⊙   Ground zero

◉   Original aiming point

– – –   Distance from hypocentre
at 500m intervals

Railway line

Tram line

Rivers, streams

0   1.5
KILOMETRES

MANCHURIA

*Sea of
Japan*

KOREA

JAPAN

Hiroshima

Tokyo

NAGASAKI

CHINA

PACIFIC OCEAN

0   500 miles
0   500 kilometres

Location of people at detonation of the atomic bomb

fireball could be seen forming in the sky. The bomb exploded with an immensely bright blue-white light like a giant magnesium flare. A powerful pressure wave followed with an explosive rumbling. To the people who experienced it, this translated as the *pika-don* (flash-boom). The view from the ground of the white vertical cloud was obscured at first by a bluish haze, then by a purple-brown cloud of dust and smoke.

Almost everything within a kilometre of the hypocentre was destroyed, even earthquake-proof concrete structures that had survived at similar distances in Hiroshima. People and animals died instantly. Heat rays evaporated the water from human organs. A boy, standing in the shadow of a brick warehouse a kilometre away, saw a mother and children out in the open instantaneously disappear. Tightly packed houses of flimsy wooden construction and tiled roofing were completely obliterated. The explosion twisted and tore out window and door sashes, and ripped doors off their hinges. Many buildings of brick and stone were so severely damaged that they crumbled and collapsed into rubble. Glass was blown out of windows 8 kilometres away.

The detonation flash only lasted a fraction of a second, but ultra-violet light coming from it was sufficient to cause third-degree burns to the skin and to bubble heavy clay roof tiles for over a kilometre and a half. Clothing ignited, telegraph poles smouldered and charred, thatched roofs caught fire. Paper spontaneously incinerated 3 kilometres away. As in Hiroshima, black clothing absorbed heat and charred or caught fire, while white and light-coloured material reflected the ultra-violet rays. Patterns in people's clothing were duplicated in the pattern of burns on their skin.

There was no firestorm as there had been in Hiroshima. Fires broke out from the intense heat for the first kilometre. Beyond that, secondary fires, burning all combustible material—wood, clothing, mattresses, mats—sprang up an hour or more later in the wake of the hot light and atomic blast that rolled inexorably down the Urakami valley and out across the bayside flatland around Dejima.

◆ ◆ ◆

With her baby lowered in front of her while she untied the strings that strapped Naomi to her back, Chiyoko Egashira heard a huge roar and felt a sharp pain in her back as if her flesh was being torn away. Only 500 metres from the hypocentre—so close that Chiyoko didn't see a separate flash of light—the innards were ripped out of the school's buildings. All that remained of Shiroyama Primary School was a skeleton of reinforced concrete. Thinking this was about to collapse, Chiyoko covered Naomi with her body, then scooped her up and began to crawl out of what was left of the school dispensary. The hair on Naomi's head stood straight up, but her eyebrows had been scorched off. Covered with yellow dust, the child was silent, eyes peering expressionlessly through a dusty mask.

Chiyoko noticed the principal get up on the overturned desk in his office, then leave the room. She tried to shout for help, but no sound came out. Somewhere nearby, a male teacher was screaming for the principal. Chiyoko decided to try to make her way home. When she looked out the window, she couldn't see anything but yellow smoke. In the hall she found that the classroom block had been completely destroyed. The dispensary was in the part of the school that had most withstood the blast. Mrs Takahashi's suggestion to put Naomi to sleep inside had saved the lives of mother and daughter.

Cement posts at the front entrance of the school had been pulled up and thrown towards the school buildings with earth still clinging to their concrete aggregate bases. The school's chinaberry and cherry trees had been flattened. The janitor came towards Mrs Egashira carrying a bag, but he didn't seem to have seen her. It was as if he was walking in his sleep.

Chiyoko became frightened and took Naomi back to the remains of the dispensary. She still hadn't noticed that her own back had been peppered with shards of glass when the bomb blew in the dispensary's windows. Looking out in the direction of her home, all she could see was a sea of flame. Shiroyama was no longer cloaked in yellow dust. Now it was alight, a mass of bright red blazing fire, extending who knew how far. The teacher had run out of options, had no idea what to do next. Holding her child close, she cowered in the part-demolished room.

◆ ◆ ◆

Fat Man was a most democratic weapon, dispatching the good, the bad, the ugly and the ordinary with equal finality and equal indifference. Anyone within a kilometre of the hypocentre without some sort of cover was vaporised instantly, reduced to ashes in a highly efficient cremation.

Father Nishida, the head priest at Urakami Cathedral, and Father Tamaya, the priest from Kuroshima who had obligingly delayed his return, were hearing confession as the bomb fell through the gap in Nagasaki's gathering clouds. About twenty of the faithful were waiting their turn, standing obediently in line. All died instantly when the bomb exploded above a point 500 metres away, about the same distance as Shiroyama Primary School from the hypocentre.

The Romanesque building had appeared to be of solid construction, but neither the cathedral nor the heavy curtain of the confessional offered much protection to those inside. Unlike the school, it wasn't built with reinforced concrete. The bomb reduced the cathedral to brick and timber rubble scattered across its foundations. Only the imposing entrance and a couple of buttresses remained upright. Two domes with reinforced concrete frames had been broken off and sat on rubble like giant bowler hats. The steeple bell lay charred and cracked under debris some distance from the remains of the building.

Placed elsewhere in the spectrum of goodness but even nearer to the hypocentre, the occupants of Urakami Prison fared no better than those in the cathedral. Three hundred metres from under Fat Man's detonation point, the three buildings of the prison were demolished in a microsecond. Only the giant concrete slabs on which they were built survived, cracked and blistered. On top of the slabs were piles of rubble that had been the prison's buildings.

All inside the prison died, burnt literally to a cinder. Ninety-five prisoners were gone—those too high-risk to be allowed out with the work party and those who gambled on the unlikelihood of a prison being bombed—as were fifteen guards and their families and the wife and small daughter of Warden Minami.

Electric trams plying their trade along Route 206 were destroyed, some crushed beyond recognition, their passengers and crew gone without trace. This was where the mobilised driver, Koichi Wada, might have been but for the derailment that morning. A train coming into Urakami railway station was no match for the frightening power of the bomb's blast and no-one survived in its crushed wreckage.

◆ ◆ ◆

In his second-floor room at Nagasaki Medical College's hospital, Dr Takashi Nagai was choosing X-ray films for a classroom exercise when he was stopped in his tracks by the blinding flash of light. He thought a bomb must have fallen on the school entrance just outside. Before he could throw himself to the ground, as he had often drilled with the Eleventh Medical Corps, window glass in his room exploded inwards. A cyclonic blast of wind forced him into the air, swirling him around with pieces of broken glass and bits of timber and cloth. The right side of his face was cut, warm blood ran down his cheek and around his neck. He felt no pain, but an overpowering sense of confusion.

Furniture, books, a steel helmet and shoes were thrown around the room in snarling reckless abandon until the madness of the beast subsided and the objects piled in a heap around and on top of the doctor, already discarded onto the floor. Dusty wind had filled his nostrils so he found breathing difficult. Surrounding him, a constant roar like a storm at sea, as sunlight faded to a bare presence. In the darkness, he could smell smoke and hear fire somewhere in the middle distance. Some shapes began to emerge in the vision of his left eye, but his right eye was filling with blood leaking from the cut on his temple.

The college precinct spread between 400 and 800 metres from the bomb's hypocentre at the tennis court. The wooden classrooms for elementary medicine lectures were closer to the explosion. They were smashed and incinerated, killing nearly all lecturers and students in class that morning at a stroke—they wouldn't have lived long enough to hear the *don* of the *pika-don*—and the rest soon after. The reinforced concrete buildings of clinical medicine were more resistant to the power of the blast and, a little further away, enough to give their occupants some chance of survival . . . not much, but some. The ailing head of radiology hadn't had much good news recently, but this day he was luckier.

In his shattered office, Dr Nagai tried to move his body. He was pinned by debris and couldn't see what was over him or where the glass shards were. Moving his shoulder slightly, something fell and his heart jumped, but nothing else moved.

'Help, help!' he cried out in a thin voice.

Nurse Hashimoto—seventeen, short and stocky, nicknamed Little Barrel—was in the X-ray room next door. Standing between a solid bookcase and the wall when hell broke loose, she watched in unbelieving horror as objects, dust and smoke flew around the room. When they settled, she climbed unhurt over the rubbish that had piled up on the floor and went to an empty window frame. The familiar spread of purple-tiled homes below the hospital had vanished. The steel and munitions factories lining the river were flattened, white smoke streaming upwards from them, sucked towards a column of smoke reaching high into the sky further up the valley. The slopes of Mount Inasa across the valley had turned from their usual lush green to bare, red rock. Trees were stripped of summer growth. There was no grass to be seen.

Looking down at the open square, where a crowd had gathered around the main entrance a short time before, the young woman saw naked and contorted bodies lying everywhere, tangled up in torn-up roots and bushes. Nurse Hashimoto closed her eyes and sank her head into her hands.

'This is hell!' she whispered to herself.

In the silence and darkness belying the time of day, she wondered if she was the only person left alive in the world. As she began to cry, she heard a pitiful voice call out. She listened and it came again.

'Help me!'

Recognising the voice of Dr Nagai, she tracked its source and tried to push her way, without success, into the next room, getting tangled in electric wires from a smashed X-ray machine. The young nurse realised she couldn't get through the piled-up debris by herself and went looking for help.

Groping her way down a dark corridor, Little Barrel bumped into something wet and sticky. She slid her hand down the smooth skin of a bloody arm and felt its pulse. There was none. Her sticky hands were held together in brief prayer, before resuming her blind groping passage.

A fire broke out by a window opening. It threw a flickering red light into the corridor, revealing the convulsed bodies of dead staff and patients. Some were on their knees, some grasping at empty air in the position they died. These were people she knew and perhaps knew well, but she didn't dare look at them. The horror of knowing they were there was already overwhelming.

Nurse Hashimoto found her way into the examination room. Five X-ray screening staff were crouching there, immobilised by shock and apparently uninjured. The young nurse goaded them into action to the rescue of Dr Nagai.

Unable to force their way into his room through the pile of debris, they tried a different approach. Outside, underneath his window, one technician stood on the shoulders of another. The group hoisted two nurses, one after the other, on top and through the window opening. With fire threatening to spread from elsewhere in the building, the nurses were able to clear the pieces of broken timber holding Dr Nagai down. He had a gash in his head, but the rest of his body had survived reason- ably well . . . apart from the illness already diagnosed. His war experience in China had taught him to remain calm. The two women helped the doctor out of the room by the way they had come in.

At the back of the medical college, behind the Department of Pharmacy where Professor Seiki and his students had been digging a new shelter, the blinding flash lit up the interior, followed by the bestial roar of the blast. Working near the entrance, Tsuneo Tomita was driven inside into the solid back of Seiki crouched over his spade. Wood, clothing and broken tiles hurtled through the air after the student. A piece of wood thumped into the back of Seiki's head and the big man fell senseless into mud.

When the professor came to, smoke and fumes were filling the dugout. Hot air was pouring in. Tomita was picking himself up, stunned but not critically injured. The entrance to the shelter had collapsed, but a shaft of pale light indicated an opening over the pile of earth. The two clambered out.

Outside, nothing was recognisable. Houses adjacent to the shelter entrance and their fences were no longer there. The green hillside sloping down to the shelter entrance had turned to brown clay. Seiki and Tomita were confronted by a sea of fire spreading across a once-familiar neighbourhood. Immediately in front of them were lifeless and near-lifeless bodies of students. They had been helping build the shelter, but had gone outside for the morning break. Okamoto was the nearest. Tomita tried to lift him by his shoulders, but his flesh peeled off and he slid back on the ground. Murayama lay alongside groaning. Tomita didn't recognise his friend. As the professor held him with his skin hanging in strips, Murayama rolled over and died. Araki was swollen like a pumpkin. His eyes opened slightly and he said, 'I'm finished.'

Blood was flowing from the ears and noses of the dead and dying. Others had frothy blood blowing out of their mouths. Tomita moved among them, giving them water and encouragement, but within a short time he and Seiki were the only ones still alive. About twenty corpses were sprawled around them.

The professor cried out, 'Someone come! Help!'

The swirling wind carried his cries away and brought back other cries for help, water, mother . . . some were just cries without words. Professor Seiki felt dizzy and passed out again.

Students started arriving in various states of injury and shock, looking for shelter in the dugout. Some were carried in. Tomita was told his friend Tanaka had been killed by the blast. Others kept on walking, up the track to Mount Konpira. Tomita stayed to help the injured although there were no medical supplies. Fires were getting closer with smoke and ashes swirling around them.

Professor Seiki revived to see a thick black cloud filling the sky. The sun was like a reddish-brown disc. It was dark as if evening had come early and it had turned cold. There were fewer voices crying out than before. Seiki and Tomita decided to seek help across at the hospital, walking barefoot over the hot earth littered with broken glass.

Back in the clinical wing of the hospital, Dr Nagai's group went looking for other radiology department staff. Many were found already dead, their bodies swollen, their skin peeled off. Others were moving feebly and crying out, 'I'm burning. Give me water.'

Nagai was in a daze. He told his group to check the X-ray equipment to see if it could be moved away from the fire. They came back and reported that all the equipment was smashed beyond repair. People in advanced states of appalling injury; crucial medical equipment unsalvageable. What was to be done? Dr Nagai's brain was numb. He couldn't formulate his next move and broke into a nervous helpless laugh. The others laughed politely with him.

◆   ◆   ◆

Having stayed in the local dugout with her sister and baby brother, some of her school friends and the one-legged Korean lady, Sakue had just taken a rice ball out of her lunch box when the inside of the shelter was suddenly awash with an intense light. A blast of wind followed closely after it, knocking the ten-year-old against a rock. She struck her head and fell unconscious on the shelter's earth floor.

Someone was shaking Sakue when she came to, with no idea how long she had been out. Even in the gloom, she sensed her world had changed dramatically. Only a few minutes before, there had been eight young schoolgirls talking quietly. Now the dugout was filling with human carnage, shadowy people with eyes hanging from sockets, fried hair and skin peeling off in strips. The smell of burnt flesh and blood hung in the pallid light, along with moans and the cry of 'Kill me! Kill me!' Sakue was overcome with terror. She noticed Ryoko sitting to one side, numbed and motionless, but she couldn't see little Tamashii anywhere.

Sakue grew frantic searching for her one-year-old charge, pushing her way through burnt, crying people. She couldn't tell if these were people she knew or not. With the sun lost in a giant cloud and dust, and with people so disfigured, she couldn't distinguish one person from the next.

The panicked search eventually revealed the baby boy pinned under a mat on which injured people sat, bereft of reason. She thought he'd been crushed to death. Somehow, miraculously, he'd survived without injury. Sakue held him tightly to her, before carrying him over to where her younger sister sat. Wordlessly she crouched beside her. Ryoko looked at her but said nothing.

Although she stayed inside the shelter, the young girl realised something terrible had happened outside. The cries of the injured reverberated off the dugout walls. A stench filled the air so strongly she could hardly breathe. Sakue saw boys from the commercial school across the road. They had been working outdoors as mobilised students. Most had died instantly, but some had survived with terrible burns. She could hear voices of teachers trying to comfort them. The boys from her class who had run out of the shelter when the all-clear sounded were nowhere to be seen.

Sakue was in a hell she didn't understand. She began to sob hysterically. She screamed out for her mother, but Miwa Takigawa didn't come.

◆ ◆ ◆

The Franciscan order's Urakami Hospital stood on a high point 1500 metres from the bomb's hypocentre. In its consulting room, Dr Akizuki had thrown himself to the floor on hearing the approaching plane, as he had been endlessly instructed in home defence drill. A blinding white flash preceded a tremendous blow to his head and body on the floor. Piles of debris poured down on his back. He grew dizzy from the pounding.

Sugako Murai, the doctor's assistant for the day, had barely got to the window when the penetrating blaze stopped her in her tracks. The sound of a deep roaring explosion followed. Covering her ears and eyes with her hands, she dropped to the ground with broken glass falling over her. She could feel and hear through the roar the crash of shelves and walls falling down around her in a pile of rubble.

A few minutes later, Dr Akizuki staggered to his feet. The air was filled with heavy yellow smoke. White powder flakes drifted through the gloomy darkness that had replaced daylight. Over near where the window had been, his temporary assistant crawled out from under broken furniture and rubble, struggling to her feet. Like the doctor, she was covered with white dust. She shook off some of the glass splinters that had caught in her clothing. Feeling her back and upper arms, she found them wet with blood. A voice said, 'Are you all right?' Nurse Murai looked around and saw a ghostly white Dr Akizuki standing beside her. Faint cries of 'Help!' could be heard coming from other rooms.

Their patient picked himself up from the debris. Only a few moments before, he was receiving a pneumo-thorax needle from the doctor. Now his face was smeared with white powder and streaked with blood. The pneumo-thorax apparatus and microscope that Dr Akizuki had been working with had gone from the desk. Moaning, the patient lurched towards the door, holding his head with his hands. He showed no awareness of the doctor and nurse nearby.

As he gathered his thoughts on how to deal with this unimagined emergency, Akizuki told his nurse they should rescue the patients upstairs. Even though he anticipated the second and third floors would be destroyed, he had to do something. Going to the stairwell, they found tuberculosis patients staggering down through plaster and timber debris. Nurse Murai picked her way around the rubble on the stairs and made her way towards the upper floors. The unexpected figure of Miss Yamaguchi, a serious tubercular case from the third floor, came tottering down the cement steps. Ordinarily, she couldn't get out of bed unaided, but somehow she'd managed to get to the staircase. On hearing the nurse's cry of surprise, shock, concern—all were intermingled in Sugako's mind—Miss Yamaguchi's reserves deserted her and she crumpled onto the steps.

The nurse hoisted the patient clumsily onto her back and staggered with her down the remaining steps and out to the hospital yard. On the way out, Sugako saw lying on the ground a young boy she had noticed playing in the yard earlier in the day. His head was crushed and his entrails hung out. Nurse Murai took a wide path around the boy so the patient wouldn't see the horror of what she had just caught in the corner of her vision.

Patients who were sufficiently mobile were able to stumble their way outdoors. Dr Akizuki was momentarily struck with inertia. He returned to the consulting room in a daze and stared out the space where windows had once been. Smoke was clearing and figures could be seen running through the yellow-brown fog that hung low. It lifted to reveal buildings on fire all along the Urakami valley: the cathedral, the technical school, the weapons factory in the distance. Power poles and trees were broken and burning. Even the leaves of sweet potatoes in the vegetable garden had tongues of fire licking from them.

Nagasaki city was in flames as far as Akizuki could see. He reasoned to himself that this amount of damage could only be caused by the carpet-bombing that Nagasaki had managed to escape up to this point, but he hadn't seen or heard the large numbers of planes necessary for this. Then he remembered the talk by Dr Tsuno about the new bomb that had been dropped on Hiroshima.

People ran about crazily in the hospital grounds, patients and staff, many with blood flowing profusely from head wounds. Akizuki came outside and was told by a panicked patient that two of the tubercular invalids were still trapped in their rooms. Fire had started in the timber of the hospital roof where tiles had been thrown off by the blast. It was spreading through the wooden attic storerooms.

Gathering Brother Iwanaga and the seminarian Noguchi with him—both had escaped with only minor injuries apparent—Akizuki went up to the third floor. There they found Sugako Murai, alone trying to move the seriously ill patients. A neighbourhood volunteer who had been helping with meals had been found trapped in a corridor, pinned under fallen shelves and unable to move. The day before, she and Sugako had worked together in the kitchen. With the help of a patient making his own way out, the heavy timber shelving was lifted. The volunteer's pelvis had been broken by the falling material, but she was able to be moved painfully to the safety of the yard.

Now the rescue team was four persons as flames spread ominously across the roof. Time was running out. They were joined by volunteer workers from the parish who had avoided the worst of the blast. Head nurse Fukahori, ill in her bed that day, had been badly injured and was taken outside by two parishioners and laid on the grass. Dr Yoshioka, the visiting physician from the city hospital, was also badly hurt in the room where she was resting. Iwanaga carried her on his back, out of the building and across to the hill opposite.

The last two patients to be rescued were found pinned under fallen beams, too heavy to lift with the weight of other debris on top. Brother Iwanaga went away and returned with a two-handled saw. He and Noguchi cut through the beams as the heat and flames grew nearer. The trapped men were pulled away in time and carried out to the yard. They were the last to be rescued. Everyone from the wards and dormitories was out of the building: the seventy tuberculosis patients, the visitors from Takahara Hospital, the staff and volunteers. Like a giant balloon, relief rose from the crowd gathered in the yard. Nurse Murai burst into tears as she watched the hospital burn.

But the nightmare was only beginning. People were coming up the hill from the nearby suburbs, crying and groaning with an unearthly sound, looking for medical assistance. They arrived with strange, slow steps. One reached the yard, croaked 'Is this the hospital?' and collapsed. Their faces were pallid masks; some were stark naked. Crying 'I'm burning!' and 'Water!', many went down to the stream in the steep valley below the hospital.

A burly half-naked man came into the yard, holding his head between his hands, gurgling sounds lifting from somewhere deep inside his body. Akizuki didn't recognise him at first. The market gardener Tsujimoto, from next door to the hospital, had been picking pumpkins in his garden when the atomic blast struck. His head and face were white, his hair singed and eyebrows scorched away. His shirt was burnt from his back.

Someone remarked that the chaplain, Father Ishikawa, had not been seen coming from the building. Brother Iwanaga went looking for him in those parts of the hospital building that weren't so engulfed in fire that entry was no longer possible.

'The X-ray machines will be burnt,' exclaimed Dr Akizuki suddenly. Nurse Murai and two patients went to check the new equipment, stored in the basement until it could be installed. Burning timber had fallen down a lift shaft to the basement near where the three new machines had been temporarily placed. While they watched, insulation oil in the trans-formers ignited in the intense heat and exploded. The X-ray machines caught fire. They were beyond saving.

Iwanaga returned with a very groggy chaplain. Father Ishikawa had left the chapel and gone to his third-floor room to get a book. Returning along the ground floor corridor, he was hurled through the air, striking his head against a concrete post. The monk found him where he had wandered back in a daze to the chapel. The chaplain was moved to a quieter part of the yard and Brother Iwanaga fetched Dr Akizuki to look at his wounds. One eye was already swollen purple, but the bleeding from his head had stopped. There was little at this point that could be done for him.

Leaving the burning X-ray machines, temporary nurse Murai went up to the green patch on the hillside where the seriously wounded Dr Yoshioka and nurse Fukahori had been taken. On the way, she saw several half-naked nuns sitting in a rice field, looking up to the sky and praying. The sky was covered with a massive black cloud. The cathedral lower in the valley was burning with a column of flame. The hospital was crackling from the fire as it burnt. The wind blew up from time to time, throwing falling sparks around like darting insects. When the bomb had exploded, the nuns had been weeding in the rice field. Some had already died and the others were dying. Sugako was deeply affected by the transcendent beauty of their piping voices at the time of their death. Unselfconsciously, they sang 'Angeles Glory'.

◆ ◆ ◆

The relentless blast wave had continued on its path of devastation down the valley, rolling over the suburbs there. Sitting at a workbench in the torpedo factory, filing the rough edges off metal castings, Mitsue Takeno's reverie about a rice-ball lunch was broken by an eye-crushing flash of multiple colours. A roar followed, accompanied by the sound of objects being crushed and an earth-shattering tremor. Everything turned dark as if evening had come suddenly. Mitsue was knocked onto the floor. This plant of the Nagasaki arms works was little more than 1500 metres from the atomic bomb's detonation point.

When Mitsue regained consciousness, factory din had been replaced by human screaming. She was unable to move, lying on her belly under something—or things—holding her down. She tried to look around, but found she was covered with debris. Her arms were pinned by her side. Wriggling frantically, the sixteen-year-old managed to get her right arm loose. The floor beneath her felt slimy. Touching her head, she realised it was her blood on the floor. She reached out in the dark and felt the foot of the silent girl from another high school who had been sitting next to her at the table. Mitsue called out her name and tugged at her foot, but there was no response. The girl was as still and silent as stone.

Screaming voices and urgent footsteps were receding into the distance. Mitsue talked to herself to keep her spirits up. Unable to move, she thought about her family back on the Goto Islands. She remembered her grandmother chanting Buddhist sutras at the family altar and chanted to herself. No-one came to her aid.

With some writhing and pushing, she finally got the heavy object on her to slide. No debris fell into the space. Instead, a dull light came through a gap that appeared above her head. Mitsue pushed her head towards the hole, wriggling her body out of the debris. She called out again to the girl, but again there was no answer. Looking around, it seemed to her there was no-one there. Apart from her silent neighbour, Mitsue hadn't registered that there were other bodies, dead or crying out over the noise of burning and collapsing superstructure in the devastated factory.

Looking to get out of the building, Mitsue staggered through the doorway out of the work area. The long wooden staircase was no longer there, its lower half blown away, its upper part torn loose and hanging. A railing was dangling in the air near the end of the stairs. Clouds of smoke were rolling out from fires that had started in the factory. Mitsue jumped and grabbed the loose railing, clambered down the hanging remnant of stairway and dropped the remaining distance to the ground. Relief on getting to the ground gave way to a surge of dread. She was in a situation totally beyond her comprehension. Sixteen-year-old Mitsue Takeno sobbed uncontrollably.

Recovering somewhat, she stumbled over the debris that was most of what remained of the weapons factory. Blood was trickling from her head on to her neck and bare shoulders. Her blouse was torn and bloodied, her *monpe* tattered and hanging like seaweed. She fell, got up and staggered further, falling again. In this stuttering fashion Mitsue found her way alone to the main entrance of the factory, where she spotted a boy she recognised from Chinzei Middle School. He had often come to her work area during lunchtime to see his friends, but she had never spoken to him. His friends had included T-kun, the object of the girlish obsession of Mitsue and her closest friend. Although it was thought improper for a young man to be friendly with female students, the boy spoke to the sniffling girl.

'Don't cry,' he said. 'You should get that wound on your head treated.' He told her there was a dispensary just past the main gate. She nodded, glad to hear a human voice, and he ran off.

Smoke was billowing about the yard as Mitsue went through the factory gate looking for the dispensary. What greeted her instead in the world outside was unrecognisable from the one she had left in going through the factory gate that morning. The neighbourhood of closely packed houses had become a wide field of broken roof tiles. Every house that had been there was now crushed to the ground. The saw-toothed roofs of the row of factories along Urakami River were now steel frames twisted and bent over, their roofing torn off. Corpses were everywhere littering the streets and lanes. People crouched silently in groups, their bodies burnt and blackened. Screams of 'Help me!' came from within crushed houses. The dispensary forgotten, Mitsue headed unsteadily towards the hills below Mount Konpira, following others dragging leaden feet in that direction. No-one turned their head towards the cries for help.

In the same factory complex where Mitsue Takeno had been working with her school friends and POWs from Fukuoka Camp 14 were used as slave labour, inmates from Urakami Prison had also been contributing to the Japanese war effort while Warden Minami attended to his daily paperwork. Minami didn't see the flash of light before the factory room exploded around him, knocking him over. He got to his feet and made his way out of the room.

Three dazed prisoners were standing about in the shattered hallway, not sure what to do next. Minami could hear cries for help coming from a nearby office. He recognised the terrified voice of Commander Kamizaki of the Fatherland Defence Corps. A short time ago Kamizaki had seemed a tedious time-waster. Now Minami's responsibility to a fellow human prevailed. The warden went into the ransacked Corps office and found its occupant under a collapsed brick wall. He tried to remove the bricks.

Concerned that more bombs might be dropped, Minami decided instead that the commander should be pulled out. He ordered the three prisoners to prise the trapped official out. They did so by grabbing a leg poking out of the rubble and tugging sharply with all their strength. Kamizaki came out roughly and without much dignity, uniform torn and bloody, but with no apparent serious injury. Minami's next move was to locate the prisoners in the factory wreckage and determine how many casualties he had among his charges.

◆   ◆   ◆

The prisoners of war who worked in one end of Mitsubishi's mid-valley factory complex were no longer there by eleven o'clock. They were back in the POW camp next door, as were those who'd been reassigned from factory labour to working on the shelter and bridge at Mifune Canal.

The three men in the room with Peter McGrath-Kerr—Les Prendergast, Bert Miller and Murray Jobling—started to run for the camp dugouts the moment Prendergast concluded the plane they heard was American. The snoozing Miller woke and made an instinctive dash after the others. McGrath-Kerr, also lying on a bed, was slowest to move. He put down his book and started towards the door. That was the last thing he remembered. He was buried under the wreckage of the former cotton factory, buried under steel girders and flimsy light pine. Jobling, just ahead of McGrath-Kerr, hadn't left the barracks when the blast wave threw him out of the building and onto the ground in the yard. The other two were knocked to the ground in front of the barracks.

Outside in the yard, some Dutchmen had been digging a new shelter to replace the one destroyed in the recent air raid. Guards called out, '*Hikoki, hikoki* [Plane, plane],' and guards and prisoners headed for a finished dugout. Allan Chick had been standing on the low roof of the storehouse, chatting to an Indonesian fellow prisoner in a lull in fire-proofing the roof. After the alarming flash of light, the Australian had no idea what happened next. When he came to, he was sprawled on a log down at ground level. The storehouse had collapsed underneath him. He had come down with it but stayed on top of the pile of broken timber.

Chick looked around, but couldn't see anything. He thought he'd gone blind until he glanced in the direction of a shaft of light cutting through the murk. Dust from the bomb had cut out the sun, but it was starting to clear away. As his eyes regained their function, he could see that there was little left of the barracks block. Its steel girders were lying flat on the ground. Small fires were starting all over the camp in the crushed timber.

Another Australian, standing behind a wall, watched in stunned amazement as paint peeled off the building opposite in the instant of the flash. Leaves shrivelled and dropped off a tree. John Marshall's protecting wall collapsed on him from the force of the blast. He crawled out of the debris with a broken collarbone to see Nagasaki in flames.

Jack Johnson, who'd also been brought back from the foundry, had been told to clean up some debris from the air raid a week before. The guards had disappeared so he wandered around the camp yard. Hearing a plane overhead, the RAAF man looked up and saw three white para-chutes moments before a brilliant flash. Dropping by instinct beside an alleyway kerb, he had barely reached the ground when he was hit by the blast like a kick in the belly. Gasping for breath and pinned under rubble, he wriggled out and stood up in thinning dust. The camp was in ruins, with only a couple of brick and cement perimeter walls standing. They probably took much of the sting out of the shock wave, but just the same three Dutch POWs and an Englishman were killed instantly.

Johnson recovered sufficiently to join a search party, finding a pair of gumboots on legs under fallen timber. Rescuers dug the concussed

McGrath-Kerr out in a hurry, aware the broken wood around him could ignite at any moment. This was the same Jack Johnson who had pulled McGrath-Kerr onto an upturned lifeboat after the sinking of the *Tamahoko Maru* on the way to Nagasaki. The rescued sergeant had five broken ribs, three bones broken in one hand, and cuts and bruises on his arms, legs and head . . . but he had survived.

◆　◆　◆

Just a short distance from the POW camp and the factory, Mitsue Tabata was under the eaves of her house when the atomic blast propelled her inside. The pregnant woman, who with her little girl had watched POWs marching daily to and from work, lost consciousness. The next thing she was aware of was lying on her swollen belly under a pile of *tatami* mats and building debris. The lower part of her body was steeped in blood from a savage gash on her buttocks. With her right arm able to move a little, she pushed the pile of rubble off herself, piece by broken piece. After an interminable period of patient removal, Mrs Tabata was able to crawl out from under the wreckage of her house.

Her arm, hips and legs were severely burnt, her head injured, her hair stiff with clotted blood, but the Tabatas' eighteen-month-old daughter had been lucky. Caught in a space created by two larger pieces of timber, she'd been spared any serious injury. Carrying the baby girl in one arm and supporting her pregnant belly with the other, Mitsue fled from the remnants of her house. She had no shoes and her clothing had been stripped off her to the waist. As she made her way with her human load towards the slope up to the ridge from Mount Konpira, she was seen by a neighbour carrying a spare *monpe*. Although she hadn't given her half-naked state much thought, she was grateful for the clean piece of clothing.

◆　◆　◆

Everything disappeared in a bluish-white blinding flash, followed by the thunderous roar as the atomic blast rolled up the valley as well as down. Sumiteru Taniguchi was thrown into the air from his red postman's bicycle, landing on the ground a few metres away. He had just looked up to see if he could find among the clouds the plane he had heard getting closer. Through the dust and darkness, he saw white shapes swept along the ground. Moments before, these had been the playing children he'd waved to. A stone, from a pile around the base of a pine tree, had been lifted by the blast and hit his scorched back. The earth was trembling beneath him.

Eventually he struggled to his feet. The skin of his left arm had been baked off and hung in shreds from his fingertips. The left side of his chest was lacerated. Running his hand across his back, he felt a sticky mess of blood and dirt. The skin on his back had been stripped and hung down from his waist. There was no pain from either the burns or the rock that had been thrown at his back. He had been out in the open, exposed, 2 kilometres from the bomb's hypocentre.

The twisted metal of Sumiteru's bicycle lay on the ground nearby, its red paint seared off. The mailbag was empty. Letters and parcels had been tossed everywhere, mixing with the debris that littered the lane. His postman's cap was nowhere to be seen. Using his twisted bike to lean on, the young man gathered up the scattered mail and put it in his bag, letters to addresses that no longer existed.

Mitsubishi's torpedo factory was next on the postman's delivery route. He told himself he had to get there or he would die where he was. Through the murky yellow light, he could see nearby buildings in flames. The houses he'd just passed were flattened. The house where he'd just delivered letters was still standing, but he couldn't move to find out if anyone was still in it. Dozens of the dead and injured were on the street. Most were burnt, some were charred black, frozen in the moment when the bomb blast struck. People everywhere were crying for help, but Sumiteru couldn't answer them.

Eventually, step by step, he dragged himself towards the torpedo factory in the Sumiyoshi Tunnels. Passing the women's dormitory, he heard loud female cries for water, saw women staggering in circles, their clothing burnt off them, their hair singed to the scalp. Sumiteru stopped. He couldn't get his muscles to work. His brain was somewhere else.

Finally, the postman somehow got himself over the last hundred metres to the factory, collapsing on a bench at a tunnel entrance. Through the gloom he could see people inside, apparently uninjured. Possibly they were working in the tunnel, protected when the bomb exploded. A woman came over to see if he wanted help. He said, 'Water! Please!'

The woman brought him some water in a small cup, apologising there was so little. The mains had been cut and there was no more water. Still uncertain of the extent of his injuries, the young postman asked if she could cut off some of his hanging skin. She took a pair of scissors from a cupboard just inside the stone entrance, wiped them on his shirt, and carefully cut off much of the hanging skin. Still Sumiteru had no feeling in the affected areas . . . and little anywhere else. The woman cut off a piece of his shirt. She dipped it in motor oil and rubbed that ever so gently over the affected flesh. He could feel no pain, but he fainted.

◆ ◆ ◆

Deputy director Yoshiro Fukuda slammed down his phone in frustration and turned to the engineer, but before he could speak he was over-whelmed by the great blinding light. With a crack like a rifle shot, a large glass window shattered behind him. When Fukuda recovered his senses, he found he was on his back. His legs were draped over an upturned chair and there was a heavy weight pressing on his chest. It was the corner of a filing cabinet.

With great effort, he managed to push it off and got uneasily to his feet, his head hurting and his glasses lost. His sight wasn't good, but he could see that the room, in which he had been holding a management meeting of the Mitsubishi Arms Factory only moments before, had been demolished. Broken plaster and timber were everywhere. He could see two bodies under debris in the corner of what had been the conference room. Feeling weak and dizzy, a burning sensation on cheek and arm, Fukuda saw a trail of his own blood on the white plaster behind him. His head ached.

The bomb's piercing light also blinded Torahachi Tagawa. The percussive force that followed threw him on his stomach under a washbasin in the toilet block of the same munitions factory at Ohashi. Tagawa's fellow foreman was thrown on top of him. With a thundering roar, the roof and the tiled walls of the lavatory fell in. In the silence that followed, the two men disentangled and crawled out from under the basin and the debris that had fallen on and around it. While Tagawa checked himself for damage, the other disappeared without a word. He was there one moment and when Tagawa looked up again he had gone.

Staggering back toward the factory's administration building, Tagawa found its roof collapsed, its machines and office cabinets scattered about, its workers lying dead or injured in among the debris. In the office, the engineer Koga was lying face down by Tagawa's desk. He was dead.

The open-plan area of the office was filled with clerical workers crying out. Nothing was articulated in their despairing voices. Some were trapped under the rubble of collapsed roof and fallen fittings, some were too badly hurt to be able to move. Tagawa was able to free some of them, trapped under timber that had crashed to the floor. He worked solo with an energy he didn't comprehend. He recognised the deputy director stumbling through the dust and smoke, bleeding from the head, having come from a nearby room.

Tagawa disappeared from Fukuda's limited vision, returning soon after with an emergency medical bag he'd located somewhere. The foreman methodically picked out glass splinters from his executive's head. He'd been carrying the splinters since the large window shattered behind him in his office. It seemed like another lifetime but was probably only ten or fifteen minutes earlier. Tagawa painted over Fukuda's pinprick wounds with Mercurochrome.

His immediate injuries dealt with, the deputy director wandered outside in a daze of myopia and shock. People were lying on the ground, staggering in circles, crawling towards the factory gate. Nothing was in focus. No building stood whole. There was a fire in the company's wooden mess hall. Fukuda shouted for fire extinguishers, but no-one responded. He walked unsteadily to the factory's main building, where weapon assembly was carried out, with a vague intention of doing something, although he wasn't quite sure what. He heard cries from people trapped in buildings. He made out figures dimly, and ordered a group to rescue the trapped victims. They set about the task half-heartedly. He knew they'd stop when he moved on. Fukuda saw that Mitsubishi's technical section was on fire. He joined the throng shuffling out the gate.

The foreman Tagawa remained in the office for a while, trying to help others after Fukuda had left. He went outside looking for medical assistance, saw that oil drums had caught fire and tried to put them out. He picked up a bucket he found lying around to scoop water from a concrete tank alongside the drums.

A voice shouted from somewhere, 'That's too dangerous!' He dropped the bucket and fled through the factory gate.

◆　◆　◆

Sitting with his friends in the tram terminal at Hotarujaya, Koichi Wada was struck by the blinding flash of light and, a few seconds later, the impact of a violent explosion. Although he was nearly four kilometres from the hypocentre, Koichi was lifted into the air before being thrown heavily onto the floor. He felt something weighty falling on his back. After that, everything went dark.

Slowly his surroundings came back into vision as dust settled, but these surroundings weren't the same. Koichi was startled to see how extensive the destruction had been. The terminal he had been sitting in a few moments before was unrecognisable. As his fellow workers pulled him out of debris from the damaged building, he heard the chilling sound of people crying despairingly for help.

He suffered shock and scratches and bruises, but Koichi was not badly hurt. The ridge running down from Mount Konpira had screened the terminal from the extreme radiation heat that accompanied the atomic blast, although not the blast itself. Koichi began to help with rescue work, digging people out of the material that had fallen from the building. Those drivers, conductors and other employees of the streetcar company who were nearby when the bomb fell were gathering at Hotarujaya. Some were badly injured. While they were attended to with what little first aid was available, the young driver decided to walk in the direction of the bomb blast to see what had happened, perhaps to see what aid he could offer he wasn't sure; his mind was in a jumble.

◆ ◆ ◆

The Yamawaki twins were sitting at the table sharing a snack when a whitish-blue light shot across the room. Following on its heels was an unearthly roar that shook the family's large house at the foot of Mount Inasa. The two eleven-year-old boys dropped on *tatami* mats and covered their eyes, ears and noses with fingers as they'd been taught. They could feel plaster and other debris falling on top of them as it peeled off the ceiling and walls.

After a while, when the room stopped trembling and the falling debris slowed to a trickle, they opened their eyes. Lying there, they could hear distant voices from the neighbourhood, people crying and screaming. Yoshiro lifted his head and looked around. His world had been turned upside down in just a few short moments. The walls had partially crumbled away; the roof had been blown off. He looked up and he could see the sky. He and Tatsuro got up cautiously. *Tatami* mats in every room were covered with dirt and rubble. Their furniture was mangled and scattered around. Pillars and what was left of the walls were speared with sharp-edged fragments of glass like an archery range for glass arrows.

The Yamawaki boys went outside through the open doorway. Other houses in the neighbourhood were also seriously damaged. They had assumed a bomb must have hit their house, but everywhere seemed to be in much the same state of destruction. There was no obvious point of greater destruction that would indicate where the bomb had exploded. In fact, the weapon's hypocentre was more than two kilometres away. Across the harbour, the central part of the city was covered in clouds of dust. Further north, up the Urakami valley, there was a giant plume of swirling cloud.

The twins' older brother had left the torpedo factory at Tomachi earlier in the morning. Because of disruption by the morning air-raid warnings, part of the production line had been suspended and Toshihiro Yamawaki had been given the rest of the day off. By the time the bomb was dropped, he was at the customs house. He would have got a ferry across the bay from Ohata, but they were damaged by the bomb and taken out of service. Instead, Toshihiro walked around the top of the bay, going up to the first bridge across the river and back down the western bank to his home.

Yoshiro and Tatsuro had gone to the bomb shelter in their substantial yard and waited for their father and older brother to come home. An hour later, Toshihiro arrived and said it was too dangerous to stay in the tiny bomb shelter. Ohata was on fire, he said. Houses were burning and everyone was fleeing. They put a sign on their gate to tell their father they'd gone to the neighbourhood shelter.

◆　◆　◆

While his department head was suggesting his brain was addled, Yamaguchi the draftsman saw a blinding flash burning through Mitsubishi's office windows. Instinctively he dived under a desk before the office interior blew inside out. His workmates and boss followed, flattened by the blast wave. Desks and chairs tumbled about. Yamaguchi's firmly wound bandages were stripped off his arms and face like socks coming off.

The boss was shouting, 'Help me! Help me!', but Yamaguchi was so confused and distraught and in such agony that he just wandered away, leaving the others to fend for themselves as best they could. With pain from the heat spearing through his body, he staggered without any conscious plan out of the shipyard and up the steep rocky hillock that marked the beginning of the rise towards Mount Inasa.

Down on the quayside, his associate from the Hiroshima experience reacted equally as instinctively to the familiar flash of intense light. Sato recognised what was happening and jumped straight into the bay alongside. He trod water for an hour before making his way back onto dry and seared land. Although the shipyards were in an unimpeded line from the bomb's hypocentre, at nearly four kilometres away they were on the outer reaches of the worst of the destruction.

Iwanaga, Yamaguchi's boarding house roommate in Hiroshima, was even further from the firing line up in the hills beyond Urakami, at

Nagayo railway station. The shipping draftsman was woken from his train-ride slumber by the flash of light to see his fellow passengers rolling onto the floor and jumping under seats. A second later, the carriage's windows were blown in with a deep 'Fuff', followed by the tinkling sound of showering glass.

The station master and his assistants came rushing through the train, shouting for everyone to get out and take shelter. Iwanaga left with them as they silently and obediently filed into the woods behind the station. He looked up and saw a cloud even more mushroomed in shape than the previous one he'd witnessed. He knew then he was in a repeat of the Hiroshima bomb. Eventually the passengers climbed back on the train. It crawled onwards along its scheduled route until it arrived at Michinoo station, where those on board were ordered off to make room for refugees drifting up from Urakami.

Iwanaga had not been heading for the shipyards on Nagasaki Bay, but to Mitsubishi's marine parts plant at Ohashi. He was now only fifteen minutes' walking distance from his workplace. On his way, he passed the five tunnels of the Nagasaki Ordnance Factory's underground works at Sumiyoshi. By now he was about two kilometres from the hypocentre. Around the tunnels' stonework entrance, he saw charred bodies of Mitsubishi workmen. Inside the mouth of the tunnels he could see badly scorched people who had made their way to shelter there. The city was a sea of fire under a brooding sky. Houses were bursting into spontaneous flame. He was only 800 metres from the marine works, but his path was blocked by fallen trees.

Akira Iwanaga turned around and started walking back to his parents' home at Isahaya. He would still be walking at nightfall.

Yamaguchi meanwhile was picking his way up the rocky incline towards a concrete watchtower. He had no clear idea why. In front of the structure, when he got there, he found a watchman lying unconscious on the ground. The man had burns all over his body. He had probably been watching the American planes as they approached and released their weapon. His large binoculars had been blown out of his hands.

Numbed by the breeze fanning the pain in his burns, Yamaguchi tugged open the watchtower's steel door. He noticed it was warm to touch, too hot to have been heated by the sun. He went inside and looked around, without registering anything he saw. He went over to a slit window and peered out over the devastated city. Tsutomu Yamaguchi stood there a long time, his brain in neutral.

◆ ◆ ◆

For some in the Urakami valley, the end was serenely surreal, belying the horror. Kazuyo Inao, a 24-year-old factory worker, had the day off work that Thursday. She decided to go to the public bathhouse at Aburagi, near the Gokoku Shrine. It would be her first bath for quite a while and she looked forward to it with relish. She undressed and scrubbed down her grimy body with cool clean water. As she stepped demurely into a steaming tub sunk into the floor, the bomb blast threw her violently over it. Her head crashed against the wall behind. Her unconscious body folded and sank to the bottom of the tub.

Twenty-four hours later, she was found by a newspaper reporter covering the story of Nagasaki's devastation. The tub was drained of water through cracks in its structure caused by the bomb. The reporter found the young woman's body wasn't blackened like most of the corpses he had been seeing. It was naked and unmarked. Her skin was bright rosy red. She looked like she was posing for a painting by a European master.

For others, the escape was wryly comical, at least to the observer looking back in time, if not to the people concerned during the ter-rifying experience. Isaburo Kubo and Tomoyo Kishi were two of the escapees. Kubo was an electrical parts inspector for the Nagasaki shipyard. He was at the torpedo factory that day, the same factory where Mitsue Takeno and her school friends worked, inspecting a one-man *kamikaze* submarine just assembled in the factory compound.

As Kubo climbed into the sub to examine its electrical work, a flash blew out the sun. Seconds later, he was rammed into the new submarine. It was turned over and he was rolled down the yard like a circus clown tumbling in a barrel. Kubo emerged, stunned and bleeding, to see the torpedo factory destroyed. The bodies of the workers who had been busy around him a few minutes before were now spread motionless and twisted across the yard.

Kishi was a fifteen-year-old in the Student Patriotic Corps. Pouring a plaster torpedo mould at the same factory when the blast rolled through, she was pinned under upended fresh plaster and its container up to her neck. The plaster was already hardening when she was found by rescue workers. It got harder over the nine hours it took the workers to dig her out. She emerged extremely distraught and still with hard plaster remnants attached to her body ... but she was alive. Tomoyo Kishi was one of the lucky ones.

◆ ◆ ◆

On seeing the flash, Junji Sato instinctively dropped off his bicycle and rolled into a shallow gully by the road, pushing his face into the earth for protection. His exposed skin began to smart just before a giant thunder-clap rolled over the top of him, followed by a continuous roar fading into rumbling. Then, silence.

After a few minutes, the reporter stood up. The entire downtown area was immersed in thick dust clouds and a purplish cloud was spread-ing overhead from the north. A black smoke geyser shot up into the sky behind the ridge. Sato straightened his bicycle handles and moved along the road. He couldn't see clearly much more than ten metres in front of him in the dust and smoke-laden air. Ghostly figures shuffled in slow motion in the opaque noon twilight, dazed men and women with clothes torn to shreds. Croaky groans and agonising cries drifted out of the gloom. When he got closer to the passing figures, they would stare at him. The skin of some of these chameleon people had turned white, some red and, later, it would go black. There were no visible signs of severe burns. Here, out of the Urakami valley and on the edge of the high-destruction zone, houses hadn't vanished, but most downtown buildings had been gutted, and some homes were flattened. Windows and doors had been blown away.

From the gate of the luxurious house occupied by the Domei News Agency, Sato saw that the glass had gone from the large French windows.

He was met at the doorway by the imposing figure of his boss, managing editor Yamanaka, in a state that was a mix of agitation and excitement. The offices inside were filled with broken glass, although none of the staff seemed too badly injured.

A police inspector had been copying a report on Hiroshima at the agency when the bomb exploded. He had gone to the window to see what the flash of light was about when the glass disintegrated, throwing slivers in his face. A stenographer was removing them with tweezers and dabbing Mercurochrome on the wounds, painting his face the colour of sunshine.

The editor was at his desk in the corner at the time of the explosion. Glass had gashed his forehead but Yamanaka, ever the journalist, had leapt for the phone, recognising what had happened. All phone and utility lines were knocked out, but Domei's private line between Nagasaki and Fukuoka remained intact. Yamanaka shouted down the line that the new American bomb had been dropped on Nagasaki. Sato was sent back out to get the story.

At the prefectural meeting that had prevented Sato getting his *sake* requisition a short while before, Mayor Koura had been speaking. He hadn't got very far upstaging Governor Nagano when the shelter interior was bathed in a bright, blue light. After a short pause, a loud unidentifiable noise roared out and the wall lights went off. A voice said in the pitch black, 'It's a power failure!' Another voice said he'd go for candles, not explaining how he would find them in the dark. However, at the same time a shaft of light appeared through the bomb shelter's door, broken open by the blast wave.

The defence meeting disbanded. Nagano and the others emerged from the shelter to see what had caused the commotion. About three kilometres from the hypocentre, they were on the leeward side of the ridge up to Mount Konpira, separating the Urakami and Nakajima valleys. A group of labourers told the governor they had seen a bright flash and heard a loud explosion in the distance. Urakami was in flames. Nagano looked in its direction and saw a stream of smoke rising beyond the ridge. However, the house in front of him seemed untouched and there was no apparent damage to the older parts of the city on the slope below him to his left, nor up the Nakajima valley.

Puzzled, the governor began to wonder if Nishioka, the newspaper publisher, had exaggerated his Hiroshima experience in his graphic description. He had said all the buildings had been flattened, yet here was Nagano surrounded by upright houses. He had described horribly burnt people moaning in agony as a result of the bomb. None of the workers Nagano was talking to were injured.

Nagano's main concern was the severity of the fire in the downtown area, facing unimpeded up the Urakami valley. It was widespread, too big for Nagasaki's fire department to handle on its own. Needing to work out a strategy, Governor Nagano went back inside the shelter.

Nishioka's advice to the governor the morning before had found at least one attentive listener. Nagano had passed it on to police chief Mizuguchi who had, in turn, told his family. Mizuguchi's teenage son was walking in the street with three classmates when he saw the flash in the sky. Remembering his father's warning, the boy grabbed the hand of a friend and pulled him into a shelter. He called to the other two to follow, but they kept on walking. Those two boys were never seen again.

Mrs Mizuguchi was standing under the eaves of their house with the baby when she saw the flash. Recalling her husband's words, she dashed inside the house, squeezed herself and her baby into a closet and pulled the sliding door shut. The house shook as the blast wave hit it. When it had passed, Mrs Mizuguchi came out of the shelter to find the room covered with shattered glass. Perhaps the police chief had a responsibility to pass Nishioka's warning on to a wider audience than his family, but then that's what the governor's morning defence meeting was to be about.

Takejiro Nishioka was nowhere near the prefecture's governor to set him straight on the atomic bomb. Chatting to the bus company's branch chief in the hot springs town of Obama, the publisher had heard the drone of a distant plane. Looking up, he saw two B-29s approach across the Ariake Sea, then disappear into the clouds that had gathered. A gigantic brilliant gold and white ball appeared above the distant city of Nagasaki. The crowd waiting for a bus gasped in shock or awe, or both.

Nishioka shouted, 'Get into the shelter right away!'

He headed for a large dugout by the bus station. The taxi-driver jumped out of his car and followed. Within a few seconds, there was an explosive roar with a sharp high wind. When the shelterers came out, the sun was dull red. A red-brown atomic cloud towered over the city to the south. Nishioka gathered his thoughts and told the driver he now wanted to go to Nagasaki.

◆　◆　◆

Chuck Sweeney had flown *Bockscar* south towards Okinawa, Fred Bock in *The Great Artiste* sitting on his starboard side. The crew got out of their flak suits and survival equipment. Radio operator, Abe Spitzer, transmitted the bombadier's report of the smoke-obscured target site, 'Nagasaki bombed. Results good.' The message was received at Tinian with surprise and relief. Sweeney's attention turned to the state of the *Bockscar* fuel reserves. John Kuharek did the calculations. There were barely 300 gallons of useable fuel left. That was insufficient for the 600 kilometres to Okinawa. If they slowed down, they might get to within 80 kilometres of Okinawa before their fuel supply gave out, but that seemed the best they could hope for.

There was a rescue process that had been set up as part of the mission. Now was the time for it to be put on alert. Sweeney told Spitzer to contact Air-Sea Rescue, advise they were leaving the area and give them the plane's position. Spitzer did so, but there was no response.

These men were trained to deal with problems calmly and methodically. Sweeney dictated a message to Spitzer to be transmitted to Tinian:

Bombed Nagasaki 090158Z visually with no fighter opposition and no flak. Results 'technically successful' but other factors make conference necessary before taking further steps. Visible effects about equal to Hiroshima. Trouble in airplane following delivery requires us to proceed to Okinawa. Fuel only to get to Okinawa.

Sweeney asked his radioman to try Air-Sea Rescue again, but again there was no answer. The rescue team had gone home to Iwo Jima.

Chapter 13

Nagasaki, Thursday 9 August 1945, afternoon

Oblivious to another major setback to Japan's cause circling over Kyushu at that time, the Supreme Council for the Direction of the War had gathered at ten thirty in the concrete-walled shelter of the prime minister's official residence. The six council members met in a mood of 'impatience, frenzy and bewilderment', according to Grand Chamberlain Fujita, who ushered them into their seats. A rumour was doing the rounds, fuelled by the interrogation of the American pilot McDilda, that Tokyo was the next target for the atomic bomb.

Prime Minister Suzuki opened discussion, arguing that Japan did not have the military strength to meet the challenge of both the atomic bomb and the Soviet attack. 'I believe we have no alternative other than to accept the Potsdam Declaration,' he said. 'I would now like to hear your opinions.'

Suzuki's remarks were so uncharacteristically blunt they were greeted with stunned silence. After an awkward pause, the perpetually cheerful Navy Minister Yonai spoke. 'We're not going to accomplish anything by keeping silent.'

Yonai's comment triggered a short exchange of tit-for-tat remarks. The army's Chief of General Staff was first. 'We won't know the full story of Hiroshima until the investigation is completed,' said General Umezu, although he knew Dr Nishina's opinion and therefore knew what inevitably would be the result of the investigation.

Togo responded, 'We know that the new weapon wiped it out and the United States president has promised more.'

'Truman's statement could easily be a lie to force a quick surrender,' cut in Admiral Toyoda, Umezu's equivalent in the navy. 'Damage by the bomb was heavy, but we don't know if America can stockpile material for these bombs.' The navy leader was talking about the new weapon as if it was an atomic bomb, while at the same time questioning that it was. 'In any case, world opinion might prevent its further use.' The Vatican had already criticised the US over Hiroshima.

'Hata has suggested countermeasures against the bomb,' said Umezu. 'We don't yet know the implications of the Russian declaration.'

It was a scattergun discussion and Yonai sought to rein it in. 'We all seek peace,' he said. 'The question is whether to accept the Potsdam Declaration as stated or negotiate more favourable terms. Are we agreed the imperial system must remain?' All nodded sombrely. 'Then what are our positions on other possible implications in the Allied demands?'

'Japan's position becomes weaker with each passing hour,' said Togo. 'The only condition we can and must insist on is continuation of the imperial system. We must safeguard the emperor.'

General Anami, the War Minister and leading voice for continuing to fight, spoke for the first time. 'We all want peace, but it must be on the basis of four conditions.' He listed the three additions. Occupation of Japan should be avoided or, if inescapable, should be on a small scale and not include Tokyo. Disarmament and demobilisation should be carried out by Japanese officers, and war criminals should be dealt with by the Japanese government. They were the demands of a military seeking peace, but not yet recognising itself as defeated.

'I concur with the War Minister's decision,' said General Umezu.

'I too agree with General Anami,' said Admiral Toyoda.

'If we make those demands,' responded Togo, 'the Allies will refuse to negotiate at all.'

At that point, a Suzuki aide burst into the room, announcing, 'Nagasaki has just been hit by another atomic bomb.' Governor Nagano had advised that the city had been attacked with a bomb like that used on Hiroshima, but that it was less powerful and a smaller number had been killed. His assessment was based on the damage done in the Nakajima valley. Nagano was unaware at the time of the extent of destruction in neighbouring Urakami. The news got scant discussion by the Supreme War Council, which moved back to its active debate.

Anami resumed his exchange with Togo. 'You are speaking of Japan as if it was a defeated nation. I'd point out that we have not yet surrendered. We have not yet lost this war. And if the enemy attacks our home islands, he will do so at his peril!'

'Can the military offer any hope of victory if negotiations fall through?'

'We can't give any guarantee of victory,' said Anami, 'but Japan still has the capacity to fight another battle and force an end to the war on more favourable terms than we're now offered.'

'Can we prevent the enemy landing on the Japanese mainland?'

'Battles are unpredictable. We might drive the enemy back into the sea, if we're lucky,' said Umezu, 'but even if they establish beachheads, we can inflict heavy losses.'

'The enemy will follow up with a second assault after we have sacrificed all to destroy their first wave. We would have no aircraft or ammunition left.'

'You want us to accept surrender, not peace,' said Umezu, the discussion heating up. 'The military code doesn't allow for surrender.'

Anami added, 'The people of Japan wouldn't tolerate occupation of their country.'

By one o'clock, the argument had become impassioned but inconclusive. A cabinet meeting was scheduled for the afternoon, where the same question would be submitted. The Supreme War Council was adjourned by the prime minister without coming to any agreement on how they should proceed. It was Japanese leadership at its most unproductive when it needed decisiveness.

◆ ◆ ◆

Major Sweeney had managed to get *Bockscar* further than expected using a fuel-saving technique that Paul Tibbets had once shown him. Power settings were kept steady on a gradual descent, so the aircraft picked up air speed without requiring more power and without drawing any more fuel. The plane eventually levelled off and was then dropped another step. *Bockscar* was able to be taken through this process because it had started at 10,000 metres. As well, Sweeney throttled back the propellers from the recommended cruise speed. Fifteen minutes' flying time out of Okinawa, *Bockscar* was still in the air.

Spitzer called the tower at Yontan Field on Okinawa several times and got no response. Sweeney took over.

'Yontan tower. Yontan tower. This is Dimples 77 . . . Yontan. Yontan. This is Dimples 77. Mayday! Mayday! Over.' There was silence.

Spitzer radioed the nearby island of Ie-shima and was able to talk to them, but Ie-shima and Okinawa towers were on different radio frequencies because they were so close to each other. Ie-shima would not be able to raise Yontan in time.

At twelve thirty, Yontan came into view. Planes of all types could be seen everywhere, taking off and landing in a continuous stream. They were running missions from Okinawa around the clock.

Kuharek said, 'Major, all gauges read empty.'

As if on cue, the outer starboard engine cut out. Sweeney instructed co-pilot Albury to increase the power to number three engine to compensate. The plane steadied but Sweeney couldn't afford a long low approach or a second attempt at landing. It had to be one short run only at the airfield, come what may. At least they no longer had Fat Man on board.

Sweeney's options spun around in his brain as he calculated the odds. He would aim halfway down the runway at a landing speed above the recommended 110 mph (180 km/h). The 600 gallons of fuel trapped in the reserve tank might explode if they crash-landed. The landing had to be steep, but not too steep.

Olivi was told to let off the flares of the day. Four red and green flares were fired through a porthole in the fuselage, but there was no response from the airfield. The traffic pattern on the ground continued unchanged, aircraft coming and going.

'Mayday! Mayday! Yontan. Dimples 77.'

The agitation was growing in Sweeney's voice. He could hear the tower talking to other planes. It was apparent they couldn't hear him.

'Mayday! Mayday!' No response.

'I want any goddamn tower in Okinawa.' Still nothing.

Sweeney turned to Olivi. 'Fire every goddamn flare we have on board!'

'Which ones?'

'Every goddamn flare we have! Do it now!'

Twenty flares curved above the plane and exploded in all colours, signalling all manner of emergency, 'prepare for crash', 'heavy damage', 'dead and wounded on board', 'aircraft on fire'. No disaster was left un-notified. The forward section of *Bockscar* was filled with the acrid smell of gunpowder from the Very pistol.

The fireworks display had its desired effect. Planes peeled away as *Bockscar* loomed over the runway at speed, charging in on a straight line. Fire trucks and ambulances raced towards the runway. The giant silver bomber descended steeply, hitting the pavement halfway down the strip at 230 km/h, bouncing once and slamming back down. As the wheels hit the concrete, the port outer engine cut out and 65 tonnes of aircraft veered left towards a line of B-25s parked along the edge of the runway.

At that moment, a welcome change of fortune came their way. B-29s made for the 509th Composite Group were the only ones with the new Curtis reversible propellers. Sweeney flipped the *Bockscar* props—the two that were still working—into reverse and hit the emergency brakes. The aircraft straightened, continuing to roll down the runway. As the end of the runway approached, Sweeney pulled on the yoke with all his strength. The B-29 came to a halt 3 metres from the end of the runway.

The pilot and mission leader was mentally and physically drained. He let the plane roll to the side of the runway and onto a taxiway. As another engine cut out, he slumped back in his seat and switched off the remaining engine. Not a word was spoken. In a plane with thirteen men, there was total silence as the distant wail of sirens got nearer and nearer. Emergency vehicles pulled alongside. A man opened the nosewheel door and poked his head in.

'Where's the dead and wounded?'

'Back there,' said Sweeney, pointing northwards to Nagasaki.

◆　◆　◆

The front of Nagasaki Medical College was littered with dead and wounded. Bodies were draped on stone walls with heads or limbs missing. Mutilated people came up looking for the first-aid station they assumed would be set up in the hospital. A mother ran past the entrance clutching her decapitated child. The wards were beginning to break out in flames. Having recovered his sense of urgency, Dr Nagai sent his staff, the nurses and technicians, to look for patients in wards where it was still possible to get in. They tied wet hand towels around their faces and plunged in, stumbling out soon after with the wounded on their backs or over their shoulders. The hilly area behind the college was free from the fires that were burning everywhere else. Dr Nagai organised for the wounded to be carried up onto a hill. Two children followed, dragging their father up with them.

Trying to minister to so many wounded, Nagai felt helpless and empty-handed. He went to the operating room in the basement to see what medical supplies he could find, but it was flooded from a burst water pipe. In the next room where emergency medicines and instruments were stored, the contents had been tossed about by the blast wave and smashed on the floor, with water from the broken pipe washing over them.

A rescuer came out supporting a distressed Dr Tsuno, his hair and face white, his white medical coat soaked in blood. The dean's glasses were gone. Dr Nagai felt his pulse and it was steady. He told the rescuer to take Tsuno up the hill. At the same time, a young doctor returned from the wards to report that an arthritis patient had refused to leave unless he got a stretcher. There were no stretchers available.

'Leave the patient,' said Dr Nagai. 'I take responsibility.' Fires were being fanned by a stiff wind that blew up at about one o'clock. It would be highly risky for the doctor to return.

Some of the staff became concerned at Dr Nagai's head wound. They stemmed the blood flow, packing the wound and binding his head tightly with dirty bandages they'd found. Now he had a red turban. Getting back to tending to the injured, the doctor had to listen to patients complaining that their wounds hurt, that they wanted to be carried up the hill slowly or they wanted someone to go back and get their things. A mother lay unconscious on the ground with a baby crying alongside and the fires closing in. Nagai took the baby up the hill and laid her near to the slumped form of a nurse. Others carried the mother up and laid the baby at her breast.

By the time Tsuneo Tomita and Professor Seiki got to the hospital, they found it wrecked and anyone who could move or be moved had gone to the top of the first hill. About five hundred refugees had gathered there at the side of a burnt-out field of sweet potatoes. A discordant chorus of moans let the student and the teacher know where the survivors could be found. They arrived to see two girls with their arms around each other in the throes of death. An old woman had a makeshift tourniquet around her leg stump. Dr Tsuno was lying in the corner of the field, curled up and covered with an overcoat. Seiki went up and gave him a report on behalf of the pharmacy section. Tsuno nodded but didn't respond otherwise.

Dr Nagai called out to get some of the rescued patients further up the hill, away from the encroaching flames. He carried two himself, but then began to sway on his feet. Matron Hisamatsu took the doctor's pulse, affected by blood loss and leukemia, and forced him to sit down.

Refugees were still drifting up from the valley. Staff were beginning to panic at the enormity of the task that confronted them. Overwhelmed, they were losing confidence they could acquit themselves well in this test of character. Nagai could sense the steel was slipping out of their spirit.

'Quick! Find a *Hi no Maru* [Japanese flag],' he shouted urgently.

One of the younger doctors looked around but couldn't find a flag, indeed couldn't think where to look for one. Nagai grabbed a white sheet blowing past. He tore it into a square and dabbed the blood-soaked bandage on his head into the centre. Others painted stripes radiating in blood around the centre blob. They now had a Japanese flag.

Nagai told the young doctor to tie it to a bamboo pole and drive it into the grassy knoll above them. The militarists had made the flag so important to Japanese life over the last fifteen years that all on the hill responded to its symbolism with renewed vigour, rallying around the ad hoc hospital headquarters. At four, heavy blobs of black rain began to fall, leaving dark streaks on the flag, but it had already served its purpose.

Tomita and Professor Seiki were inspired by the Rising Sun in blood, but could find no-one to help them. They returned to the shelter to discover more dead and none of the living with much strength. A water tank had two dead bodies lying in it. Tomita took water in a helmet back into the dugout for those still able to drink. They gulped it down without drawing breath.

Back on the hill behind the college, Nagai reported to the incapacitated dean on what was being done. He felt dizzy, with his legs getting rubbery. In pausing to talk to Dr Tsuno, his mind had drifted to the subject he had subconsciously held in check in the immediacy of the moment. Since realising that all of Urakami was burning, he had wanted to search for Midori, but he knew his responsibility was to remain at the hospital and provide what aid he could. Now it occurred to him that if his wife had survived, she would have made her way to the college. He tried to distract himself by taking the pulse of a technician lying soaked and streaked on the ground. His pulse was strong. Nagai put his coat on the man, took a few steps backwards and collapsed on the ground.

'She's dead. She's dead,' he whispered mournfully and passed out.

◆ ◆ ◆

Kyoto Hashimoto was in the same year at Nagasaki Girls High School as Mitsue Takeno and had been mobilised to work in the same arms factory. Climbing the hillside with others escaping the conflagration in Urakami, their paths crossed once again. Apart from the brief meeting with the boy from Chinzei, Kyoto was the only familiar face Mitsue had seen since the atomic bomb exploded on this most unfamiliar of days. They'd been on talking terms, but never close. Just the same, when their eyes met they wept and embraced. Each was a secure anchor for the other when the world was drifting so uncomprehendingly. They grabbed each other's hand instinctively and continued their careful negotiation of the narrow footpath between terraced fields.

Approaching aircraft could be heard. People shouted, 'Enemy planes!' The two girls fled across garden patches, but they couldn't see anywhere practical to hide. A young man sheltering under an embankment called out and they ran over to where he was, crouching alongside him. Tied tightly around his head was a headband with a rising sun on it. The young man looked to the girls like a samurai of old. It was as if they had stumbled into some story from Japan's mythology.

The sound of planes faded into the distance. 'They must have been our planes,' said the samurai.

The girls followed him silently as he climbed further up the pathway to a graveyard and rested in the cool shade of lush green trees. He didn't shoo them away so they stayed near him. They'd reached a height above the bomb-ravaged area. Other refugees had gathered in the glade and were watching the sea of fire in the valley below. The only person who spoke was a half-naked young man.

'We've lost the war,' he said.

So effective had Japanese propaganda been that Mitsue believed losing the war meant death. She wondered if she had already arrived at that point. Wooden power poles had been blown over. Electric cables dangling from tilted poles moved about in the breeze, sparking as they came in contact with each other. Any poles still standing glowed red. Periodically, pillars of flame darted in the air around the arms factory. Mitsue looked down and saw that Mezane-cho was blazing. Her friend N-san lived there. Mitsue wondered whether she had survived the inferno.

Mitsue and Kyoto scooped up dead cicadas that were lying around, putting them in a pile and covering them with sand. When the young man wiped sweat off his face with his headband, Mitsue saw that the rising sun was actually a bloodstain from a wound on his forehead.

'Nothing serious,' he said. 'It's already stopped bleeding.'

The young man said he was from Tokyo, but Mitsue had already worked that out from his accent. He told them he had been drafted to the

Nagasaki factory of Mitsubishi's steelworks. Since he wasn't conscripted, Mitsue guessed he must be a key technical person. He re-folded the cloth and tied it back around his head.

◆ ◆ ◆

The crew of *Bockscar* dropped out of the plane onto the Yontan taxiway. Sweeney drew them together and told them to get something to eat, but to say nothing about their mission. They climbed onto a waiting truck while their leader and Ashworth, the weaponeer, got into a jeep. Sweeney told the driver to take them to the senior ranked unit commander at the base. He wanted to make a detailed report.

The crew went to a pristinely white mess hall for 'chow' while *Bockscar* was serviced. There was a buzz of excitement there, with reports that a second atomic bomb had been dropped on Japan. A GI told the visiting crewmen that a new special bomb was being used against Japan, carried by P-38s and dropped by parachute. Another said the bomb was no bigger than a baseball. The boys from *Bockscar* didn't comment.

They told the mess sergeant they were hungry. Surly, he asked why combat guys could never get to chow on time.

'We were busy,' said Gallagher.

'Busy?' snarled the sergeant. 'I'm busy eighteen to twenty hours a day.'

He finally produced a bologna sandwich for each of them between thick pieces of day-old bread.

In the meantime, Sweeney and Ashworth were shown into the head-quarters of General Jimmy Doolittle, commander of the Eighth Air Force, based on Okinawa. He had led the first American air strike on Japan's mainland back in 1942.

Doolittle gave the visitors access to communications and arranged for Sweeney's report to go to Tinian. The three talked briefly about the mission, the general responding without emotion. He wanted only the facts.

Silent, serious, ruminating, he said, 'It's been a long time coming.'

'Yes, sir,' said Sweeney. 'I hope it means the end.'

Out on the runway, *The Great Artiste* had landed a few minutes after *Bockscar*. It wasn't until an hour later that the missing camera plane, *The Big Stink*, finally appeared and landed. The crew of the late arrival were greeted with good-natured banter. While all this was going on, John Kuharek measured the fuel remaining in the main tank. There were seven gallons left, not even enough for one minute of flying.

◆ ◆ ◆

After the unproductive Supreme War Council meeting, Prime Minister Suzuki hurried straight to the Imperial Palace to see Marquis Kido, the emperor's chief adviser. Former prime minister Konoye was already in the room when he arrived. There was no discussion about the Nagasaki bomb. They were more concerned about what was happening in Manchuria. For some inexplicable reason, Suzuki told them that the Supreme War Council had agreed to accept the Potsdam demands with four conditions, which he listed. The inscrutable Kido had a meeting with Hirohito at three at which he said he would pass on the council's decision. A long-time supporter of the peace initiative, Kido wouldn't have thought this a good result.

Konoye was horrified. He could see a disaster looming with what the Allies would regard as a refusal to surrender. He left to phone Prince Takamatsu, the emperor's younger brother, a strong advocate for ending the war. Konoye persuaded the prince to phone Kido and press him to drop three of the conditions, hanging on only to the stipulation of retention of the imperial system. Kido listened to Takamatsu's argument. He had no choice, he said, but to accept the four conditions if that was what council decided.

Meanwhile General Anami had returned to the War Ministry and assured high-ranking and junior officers that nothing had changed regarding the war's direction. He gave no details of discussion at the council meeting. Anami's brother-in-law, Colonel Takeshita, quipped, 'If you are going to accept Potsdam, you'd better commit *hara-kiri*.'

Anami returned to the vice-minister's official residence, which he'd taken over after his own residence had burned in the Tokyo raids. The vice-minister had moved to the Peers Club. At the meeting with officers Anami had seemed buoyant and confident, but in the car with his secretary, Colonel Hayashi, he seemed tired and dispirited. He said he resented Takeshita's remark. The delicate balancing act between national reality and the unreal aspirations of the military was wearing him down. He was in no mood for throwaway gags, particularly when there was a core of truth in them.

Hayashi suggested that if the nation was moving towards peace, Anami's duty was to disarm and repatriate the army carefully, not to take his own life. The war minister gazed out of the window, mulling over these words.

'I believe you're right,' he said.

Arriving at his temporary home, he went into the garden and practised his archery.

◆　◆　◆

Throughout the afternoon, refugees from the horror of the bomb drifted up to Urakami's Catholic hospital. The white ghosts of the morning had turned purple and black. Their hair was burnt, their skin charred, they were blistered and peeling. Their faces were swollen like pumpkins. On their way up the valley, they would stop to wash in the river. They would start walking again, then stop to wash again. Some fell flat on their faces and didn't get up. Blackened corpses lay by the river's edge.

Dr Akizuki, with nurse Murai at his side, tried desperately to give some assistance to the victims, moving from person to person. He had no means of medical intervention. By staying on the move, the doctor was able to avoid confronting his inability to do much other than deal with the human devastation with words of comfort, hollow assurances in the absence of medicine. A father stumbled up to him with a baby in his arms, begging for help. The wall of the child's belly was torn open, his intestines protruding. His face was purple. He had no pulse.

Akizuki shook his head. 'It's hopeless,' he said.

The father laid his baby on the ground.

'Would you do what you can?'

The seminarian Noguchi took Dr Akizuki up the hill to where the visiting doctor from Takahara Hospital was lying. They passed a stream by a steep forested hill. People crouched by the rushes at the water's edge, mostly naked or near naked, one side of their bodies vividly inflamed. The neighbouring market gardener, Tsujimoto, was there, his face now blackened and his lips swollen. His wife was with him, face and body charred, moaning incoherently.

Akizuki shouted, 'Don't drink the water,' but people just looked at him. All along the path the two men followed, voices cried out. 'Doctor . . . Doctor?' The doctor promised to return with medicines. He had no idea where he would get them.

Noguchi brought him to a stand of oak trees where the air was cooler. Lying on the ground near the injured head nurse, Dr Yoshioka's head was wrapped in cloth. A single eye peered out.

Akizuki said, 'She's not in danger. I'm afraid there's not much else I can do.'

Kinoshita, a local teacher, lay under the trees with his wife and baby, breathing with difficulty and gasping for water. Akizuki said he would get some medicine when the fire eased. The teacher's wife gave the doctor one of the cucumbers she had brought up from their farm. It occurred to him while he ate it that it was the first food he'd had that day.

Returning to Dr Yoshioka, he told her to keep her spirits up and continued down the hill. Back at the hospital, a medical student was pacing in the yard with a towel around his head and a young boy in his arms. Sakao Kawano had been in a group of students examining a patient at the medical college when the blast struck. Fleeing the burning shell of the college building, he found a small boy with a bleeding head crying beside a wrecked house. As he took the boy's hand, a strangled voice came out from under roof tiles and timber.

'Please save my child.'

Kawano looked for the source of the voice and saw part of a woman's legs. Most of her body was buried under rubble. He tried to dig her out, but no-one was there to help him and flames were closing in rapidly. The scorching heat became too much.

'I'll take care of your child,' the student shouted and fled to higher ground with the boy, leaving his mother with the roar of flames and the screams of others burning alive.

Sakao Kawano had made his way up Motohara Hill to the Franciscan hospital, past the burning cathedral and across a creek with bodies piled in it. Akizuki asked the student why he'd brought a child there when so many were already needing care. Kawano said nothing. He put the crying child on the grass, and some female in-patients immediately took charge without a word being spoken. Kawano declared himself available to help care for patients and fight fires.

♦ ♦ ♦

Coming through the gate of the Mitsubishi factory that was his working life, Torahachi Tagawa was stunned to see all trace of the familiar green gone from the countryside. Trees were stripped and blackened. Like the telegraph poles all around, many had been uprooted or snapped in two. Houses were crushed, some into non-existence. Recognising the extent of the conflagration for the first time, Tagawa began to worry about his wife and daughter. He walked over a bridge, past bodies of the dead and injured. On the other side, he looked for his house where it should have been, but all that was there was burning rubble. Like the other homes of his neighbours, it had gone.

Tagawa went on to his parents' house nearby. It too had burned to the ground. He noticed a neighbour lying in the shade and asked her if she knew what had become of his family. He was losing momentum, not knowing where to look next, but he couldn't give up. He'd cling to any thread of hope. The neighbour gave him one. She told him his wife had gone to weed a paddy field just before the air attack happened.

The shell-shocked factory foreman ran to the rice paddy, knowing which one it would be. As he approached, he saw another neighbour comforting a woman lying at the foot of the railway embankment. The front of her body was burnt black, with strips of skin peeling off like old paint.

There was a slow awakening in Tagawa that the charred body was his wife. Her eyes looked blankly into space. At first, they didn't register that he was there, but slowly they turned, focusing on him.

'Water!' she whispered hoarsely.

Her husband rushed to a nearby creek. Picking up a helmet abandoned on the bank, he scooped up what he could of the water trickle. While she drank with resignation, the agitated Tagawa asked about their daughter.

'Yaeko . . . died in the paddy. Body still there.'

She was in such a shocked state, she could only provide the information in short croaks. The spark had drained out of her.

Tagawa picked up his wife gingerly, and carefully draped her over his shoulder, carrying her about a kilometre to the nearest railway station. She was light, lighter than he remembered for whatever reason. It wasn't too hard physically. By being in the factory toilet at the time of the bomb blast, he'd escaped virtually unscathed even though he was less than 1500 metres from the hypocentre. So traumatised was his human load that she endured the bumpy journey without complaint.

◆ ◆ ◆

In the downtown area, outside Domei's agency building with instructions to get the story of the atomic bombing of Nagasaki, Junji Sato wasn't sure where to start. The story surrounded him in such wretched abundance that there was no clear focal point. As his bicycle was battered but still serviceable, he decided to pedal up to the Defence headquarters shelter.

He arrived to find the generator chugging noisily and electric lights on in the shelter. The local governor, Wakamatsu Nagano, was there with staff and some of the reporters who had come for the scheduled press conference that Sato had completely forgotten. The conference had been overtaken by events. There was no communications network operating, however, no information coming from anywhere and no means of contacting Tokyo. Sato told the governor that Domei's line to Fukuoka was still open. Nagano grabbed the opportunity to appear decisive and instructed his staff to draft an emergency report for Home Minster Abe in Tokyo.

Outside, refugees from Urakami were starting to appear over the ridge up Mount Konpira. Their skin was pasty grey, badly burnt and often peeling. A Korean worker with a purple bloated body staggered into the shelter and collapsed in the passageway, begging for water. At first, Sato froze in shock at the sight of such damaged people. He'd had only the barest inkling from the sketchy reports he'd read of Hiroshima's experi-ence and was poorly prepared for what he now saw.

A man in overalls had come all the way from Mitsubishi's steelworks. He was badly burnt, in desperate need of medical attention, crying out for a doctor. The steelworks had been destroyed, he said, Urakami was in flames, there were bodies everywhere. Sato asked about the munitions factory where his younger sister worked. What had happened there? The workman could only repeat that Urakami was in flames.

The head of a neighbourhood association arrived at the shelter, breath-less and jabbering. He reported to Nagano and his staff that hundreds, or even thousands, burned by the flash or injured by the blast, were fleeing to the hills and over the ridge to the Nakajima valley. The stream of wounded people had become a flood. They were coming down the other side of the ridge like a plague of grasshoppers, begging for help or water from anyone they passed.

Nagano felt the demands of the crisis were getting beyond him. He began screaming in excited panic.

'The situation is critical!' he shouted. 'What are the police doing? Have local officials been sent to see what is going on?'

The reality was that it was difficult to see what was going on when the whole area was flattened and on fire. The dead and wounded were piling up around Nagasaki's main railway station and in the hills overlooking the medical college. A rumour that the enemy had landed at Moji in the north of Kyushu and would soon reach Nagasaki was prompting even more people to get out of the city. The place was in turmoil and confusion as everyone sought doctors, nurses and medicine. The civil defence corps, police and fire brigades were out of their depth. About all the governor could do was order the prefecture health department to mobilise doctors and nurses from the southern end of town and from surrounding districts. They were to form a medical team and make their way to the burning valley.

◆ ◆ ◆

Koichi Wada, the tram driver, made his way up Urakami's Route 206 on foot, dodging the rubble that had piled up at intervals along its path. Fires were burning everywhere on both sides. Breathing was difficult whenever he passed through the streaming smoke. Without buildings, it was hard to work out where the road actually was. He had to rely on the line of refugees, the bulk of them moving in the opposite direction towards the city. They were so hideously injured that Koichi couldn't bear to look at them. He passed a mangled and scorched streetcar with a number of dead bodies in it. He couldn't tell if they were men or women or if they included any of his friends. A charred horse lay on its back, its legs sticking up in the air. A blackened corpse sat upright on its bicycle, holding onto a bridge rail, a stark frozen moment.

Eventually Koichi got to the remnants of the tram terminal at Ohashi. Chaos reigned as employees who were in the valley when the bomb was dropped and local residents wandered about dazed, not knowing where to go. One by one, they gathered their wits and moved to the top of the valley, away from the fires and destruction. None of Koichi's missing friends were there. Among the aimless wounded was Tatsu, the older Noguchi sister. The thirteen-year-old had been working on a tram that had reached the arms factory down the valley when the bomb exploded. Half her body was burnt badly.

The younger Noguchi had been even nearer the hypocentre, hanging around in her conductor's uniform at the back of the Ohashi terminal. Haruko must have been in the shadow of the building because her body was found looking very intact and still in the uniform she hadn't needed that day. She was unconscious, bleeding from the head and mouth as if she had been thrown violently against some brickwork or the ground. She was taken up the hill to Urakami Hospital, but by the time she got there she was dead.

◆ ◆ ◆

It took some time for Warden Minami to put together a rough rollcall of the prisoners at the Mitsubishi factory. Ten had been found dead, several were severely injured. Minami sent one of his guards back to Urakami Prison to check how it had fared. It wasn't yet clear to him how widespread the damage had been. Like many, he assumed the bomb exploded very close to where he was.

Fires were breaking out all over the factory. Under the warden's supervision, able-bodied workers and prisoners tried futilely to bring them under control, at the same time helping the wounded and outsiders who had drifted in. The factory was one of the few buildings still partially standing, a magnet for those seeking shelter.

In the late afternoon, the guard returned with news that all of Urakami was in flames. He'd been unable to get near the prison. Minami now knew the grim likelihood of survival for his wife and daughter, at home that morning in the prison grounds.

◆ ◆ ◆

When Sumiteru Taniguchi came to, he found himself on the floor of the tunnel in which Mitsubishi had relocated its torpedo works. The man bending over him said he should be moved out of the tunnel. It was too dangerous, too full of explosives.

The woman who'd trimmed his hanging shreds of skin helped hoist the badly burnt postman onto the man's back. Sumiteru was carried up a steep hillside above the tunnel entrance. His carrier was well built, probably a factory worker from inside the tunnel, and appeared uninjured. One of the lucky ones. Although it was a rough track, the factory man didn't have much difficulty getting the slightly built teenager high enough to be above the wide stretch of destroyed vegetation.

Sumiteru was laid gently on his largely unburnt stomach on grass near a copse of trees still standing. The sky was obscured by dust and smoke, the sun visible as a dark red disc. A breeze sprang up, pushing into the next valley the clouds of black rain that were building up. The postman was thirsty, but there was no-one to bring him any water. The factory worker who carried him up had gone back down to the tunnel.

Lying on the grass, Sumiteru was conscious but remained face down. After a while, he sensed others were joining him in his sanctuary. Painfully he raised his head and saw about thirty men and women—it was hard to tell which was which—coming in a ragged line up the slope. They dropped on the grass around him, groaning for water, with no acknowledgement of his presence. As time passed, the cries around him grew less and less. Sumiteru realised that some of the group had died and others were dying. Like them, he craved water and food, but there was none.

Towards evening, he heard a train puffing down the track past Michinoo to somewhere past the torpedo factory. One of the voices on the hill murmured that the train would evacuate them. He had no idea whether the person knew or was guessing, but he couldn't move anyway.

The train backed cautiously down the railway line, testing each section of track to make sure it could hold the train's weight. It came to a halt north of Urakami station at a creek bridge that had been demolished by the blast. The train was taking the injured to the naval hospital at Omura. People rushed to get on board, but they were pushed back by railway officials, yelling, 'Let the wounded board first!'

Those who got on were packed like sardines. Tagawa, the factory foreman, arrived at the stop carrying his badly burnt wife. He rolled her off his shoulder as gently as he was able onto the rear platform of one of the carriages. He was clambering onto the car when a conductor came out and blocked his passage.

'This is a special train for the injured,' Tagawa was told.

Pleading to be allowed to be with his wife, he tried desperately to climb aboard but was pushed backwards, falling in an undignified heap on the ground alongside. The train started moving. He got up and ran alongside it, but it had already gathered too much speed. Torahachi Tagawa would never see his wife again.

Up on the hillside, a few on the grass with Sumiteru Taniguchi had got up and tried to walk down to the railway line, but they had taken a few steps, stumbled and fallen. No-one managed to get further than a few metres. By then, much of the dust in the air had blown away. Sumiteru could now see down into the valley. It was a sea of flame all the way to Nagasaki city.

◆ ◆ ◆

Dr Nagai regained consciousness up on the hill behind the medical college to hear the voice of Professor Fuse.

'Press the carotid artery. Put pressure on the neck.'

He opened his eyes and saw Fuse, along with nurses Hisamatsu and Hashimoto and the technician Kaneko, above him in a circle. The professor was without his glasses. He had washed an X-ray film and was putting it in the fixing tank when the atomic blast struck, knocking his glasses off. He hadn't been able to find them and now couldn't see clearly, but Nagai's head gash needed attention so he just put his face closer to it than he would ordinarily.

Nagai could hear the cold metallic click of haemostats to pinch closed the severed artery. The pain of the instruments poking in his wound was acute. Warm blood spurted over his cheek.

'The end of the artery has fallen behind the bone,' said Fuse.

Someone spotted the surgeon, Dr Shirabe, down the slope where Dr Tsuno was lying. They called out, 'We can't stop Dr Nagai's bleeding!'

Shirabe came up and, seeing several haemostats hanging from the wound without stopping the bleeding, decided to try a different approach. He pressed tampons into the wound and sutured the skin over them.

'The bleeding has stopped.'

Dr Nagai lost consciousness again.

◆ ◆ ◆

The young man they had followed suggested to the two sixteen-year-olds that they should all move on from the glade where they had paused on the eastern slope up from Urakami. Mitsue and Kyoto tagged behind as he continued along a path winding through terraced crops, passing victims with bodies completely burnt, faces disfigured beyond recognition. People were huddled everywhere, begging in faint gasping voices, hands extended.

'Water . . . Give me some water. Please . . .'

Staring blankly, all practically naked, those still able to do so trudged wearily along tracks and grassy banks over the ridge that ran down from Mount Konpira, a herd of migrating animals moving from one valley to the next.

With no clear idea of where they were—the engineer from Tokyo might or might not know, but they followed him faithfully—the girls came down the other side of the ridge to a house with a well in front. A lady was serving cold well water to the people passing by. It was delicious, but soon after drinking Mitsue felt nauseous. Unable to continue walking, she knelt on the ground and vomited, watched by Kyoto and the young man. She got up again, walked and vomited repeatedly, silently following behind the other two.

In this stuttering fashion, the three made their way through the commercial sector of Nagasaki city. Although extensively damaged, it had been spared the utter destruction of Urakami by the mountain ridge from Mount Konpira. Nakajima River had halted the fires that had spread. The two girls and their guide came to the side of the river where Kyoto Hashimoto lived. The young man and Mitsue accompanied her to the front gate of her home.

Mitsue said weakly she could make her way home safely from there, but the young man wouldn't hear of it. He insisted on going with her to make sure she got home. They followed a street along the foot of the hill, past a graveyard, and moved haltingly up from the valley towards Junin in the elevated section of the city, up the winding stone-paved lanes and flights of stone steps around each corner.

Alternately running and vomiting, Mitsue heard the sound of planes and was overcome with dread. The young man took her hand and they ran desperately, but all her willpower had left her. Defeated, she stopped.

'Leave me here and please go on alone.'

He stood there watching the sky as she sat on a patch of grass retching milky liquid in painful spasms. When she paused, he lifted her up by her arm, encouraging her to continue walking, helping her up Junin's long flights of stone steps until Mitsue found herself standing in front of the building where Mrs Hirai and Chi-chan lived. Mitsue's head drooped, all energy gone.

From inside her home, Mrs Hirai had seen her boarder approaching. She came rushing out, followed by Chi-chan.

'You've come back alive!' exclaimed Mrs Hirai and burst into tears. Chi-chan put an arm around Mitsue's shoulder. Mrs Hirai gabbled with relief that she had been so worried about what had happened ... she didn't know how she could tell Mitsue's parents if something had happened to their child while her own daughter was safe. The young man stood by silently while the three women all embraced again.

'Please take good care,' he said eventually. He bowed deeply and disappeared into the gathering dusk.

'Thank you very much,' said Mitsue politely, although she was overwhelmed with gratitude.

At no time in their odyssey that afternoon had the young man told her his name. He was from Tokyo, a steelworks engineer and he seemed about twenty-five. That was all she knew. Now it was too late; he was already gone.

◆　◆　◆

Up in the concrete watchtower on the slopes of Mount Inasa, Tsutomu Yamaguchi was recovering his equilibrium. The naval draftsman had now survived two atomic bomb attacks, but was still badly burned from the first attack. The second had stripped his bandaging off inside the Mitsubishi office building but he'd been protected from further burning. Eventually his racing thoughts settled and he walked slowly down the hill and home.

Yamaguchi's new house was now a pile of broken timber and smashed furniture. There was no sign of his wife and newborn son. He searched fearfully among the wreckage for them but found nothing. Finally, he went to the nearby air-raid dugout and to his overwhelming joy found them sheltering there, frightened but unharmed. His burns were raw and painful, but his mind was at last able to rest. His body did likewise. Yamaguchi curled up in the shelter and slept.

◆ ◆ ◆

When Peter McGrath-Kerr regained consciousness in Camp 14, he was lying on a stretcher under a canvas awning that had been rigged up after the bomb blast. He looked around and everything had been flattened. The only thing standing within the perimeter walls was the transformer. He had no idea where he was. A Dutchman came up to him and offered him a bowl of rice, but the Australian was not interested in food. His dentures had been smashed. There was a stinging cut on the tip of his tongue. Flesh had been turned up on his chin and his chest, and there were burns on his face. His left hand and his chest were throbbing, the hand swollen. McGrath-Kerr's head was spinning and he was still unsure how he had got to the stretcher.

The Australian sergeant got up and moved round on autopilot, trying to take charge of a group of his countrymen. The Japanese were in a panic. It was still very gloomy and the air was hot and stifling, full of dust. The guards tried to round up the POWs, more out of duty than any sense of being in command. A guard came over to Allan Chick in a group of Australians and said to them, 'Go, go, go,' gesturing towards the open entrance with its gates knocked out.

The group went out on the road heading towards Inasa Bridge. It had withstood the bomb's impact enough to be crossed on foot. The Japanese guard went with them, pointing towards a patch of grass up on the hilly slope. Others followed, but they were no longer guarding the prisoners. Guards and prisoners now had a common purpose.

In the heat of the moment, POWs stuck with their compatriots. Australians went as a group over the river and up the slope towards Mount Inasa. The Dutch on the other hand—those in the camp that day, since many had been working at the Nagasaki shipyards—headed up towards Mount Konpira on the other side of the valley.

On the far side of Inasa Bridge, a horse stood by a cart, both having miraculously escaped death and destruction. Allan Chick harnessed the horse, a skill from his days working on a Tasmanian farm. Red Cross parcels found in the camp's wreckage were piled on the cart and the horse was led behind the group, pulling its load. On the way, large blobs of black water started to rain down, but fortunately the shower was very brief. A few dark brown streaks were left running down the bodies of both prisoners and Japanese.

Having climbed the hilly road some distance, fallen trees prevented them going any further with the cart. The horse was unharnessed, but the animal by itself was not of much use. The Australians let it run free and discussed what to do with the cart and its cargo. They had eaten raw vegetables found in an undestroyed garden on the way up, planning to open the food in the parcels later.

Before the question of the parcels could be resolved, they were found by guards and hustled across to join another larger group of POWs making its way up the slopes. The parcels were left behind as the party of prisoners and guards reached a partly flattened bamboo grove where the wounded and dying from nearby were gathering. From the hill they could see nothing standing in the factory area that surrounded Camp 14.

◆ ◆ ◆

Mrs Tabata climbed with her human load, born and unborn, towards the ridge on the opposite side of the valley to the Australian POWs she had watched in the preceding days being marched to work. She came across a foreigner, another prisoner of war, carrying a large bundle and a canteen.

'You must be in much pain,' he said in passable Japanese. 'Would you like me for you to carry baby?'

She greeted him with silence.

'I give you some water,' he continued. 'It nice and clean.'

Mrs Tabata looked at the man with no idea what part of the world he came from, possibly the Netherlands. He might have been part-Indonesian. He looked so gentle and sincere, but remembering how roughly the POWs had been treated by their Japanese guards, she couldn't bring herself to accept his offer, afraid he might take revenge on her for the harsh treatment he'd received from her country's soldiers.

'No, no, I don't want it,' she cried, running away with her baby girl clutched tight.

As she climbed higher, she could see that the whole of the Urakami valley was filled with dark smoke. Injured and burnt people staggered up the slope alongside her. Coming down the other side towards the city, B-29s circled in the sky injecting panic into the numbed silent figures fleeing the horror.

'Cover your heads with yam leaves,' came the panicked instructions.

'Don't let any children cry.'

The planes left and the people on the hillside returned to numbed silence. Mitsue wondered what her daughter made of the terrifying day's events. She seemed so uncomprehending, but what memory was she storing away of this hellish day? The mother was shocked to notice a group of soldiers from the barracks on Mount Konpira hiding under a little stone bridge.

Carrying a lingering sense of shame at rejecting the foreigner's offer of help, Mitsue Tabata headed towards her parents' house in the south of Nagasaki city. Her journey followed a path very similar to that of Mitsue Takeno, Kyoto Hashimoto and the engineer from Mitsubishi steelworks. Vaseline was put on the burns on her arm when she stopped at a rescue station in a school. In the short time mother and child were there a number of people died in front of them, each carried away to another room. Mitsue's daughter watched it all with the same impassive stare.

By the time they got to her parents' house, Mitsue was no longer able to move. She lay groaning from the pain of the burns for several days, while her parents looked after their granddaughter.

◆ ◆ ◆

Temporarily residing at the home of an elderly doctor, Yoshiro Fukuda decided to return there to get his head wounds treated. The house was set among trees on the slope rising up from the Urakami valley, but when the factory director got there, the familiar leafy stands were gone. Only smoldering remnants remained, reduced to splintered sticks. The doctor's house had disappeared as well.

Fukuda slumped in the middle of a field. People passed by, some calling out. They got no response. In the intense heat of the scorched field, he drifted in and out of consciousness. A junior manager from the factory found him. He refused Fukuda's request for water, saying it would kill him. Instead, Kubo built a sunshade from his own shirt.

After a while, Kubo and a technician who had joined him assisted Fukuda, half-carrying him as he staggered haltingly to what remained of Michinoo station. They helped him aboard the emergency train that would take him to the hospital at Omura. Kubo told Fukuda the technician would stay with him all the way to the hospital, shook Fukuda's hand and left.

The deputy director of the Ohashi arms works lay in the middle of the carriage aisle as people stepped or shuffled around him. All the while, the technician stood over him, providing protection from the constant stream of refugees.

◆ ◆ ◆

The reporter Sato had left the government shelter and made his way towards Urakami, taking notes as he went. He noticed that the prefectural building in the downtown area was now on fire, although it hadn't been when the bomb first struck. When he got to the valley, he found a burning wasteland. Houses and other structures had been crushed, the strong steel beams of factories were bent and twisted, the roofs of reinforced concrete buildings crumpled and collapsed. The dead and dying were lying everywhere, some charred beyond recognition. Anyone who could move had done so, fleeing out of the valley. It was eerily empty of active life.

Following the exodus out of the valley, Sato went to his home in the southern part of the city. His mother was inside, returned from her overnight stay and cleaning up broken glass inside the otherwise intact house. She didn't know what had happened to his sister Teruko. Working at the same factory, a girl from down the street had returned with only slight injuries, but she had also said many were badly injured and killed. Mrs Sato wanted to go and look for her daughter, but her son insisted she wait until morning when they might be able to find their way through the fires and wreckage.

The reporter resumed his observations in the dockside and downtown areas and returned to the Domei office in the late afternoon. The staff there were outraged at a public announcement that had just been made about the Nagasaki bombing:

> The West Japan Army Command announced at 1415 on August 9 that at about 11:00 a.m. on August 9 two large enemy planes invaded Nagasaki City and used something like the new bomb. The details are still under investigation, but damage is believed to be comparatively light.

The Nagasaki Fortress Command was located near the mouth of Nagasaki Bay, 7 kilometres from the hypocentre and behind two hills. It had suffered little more than broken window glass and, with communications severed, was unaware of the actual situation in the northern part of the city. The command generated its own power and so was able to send its version of the event to the West Japan Army. This was passed on to Tokyo as an official report.

◆   ◆   ◆

After two hours on Okinawa, the three B-29s of the second atomic bomb mission took off on the last leg back to base on Tinian island. On *Bockscar*, there was scant conversation and little jubilation among the crew as the aircraft flew into the gathering dusk. Some slept, their work for the day finished. The plane was able to pick up Armed Forces Radio. No mention of the Nagasaki bomb or any offer of surrender. The news was of the Soviet Union's declaration of war on Japan and the Soviet drive into Manchuria. After that, music by Tommy Dorsey and Glenn Miller.

'If the Japanese don't surrender,' thought Sweeney, 'I'll be flying more of these missions.'

◆ ◆ ◆

The fifteen members of the Japanese cabinet met at two thirty in the reinforced conference room of the prime minister's official residence. Togo opened discussion detailing the lapsed negotiations with the USSR, the atomic bomb and that morning's Soviet attack on Manchuria. The atomic bomb was mentioned in the singular without much comment. Those present knew something of the Hiroshima bomb, and the attack on Nagasaki only a few hours before had made little impression. Togo went on to outline his argument for accepting the Potsdam Declaration with the one 'indisputable' condition.

Next, Anami argued his case for four conditions on accepting Potsdam. The army, he said, was confident it could inflict prohibitive losses in any decisive battle for the Japanese homeland. There was no certainty of victory, but Japan was not yet defeated. Admiral Yonai countered that domestic conditions made continuing the war unfeasible. This was the time for cold, rational judgment, not wishful thinking.

Anami told the meeting of the interrogation of the American pilot and that the next target would be Tokyo, ignoring the news of that day's attack on Nagasaki. He said the US had over a hundred atomic bombs in waiting, while still arguing for continuation of the war. He was either rattled by events and losing his grasp on what had happened or was deliberately making the position he proposed less palatable to any waverers.

Suzuki asked other members of cabinet for views from their portfolios. Home Minister Abe reported that the morale of the people had declined considerably, although they still anticipated a Japanese victory thanks to the military's propaganda. However, if Japan surrendered unconditionally, an irate public might rise up and even assassinate members of cabinet. Abe was clearly worried for his personal safety, but his colleagues reported other problems to distract the public from the ignominy of defeat. Agriculture Minister Ishiguro said his advisers were predicting the worst rice harvest in fifteen years. What's worse, reported Transportation Minister Kobiyama, the US navy's blockade was preventing use of Korea and Manchuria as food sources. To top off the litany of gloom, Munitions

Minister Toyoda said factories were closing through lack of raw materials and rising absenteeism among the workers.

◆   ◆   ◆

When she heard a voice calling out her name, Chiyoko Egashira was still crouched foetus-like with her baby daughter in the remains of Shiroyama Primary School's first-aid room. At first she didn't recognise the voice in its croakiness and her disassociated state, then moments before he appeared she realised it was Ukichi, her husband. He had walked over the hill from the devastated Ohashi weapons factory, knowing it was likely she had been at the school. There was a slim chance she had survived the blast there. The destruction of the factory where he worked was profound enough, 1500 metres from the hypocentre, yet three times the distance of the Shiroyama school.

Chiyoko held tight to Ukichi, unable to register in her mind any feeling apart from blessed deliverance and the belief she would somehow get through this nightmare. Neither happiness nor sadness was a response she was capable of at this point.

Ukichi had lost his shoes and his air-raid hood in either the blast or its aftermath. His bare feet were bloody from walking over the remains of the factory, including its shattered windows, and then over the hill between Ohashi and Shiroyama.

With the possibility of the surviving structure of the school building collapsing, the Egashiras moved to a nearby shelter. When the three of them got there, it was crammed with jostling and motionless people. Some were already dead, some crying out pitifully and ceaselessly for water. Here was such an air of despair that the couple decided to move on with their child. They climbed up an embankment to an athletic field that had been turned into a garden growing squash. People in various stages of decline were escaping the ravaged valley. Some recognised the schoolteacher and called out, but Chiyoko couldn't tell who they were even when she saw their faces. The trauma of the day's events had erased any capacity for recognition.

Finally the Egashiras got to a less crowded shelter at Tateiwa Shrine in the backblocks of Shiroyama. Chiyoko lay on her front, unable to move. The glass pieces in her back were becoming increasingly painful. Naomi continued to utter no sound, unable to cry, unable to be nursed. Lacking the strength to even drink water, her mother vomited throughout the night.

All night, people came to the shelter with lanterns looking for relatives, calling out names. Mrs Egashira could hear the crackle of burning trees outside and the spasmodic roar of flames. She could see a bright red glow through the shelter entrance, but didn't know whether that was reflected from fires outside or the setting or rising sun. Chiyoko Egashira now expected to die.

◆ ◆ ◆

Dr Akizuki's parents had been living near the hospital for a couple of months. His father worked in the city. His mother was alone in the house during the day, but would seldom see her son because of his workload. During the afternoon, nurse Murai had asked if he knew what had become of his mother.

'Don't know,' he'd answered curtly, although it was something that was preying on his mind. Having seen the completeness of destruction of the surrounding neighbourhood, he was dubious about her chances of survival. Later, the new nurse had suggested they look for his mother.

'If she's dead,' he said, 'I'd rather know about it as late as possible.'

When Noguchi took Akizuki up the hill to tend to Dr Yoshioka, Sugako decided to search for his mother. She returned some time later, after Akizuki had come back down to the hospital. Trailing behind her was, to the doctor's great surprise and relief, Mrs Akizuki . . . uninjured.

Nurse Murai had found her in a shelter where, because her eyesight was poor, she had stayed nearby when the all-clear sounded. Alarmed at the sound of a plane at about eleven, she'd hustled back inside. It had saved her life.

'You're not hurt either,' said the doctor's mother to her son.

Survivors in the atomic wasteland, they smiled at each other in silence. Each had believed with certainty that the other was dead. Mrs Akizuki's joy was tempered though by having heard no word yet of the fate of her husband or her other son and daughters.

In the late afternoon, when people began to talk ravenously of hunger, Sugako realised she hadn't eaten since the night before. A group set out to investigate the hospital kitchen which, being in the basement, had escaped much of the conflagration. Nurse Murai, whose domain it had been up to that day, went with them. Climbing down across broken brickwork, they found food scattered about and mixed with dirt. It was the meal that had been standing by to serve to Dr Akizuki, his new nurse and other staff when the bomb fell. Looking at it increased their hunger, but not as much as the salvageable food in the pantry next door.

An iron cauldron was brought out and set up on broken bricks gathered from the ruins. Nurse Murai returned to her former role as cook Murai, and on the makeshift cooking platform unpolished rice was boiled, made into rice balls and flavoured with pickled plums from the basement storeroom. Patients and injured workers, students and residents from the town below, and staff and visitors in the rescue teams all joined the modest feast in the dying day.

Fortune's small reversal continued. The city administrators had used the former theological college's gymnasium as a storehouse for rationed food. Away from the city centre, it was thought to be safe from enemy raids. The atomic bomb had broken open its door. Inside, hospital workers found bags of unpolished rice, bean paste and other food supplies, sufficient to keep workers, patients and refugees in miso soup and rice balls for days to come. The assembled group drank hot tea and congratulated themselves on rescuing every single person from inside the hospital, a moment of cheer as night fell.

◆　◆　◆

The Keeper of the Privy Seal conferred with the emperor twice during the afternoon. Kido had been visited at Konoye's prompting by Mamoru Shigemitsu, a former diplomat and previous foreign minister and an old friend. Further pressure had been brought to bear to support a single condition attached to acceptance of Potsdam. After the second, longer conference with the emperor, Kido returned to the library where Shigemitsu was waiting.

'The emperor understands with firm resolve,' said Kido. 'An imperial conference should be arranged so that when everyone has put his view, the emperor is asked for his opinion.' Shigemitsu dispatched Foreign Vice-Minister Matumoto to cabinet to pass this on to Togo.

The cabinet meeting was recessed at five thirty without any agreement on the Potsdam demands. Three ministers had spoken in support of the military's position. The rest either agreed with Togo or were too vague for it to be clear where they stood. There had been no unanimity as convention required of Japan's decisions of government.

In the hiatus, the prime minister and the foreign minister went to the Imperial Palace. At Suzuki's request, Togo outlined to the emperor the discussion at both the Supreme War Council and cabinet meetings and the thrust of the arguments for one and for four conditions to agreement on Potsdam. Hirohito listened without comment. Suzuki then asked the emperor's sanction to call an imperial conference for later that night. He agreed.

On the way back to the cabinet meeting, Suzuki called on the cabinet secretary on the third floor and asked him to summon members of the Supreme War Council to an imperial conference at 11.30 p.m. Suzuki put his stamp on the petition. With the petitions finessed from the military chiefs of staff earlier that day, Sakomizu had the full authority necessary to call such a meeting. He didn't bother to make the confirmatory phone calls to Umezu and Toyoda he had promised.

On resumption of the cabinet meeting, the Education Minister, Kozo Ota, proposed that cabinet should tender its resignation *en masse*, since it had failed in its responsibility to resolve the stand-off over Potsdam.

'I'm fully aware of our responsibility,' Suzuki responded tartly, 'but this is no time for cabinet to argue about responsibility. Rather, we should take steps to remedy the situation.'

It was an opportunity for General Anami, should he choose to take it. He could resign. Even if the rest of cabinet stayed put, he was in a position to ensure the army did not appoint a new war minister. In that event, cabinet would have no alternative but to resign.

'I do not agree with the opinion of Mr Ota. In my opinion, the cabinet should not resign,' said the war minister.

A poll of the cabinet revealed it to still be implacably split. Suzuki cut off discussion and closed the meeting at ten.

Chapter 14

Nagasaki, Thursday 9 August 1945, evening

In the late afternoon when the fires had eased, rescue workers were able to move around more freely in the valley. Trucks and other vehicles were brought in to pick up the wounded and get them to medical aid stations that had been set up within the city, or to railway stations for transport to medical facilities at Isahaya and Omura. A medical relief centre had been set up at Shinkozen Primary School, another at Katsuyama School. Four relief trains shuttled to Sumiyoshi and by midnight had carried 3500 wounded to safety.

People in tattered clothes, skin black from burning, were sitting or lying in shelters, crying in pain and for water. Children were crying for their mothers. One aid team found a body jammed in a concrete fire cistern, so swollen he looked like a sumo wrestler. The only way they could get the body out was to break open the concrete.

Rather than go to shelters in the stricken valley a large number of the refugees from Urakami joined the exodus up the slopes on either side, the lower reaches of Mount Konpira and Mount Inasa. Above the blast-cleared areas and the fires, the slopes offered glades that had not been burnt out. Others diverted in their migration to one of the two hospitals on the eastern side below Mount Konpira. They could get medical expertise there, but medicine and equipment were in extreme short supply.

The sun was setting as Dr Akizuki returned to Dr Yoshioka and the others up on the hill overlooking Urakami Dai-ichi Hospital. Yoshioka seemed to be dying from blood loss, so he decided she should be brought back down near the hospital for closer observation. Taking turns, brother Iwanaga and seminarian Noguchi carried her on their shoulders. The head nurse was brought down next. The teacher, Kinoshita, had turned black and was gasping for air. Kawano, the medical student, carried him down the hill on his back. Mrs Kinoshita followed, sobbing with her baby on her back. Tsujimoto, the local farmer, was carried on a sliding door that had been salvaged from the wreckage somewhere. He was too heavy for either Iwanaga or Kawano to carry far by themselves. His wife was carried down next on the same ad hoc stretcher.

Darkness had set in when Dr Akizuki's father appeared. Destruction had been limited around the law courts in the city centre. When he heard the bomb had been dropped in the Urakami district he tried to make his way up the valley, but the route was blocked by flaming wreckage. He detoured over Konpira ridge. Looking down on Urakami's destruction, he was convinced his wife and son were dead. Expecting his task to be finding their bones, he picked a path through the smoke, past staggering evacuees and through the stench of burnt flesh. To his surprise and great joy he found camped among victims and rescue workers at Urakami Hospital both his son and his wife still alive.

Others arrived looking for their loved ones, calling out names in the growing darkness. Noguchi had just lowered the heavily bandaged Dr Yoshioka onto a mat he spread on the basement's bathroom floor when her elderly mother arrived with her brother to find their daughter and sister still among the living. They had walked over the mountain pass.

Because the in-patients were inside at breakfast when the bomb exploded, few were badly injured and none with the massive burns of people out in the open. As they could fend for themselves, Akizuki told them to wrap up for the night in anything they could find.

They chiacked him, 'We don't have any mattresses!'

When they were evacuating from the hospital building, some picked up their clothes and other belongings. Akizuki had said not to take clothes and mattresses, they might catch fire. Those who ignored him had a mattress for the night, those who obeyed didn't. Akizuki scratched his head and smiled sheepishly.

It didn't matter much in the end. The uninjured handed over their mattresses to the injured. The inside of the gymnasium was cleared and seriously wounded patients were laid down there. Others slept curled up under trees in a corner of the playground in sight of the burning hospital and cathedral. The fire had spread up the hillside in places. From time to time, mountain trees would burst into flame. Planes flew overhead, playing their searchlights across the terrain and dropping firebombs. All through the night, the voices of people coming along the side of the valley could be heard, calling out the names of their loved ones and friends.

'Is such-and-such there?' they would cry out.

A short distance down the valley, on the hill overlooking the other hospital at Nagasaki Medical College, Dr Nagai revived once more. On opening his eyes, he saw a dark cloud with a red glow covering the sky. The thin crescent of the moon was visible over Mount Inasa across the valley. Nurses had gathered pumpkins from gardens on the hilly slopes and were boiling them in air-raid helmets. Men were making lean-tos for the injured to shelter for the night. Nagai could see fires still burning across the district.

Professor Seiki returned, the big man using a length of charred timber as a walking stick. He wanted help for the students who were dying in the pharmacy school's shelter. Offered some pumpkin to eat, he turned it down and returned to his students.

Some needles and a few medicines had been found in the hospital wreckage. Two nurses came over to the pharmacy dugout and gave injections to some of the wounded sheltering there. Others were a lost cause, they said, and medicine was in short supply. There was little more they and the people in the shelter could do.

When night had closed in, Tsuneo Tomita went for a cautious walk in the debris-strewn grounds of the college to clear his head and gather his thoughts. He could see the burning ruins of Urakami Cathedral on its hillock. Its fiery beacon brought back memories of the lazy days, even in the middle of a war, when Tomita and his friends lounged chattering on the grass nearby. He thought his mother and brothers were probably now dead.

That night, Tomita and the professor shivered on the cold mud floor of the dugout. The only comfort was that bugs and mosquitoes, usually an unavoidable nuisance in summer, had been eradicated by the atomic blast.

In the middle of the night enemy planes flew over, dropping bundles that hit the ground with a hefty thud. They were the leaflets warning citizens to leave the city before destruction was rained on it by the all-powerful Allies.

◆　◆　◆

The walls of the dugout, where traumatised Sakue waited with her younger sister and baby brother, reverberated with the cries of mutilated people. The smell of burned flesh and blood filled the air. A voice cried out, 'Who's there? Somebody kill me!'

In the evening, a voice called through the collapsed entrance, 'Is anyone from the Komaba Eighth group here?'

Masaru Takigawa, the young girls' adoptive father, had come looking for them. On recognising his voice, Sakue and Ryoko called out with all their strength, crying at the same time, fearful he might not hear them and go away. He pushed his way through the listless crowd and came over. The shelter was not a good place for them to stay, he said. They should leave with him.

Picking up the baby, the three made their way to the entrance, stepping apologetically around the injured on the ground and pushing their way delicately through the crowd of standing and squatting victims. Outside was littered with corpses, some piled up, and people who had been unable to get into the crowded shelter. The commercial school nearby was in flames, the flickering light cast spasmodically over the waiting throng.

Planes could be heard flying low over the district. Fearful they might be enemy bombers, the family fled back into the shelter, settling down breathlessly alongside a pile of corpses. They ventured outside once or twice more during the night, but they had nowhere to go in the dark and there were always planes overhead to scare them back to the shelter.

Further down the valley, the neighbourhood bomb shelter where the Yamawaki twins had moved with their older brother was a tunnel carved into the hillside as most of them were. It was filled with mothers and children. Some of the children suffered debilitating and agonising burns on the exposed parts of their skin. Others had been peppered with slivers of glass from windows blown in by the blast. The crying created an unearthly cacophony echoing inside the dugout. The two eleven-year-olds realised that had they stayed on the verandah, they too would be suffering those dreadful wounds.

That evening, rice balls were handed out by a neighbourhood group. Yoshiro Yamawaki was about to eat his when he noticed its strange musty smell. Looking closer he found fine threads of mould. On breaking the rice ball open, he found the mould even more plentiful inside and its odour more striking. It had been tainted by heat, from either the atomic explosion or the fires.

One thing worried all three Yamawaki boys: the non-appearance of their father. Late into the night, they still hadn't seen or heard him . . . or even heard of him. He'd had plenty of time to find his way through the devastation and, even if the note had disappeared from the front door, he would know where to look for them. But, Yasuo Yamawaki, the Mitsubishi engineer, did not come.

◆　◆　◆

A devout Buddhist who chanted sutras each morning and evening, Mrs Hirai was convinced the Dainichi Buddha had protected Mitsue, her guest, and her daughter Chifusa. Chi-chan told Mitsue why she turned back on the way to work that morning.

'I had a premonition, Takeno-san,' she said. Like all of the factories, hers had been heavily damaged and many students and workers had died.

On a steep slope with panoramic views, there was little to protect the house in Junin from the power of the blast, even at over four kilometres away. Windows facing the north-east were shattered, the eaves were tilted and Mitsue's desk had been crushed under a fallen pillar. Half the kitchen was destroyed.

The next-door basement was serving as a refuge. Mrs Hirai made *okayu* there and brought it back with pickled *ume* (Japanese apricot). Mitsue had no appetite and the porridge brought back her nausea, but she found the salty sourness of pickled *ume* refreshing. She nibbled at a few pieces, sipping tea between bites. She would eat nothing else for several days.

The landlady and her sixteen-year-old charges evacuated that night to a shelter. Mitsue's nausea had subsided. She followed Mrs Hirai and Chi-chan along the sloping stone-paved roads, panting and dragging her feet, on her back her rucksack rescued from the closet.

The small shelter was packed with people, leaving no room even to stretch their legs. Mentally and physically exhausted, Mitsue couldn't sleep. She wandered out of the shelter full of strangers into the cool night breeze, her rucksack still on her back. The young girl looked up at the sky, so brooding through the day, and saw stars twinkling in the direction of Goto Islands calling her. Calling her home. Mitsue wondered what her family were doing on their island—her grandmother, parents, her sister. Had they heard news of Nagasaki? She longed to be back with them, enjoying the simple pleasures of island life in their small seaside village.

In her melancholy, Mitsue remembered an incident as a young girl. Although not a Catholic, she had wandered into the church grounds at a time when a priest from Nagasaki was staying on the island. Seeing a beautiful flower in the church, she couldn't resist picking it, even though she knew that was wrong. She looked around guiltily and saw she was observed by the visiting priest, but instead of reprimanding her he smiled in understanding. Although she never saw him again, the gentle look on his face was indelible in her memory.

That was the past. Now in torn blouse and tattered *monpe*, Mitsue took clean clothes out of her rucksack and changed in the darkness. Her dirty clothes were pushed into a bush by a stone wall. Exploding gas tanks could be heard in the distance. It was the first night that month without any air-raid sirens sounding. Alone in the darkness, she noted the red sky over Urakami and the western sky reaching over her home town. She wondered what would become of Japan. She wondered if she was a burden to Mrs Hirai and Chi-chan. It was unlikely the ferry service would be operating to the Goto Islands in the current circumstances, but she wanted desperately to be there, more than anything.

◆ ◆ ◆

Having spent the afternoon searching fruitlessly for friends in Urakami, Koichi Wada came home. His grandparents had been inside their house when the bomb struck. Four kilometres away and up the slope, they were out of the line of fire. The house was slightly damaged, tilted by the impact of the blast, but they weren't injured. Koichi's younger sister had been working in an office in a relatively unscathed downtown quarter. A note pinned to the front door let him know the three of them had gone to a town further out.

Koichi stayed in the tilted house for the night. Wandering up the hillside behind, he saw both City Hall and the prefectural office in flames at the bayside end of downtown Nagasaki. Further north, the valley where he had been that afternoon was a vast field of fire in the night dark. In the prime of his youth the world had been turned upside down.

The prisoners of war from Camp 14 also spent the night in the foothills of Mount Inasa. Among the Australians in the bamboo grove were Allan Chick and the concussed sergeant, Peter McGrath-Kerr, who later wouldn't remember any of it. From their vantage point they too watched the fires burning across Nagasaki. They were disturbed to hear planes flying overhead during the night, presumably American since they were dropping incendiary bombs on the already demolished landscape.

The army had brought trucks up from the relatively undamaged southern end of the city to help evacuate the wounded. The prison's warden persuaded a driver to transport uninjured inmates and guards from the crushed factory to the prison at Isahaya. None of the prisoners seized the opportunity to dash to freedom. In the confusion it was no longer clear where freedom lay.

Warden Minami of Urakami Prison spent the night in a cell in Isahaya Prison, still uncertain of the fate of his wife and two children. He was woken by Warden Takahashi of Isahaya Prison from a deep slumber after his day in hell. Takahashi brought the news that Minami's son had been reported safe and well. Minami felt some relief, but was still fearful of the worst for his wife and daughter.

◆ ◆ ◆

Noguchi found a bottle of *sake* in a corner of Urakami Hospital's basement. Sprawled on the grass in the yard, he and Dr Akizuki and one of the patients drank from a rice bowl.

'This tastes wonderful,' said Akizuki.

It was only a brief moment of relaxation for the doctor. Mrs Kinoshita kept coming to him, saying her husband was in pain. There was nothing Dr Akizuki could do except promise them medicine when some arrived.

Akizuki's older sister had arranged to meet him that day at the hospital. After dark her husband arrived, concerned at her disappearance. He'd been in town when the bomb dropped, but by then she would probably have been on a tram going up the valley. Akizuki's brother-in-law had searched all the places where she might be, even as far as Omura Naval Hospital where the injured were being taken. He was frantic, but the doctor hadn't seen her.

Mr and Mrs Tsujimoto lay moaning alongside the Kinoshitas. The eldest Tsujimoto son had joined them, but there was no medicine available. About midnight, Tsujimoto's breathing became harsh and his pulse faded. Prayers were offered by the family to Jesus, Mary and Joseph and Tsujimoto went into a violent fit of convulsions, his eyes bulging. His son wept and wailed. Akizuki wasn't a *kirishitan*, so he chanted a Buddhist prayer, '*Namu Amida-butsu* [May your soul remain untroubled].'

About midnight, up on the hill over Sumiyoshi Tunnels, Sumiteru Taniguchi heard a plane approaching. It circled. Below, as in many other places around the rim of the devastated valley, people were searching through the groups of refugees, looking in the pulsing glow of surrounding fire for relatives and friends, calling out their names despairingly. The plane picked out a target of moving specks, dived with a sweep of machine-gun fire over the ground, then swept up and away.

In the pre-dawn, rain began to fall. The young postman wriggled in his scorched state to a bush, pulled off a large leaf and shaped it into a cup. He caught a few drops to trickle down his parched throat. With that relief, Sumiteru fell asleep.

◆   ◆   ◆

The offensive of the Red Army's Far Eastern Command had continued its relentless drive into Manchuria on three fronts throughout the day of 9 August. Its Trans-Baikal Front on the western side of Manchuria had encountered minimal resistance. By nightfall, tank units had penetrated 100 kilometres into the Gobi Desert, sweeping aside small detachments of Inner Mongolian cavalry. Further north, the Sixth Guards Tank Army had advanced even further across desert and steppe and was in the foothills of the Grand Khingan Mountains by evening. The units that had crossed the rain-swollen Argun River had taken key bridges north of Hailar by late evening and had started a night attack against their first substantial resistance to surround and capture the town.

On the eastern front, the main force of tanks and mobile artillery had pushed past isolated units of the Kwantung Army, leaving following units to mop them up. The lead units advanced on the fortifications of Suifenho, seizing critical rail tunnels on the main line into Manchuria. By night on 9 August a hole 35 kilometres wide had been punched in the Japanese defensive lines set back from the border. The southern city of Tungning was under attack, threatening to close off Japanese movement into and out of Korea. To the north, the advance was slow through the marshland around Lake Khanka, but it was still breaking through what resistance the defenders offered.

In northern Manchuria, progress by the Second Far Eastern Front was slowest. By the end of the day the Soviet army was still taking on well-fortified defensive posts along the Amur River and ferrying tanks across the river. It was on this front that the Japanese had detected Soviet attack preparations, so their resistance was better organised. Although the advance of the Red Army here was not fast, it was nevertheless serving its intended purpose of tying up a substantial portion of what remained of the Kwantung Army.

After the pre-dawn air attack on the capital, Changchun, the Kwantung Army's General Staff concluded that the Soviet Union had begun a full-scale invasion. In asking Imperial General Headquarters how to respond, it got an evasive answer. A strategic conference in Tokyo that morning had decided that, since the Red Army would soon realise how weak the Kwantung Army was, Japan would be better to negotiate with the USSR and try to exploit its souring relationship with the US and Britain. In the meantime, the need was to restrain the Kwantung Army's military operation. Tokyo proposed a self-defence response against the Russians without declaring war. By the afternoon, Imperial Headquarters had released a statement for public consumption that 'the scale of these attacks is not large'.

During the day, the commander of the Kwantung Army, General Yamada, visited the Changchun palace of the head of the puppet state of Manchukuo, Pu Yi. Normally a solemn, deliberate speaker, Yamada was tense and jumpy. He gave an incoherent account of the Soviet incursions into Manchuria and assured the puppet emperor the Kwantung Army would prevail. An air-raid warning during the meeting moved them to the cellars, where they listened to Russian bombs exploding outside. There was no reference to a Japanese victory after that. Pu Yi slept that night in his day clothes, ready to be moved out at a moment's notice.

Back in Tokyo, an officer from the War Ministry rang Cabinet Secretary Sakomizu demanding to be told how an imperial conference could be called when the army chief of staff had not given his endorsement. The caller was one of Anami's staff, not Umezu's.

'General Umezu's signature is on the petition,' said Sakomizu.

Shortly after, several young army officers in full uniform burst into the cabinet secretary's office, hands on samurai swords at their side. Sakomizu was at his desk in his drab 'national uniform', dealing with paperwork. Led by Lieutenant-General Yoshizumi, chief of Military Affairs at the War Ministry, the intruders angrily challenged the calling of the conference, accusing the bureaucrat of double-dealing in a plot to surrender.

Sakomizu responded with apparent calm. 'It's just a routine meeting to give the Emperor a chance to hear the views of all the members.'

'The purpose of imperial conferences is to inform the Emperor of decisions,' said Yoshizumi, 'not to make him listen to arguments.'

Sakomizu replied that the emperor had apparently decided he wanted to hear the arguments and, sensing he should not allow the discussion to continue, got up from his desk. He waved a piece of paper in his hand, an unconscious parody of Neville Chamberlain.

'Gentlemen, here is the order for the imperial conference. It's now time to go to the Palace.'

With that, he walked through the middle of the group and out the door. No-one touched him.

It was the action of a man able to remain cool under fire, although historian Tsuyoshi Hasegawa has suggested Anami, Umezu and Toyoda were not tricked. They had allowed the imperial conference to take place, arguing the position they took to appease the radical officers pressuring them.

◆   ◆   ◆

At 10.30 p.m. on Tinian, a giant silver aircraft swooped out of the dark and landed on North Field's Runway A after twenty hours away from base. *Bockscar* taxied to its hardstand, but this time there were no lights, no cameras and microphones, no medal ceremony. They were met by a ground crew and one photographer. Colonel Tibbets and Admiral Purnell stood to one side in the dim light.

Tired, hungry and worn out, the crew emerged through the nose-wheel hatch, one by one. Sweeney was the last to climb out, so exhausted he was incapable of sleep. Tibbets, who had been first out of the plane after the Hiroshima mission, came across to Sweeney.

'Pretty rough, Chuck?' he asked.

'Pretty rough, boss.'

Sweeney noticed an admiral trailing behind Tibbets. It was the fellow who'd given him the homily the night before about the cost of the bomb. Purnell said that when General Farrell had read Hopkins' truncated transmission, the general had been violently sick.

'Tibbets said if anyone could get it done, you could. I see he was right,' the admiral added.

'It was close,' said Sweeney. Who was this guy?

Sweeney proposed a beer, to be told that beer had run out on Tinian base. Tibbets suggested the medics might have some medicinal whisky left. The kitchen had closed for the night and nobody had thought to keep anything for the returning crews. The bologna sandwiches they had had in Okinawa would be their meal for the day. No pie-eating competition for this mission!

Trucks dropped the crew at the medical hut, where they were quickly declared fit, and on to Intelligence. They recited the events of the day to General Farrell, Admiral Purnell, Dr Ramsey and Colonel Tibbets with minimal questioning, and handed over their log books.

Tired and winding down, the officers and enlisted men went to the officers' club where a range of spirits was turned on: sour mash bourbon, Scotch and overproof grain alcohol. Kermit Beahan went to bed exhausted. It had been his twenty-seventh birthday that day, but he didn't care. Some of the others were too tense to rest and they drank through to sunrise.

At one stage during the night, some of the crew of *Enola Gay* joined them. The mood contrasted strangely with that after the Hiroshima mission. No-one was sure quite what they were celebrating, if indeed they were celebrating at all. In reality, they were just winding down. General Farrell appeared briefly to congratulate them (again) then went to the communications hut to send a cable to Washington.

Sweeney and Tibbets chatted to one side for a while. They were the only two pilots to have dropped a nuclear bomb in battle—and still are. The conversation held a sense of significance for Sweeney that Tibbets didn't share. Assuming this was the new face of warfare and that others would inevitably follow, Tibbets saw greater celebration in being the first. To him, talking to Sweeney was doing his job as command leader, not marking an occasion of shared history.

◆ ◆ ◆

The imperial conference was held in the emperor's personal shelter under the Imperial Palace's Fukiage Garden, a classic garden with lotus pools, arbours, manicured paths and traditional bridges. Stepping out of chauffeured cars, those attending were escorted by chamberlains down a steep mat-lined stairway, through steel doors and double wooden doors into the conference room 20 metres underground. Military men wore full dress uniform; civilians wore formal morning dress.

In the small room, the air was musty and humid from a malfunctioning air-conditioner. Walls were panelled in dark wood, the ceiling supported by steel bars. Both were clammy with condensation. As they arrived, participants were shown to seats along two parallel tables with checked damask tablecloths. On a dais at the head of the room stood a small table covered with gold-lined brocade. Behind that, a chair and gilt-panelled screen.

In addition to the inner cabinet of six, those present included Sakomizu, the Chief Secretary of Cabinet, and Lieutenant-General Yoshizumi, who had confronted him half an hour before. Ironically the two had been placed next to each other at the end of one table. Opposite them were Vice-Admiral Hoshina of Naval Affairs and General Ikeda of Combined Planning. At the front, opposite Prime Minister Suzuki, was Baron Kiichiro Hiranuma, President of the Privy Council. Some of the military questioned the presence of a participant from the Privy Council and were told by Sakomizu there was a precedent over the last fifty years for it. They weren't in a position to dispute that.

Eleven men sat silently with their hands on their knees, in front of each a copy of the Potsdam Declaration and summaries of the Togo and Anami positions. At ten to midnight, the emperor entered with his military aide. Neatly dressed in army uniform, Hirohito looked tired and preoccupied. All rose and bowed stiffly from the waist. The emperor lowered himself heavily into the chair on the dais. Some coughed nervously in the tense silence.

Suzuki asked the cabinet secretary to read the Potsdam Declaration. That done, the prime minister formally announced that they were now starting a second meeting that day of the Supreme Council for the Direction of the War. After three hours that morning, they had come to no conclusion. In the afternoon, cabinet had been unable to reach unanimity after seven hours. The decision couldn't be postponed any longer. Suzuki asked the emperor to hear personally the opposing views.

Togo was first. Japan was compelled by circumstances, he said, citing the military situation, the destruction of its cities, the low morale of its people, the paralysis of its industry, the danger of Russian invasion and the threat of the atomic bomb ... compelled to accept Potsdam with just the one condition: preservation of the national polity or, in everyday language, retention of the emperor. Admiral Yonai said he agreed with the foreign minister.

War Minister Anami stood up. 'The only honourable course,' he said, 'is to continue the war and drive the enemy back or fight to the last person. But if we seek peace, let's seek it honourably.'

He asked the peace faction if they would continue the war if the enemy rejected their one condition. The three mumbled that they would. Anami replied that he believed they should continue the war then to push for the four conditions, which he enumerated once more.

'I don't object to seeking peace,' said General Umezu when his turn came to speak, 'but I agree we should hold out for four conditions.' Some of the pugnacity had gone out of his manner.

For some reason, Suzuki skipped the chief of navy staff and asked Baron Hiranuma for his view. The ultranationalist privy councillor rambled on for over half an hour. First, he asked Togo what had become of the peace initiative through Russia and whether Japan had rejected the Potsdam Declaration. Togo said it hadn't. It had, of course, but not with his agreement.

Next, Hiranuma questioned whether the army and navy were able to continue the war. 'Is there anything more you could do that you are not doing now?' he asked. He was told the military were doing the best they could under the circumstances.

'That is no doubt true,' said Hiranuma, 'but it is now quite clear that your best is not good enough, and has not been good enough for some time.'

An uneasy silence followed. Finally, the baron arrived at his view. He said he agreed with the foreign minister that Japan must fight on if its national polity was threatened, but if it insisted on the three further conditions it was not necessarily doomed to failure. He concluded with a homily: the emperor was 'responsible for preventing unrest in the nation' and in making any decision should bear that in mind.

While those present were trying to work out how the baron had arrived at his opinion in such a circumlocutory fashion and where this coda applied—how do you prevent unrest in a nation already devastated by an ill-judged war?—Admiral Toyoda got his opportunity to put his view.

'We cannot say that final victory is a sure thing, but at the same time we do not believe that we will be completely defeated,' he said.

Toyoda supported the position of Anami and Umezu and added that an order for Japanese forces to disarm, except by Japan, might not be obeyed.

Suzuki resumed the floor. It was nearly two in the morning. After two hours of discussion, he said, they were still not in agreement. He proposed to ask His Majesty for his opinion on the issue. While ten men rose, the ageing prime minister shuffled up to Hirohito and bowed deeply. Suzuki remained standing in front of his emperor.

Hirohito said, 'You may go back to your seat.'

'Pardon?' said Suzuki, cupping his ear.

Hirohito gestured with his hand. 'Go back to your seat.'

All bowed and sat again as the emperor rose. He spoke slowly. Ending the war, he said, would restore world peace and relieve the nation of its present terrible distress.

'The time has come when we must bear the unbearable. I swallow my tears and give my sanction to the proposal to accept the allied proclamation on the basis outlined by the Foreign Minister.'

All in the room were weeping as Hirohito stiffly wiped an eye with a white glove and quietly left the room. For a time nobody moved or spoke, stunned at the enormity of the point they had just reached. This was the end. This was the end of the imperial dream. What was to become of Japan? What was to become of them? In over two hours of debate, the atomic bombing of Nagasaki that morning had not featured as part of anyone's argument nor been a factor in framing anyone's opinion. All those in the room knew about Nagasaki was what they had obtained from Governor Nagano's woefully inaccurate early report.

'The imperial decision has been expressed. This should be the decision of the conference,' said the prime minister. Nobody argued with that and nobody agreed.

Eleven men filed slowly, silently out of the double wooden doors, along the narrow hallway and up the narrow stairway.

Outside, Yoshizumi turned on Suzuki. 'Are you happy now? Are you satisfied?' he snarled. Anami stepped between them.

'I understand your feelings, Yoshizumi. Now is not the time.'

◆ ◆ ◆

At a meeting of cabinet at 3 a.m., Suzuki ran through the outcome of the imperial conference. He asked if the ministers agreed that the government should accept the Potsdam terms with one condition. Everyone raised his hand.

As the written motion was passed for signing, Home Minister Abe said, 'I don't see the necessity of signing this.'

'You must sign,' said Education Minister Ota. 'The procedure is necessary.'

Abe dipped his brush in ink and slowly placed his signature on the document. Anami asked if the prime minister would continue the war if the Allies rejected the one condition.

'Yes,' said Suzuki.

◆ ◆ ◆

At five in the morning on Tinian base, a very drunk Major Charles Sweeney staggered out of the officers' club, trying to find his way to his

Quonset hut. He left Tom Ferebee and Jimmy Van Pelt at the bar, still drinking. They didn't stay much longer.

Reeling out of the club, the two spied General Farrell's jeep with its key still in the ignition. 'Borrowing' the jeep, they took a joyride around the compound. The adventure came to an abrupt halt when they drove the jeep into the crew quarters where Kermit Beahan and Don Albury were sleeping.

Soon after, Sweeney came across the abandoned jeep. A solitary figure swaying in a standing position, he tried to work out how it had got there. He lay down in the wreckage and fell into a deep drunken sleep.

Chapter 15

Tokyo, Friday 10 August 1945 and after

Shigenori Togo hurried from the overnight cabinet meeting to the Foreign Ministry and drafted a telegram notifying the Allies of the imperial conference decision. The message, sent through the governments of Switzerland and Sweden at seven in the morning on 10 August, said that:

> The Japanese Government is ready to accept the terms enumerated in the tripartite joint declaration which was issued on the 26th of last month, with the understanding that the said declaration does not comprise any demand which prejudices the prerogatives of His Majesty as a sovereign ruler.
>
> The Japanese Government sincerely hopes that this understanding is warranted and desires keenly that an explicit indication to that effect will be speedily forthcoming.
>
> August 10, the 20th year of Showa [era of Hirohito's reign].

Senior personnel in Japan's Ministry of War met at nine thirty to be told by their minister of the outcome of the conference. They were dumbstruck. Even though they knew discussion was taking place, it was still a shock when the news emerged.

General Anami said, 'You must remember you're soldiers and obey orders, not deviating from strict military discipline. In the crisis facing us, the uncontrolled action of one man could bring ruin to the entire country.'

A younger officer asked, 'Is the War Minister actually considering surrender?'

There was silence. Anami cracked his swagger stick across the table. 'Anyone who isn't willing to obey my orders,' he said, 'will have to do so over my dead body.'

At seven thirty, Domei began broadcasting the message to the Allies on short wave. At the same time, US intelligence intercepted the diplomatic notes. Translations were delivered to the US secretaries of State, War and Navy and to the chiefs of staff by 7 a.m., Washington time. The president called a meeting of his civilian and military advisers for nine.

A car was waiting at the time to take Henry Stimson and his wife to the airport, on their way to the Ausable Club in upstate New York. Although his leave was on doctors' advice, the fact that Stimson took it immediately suggests he didn't expect Japan to surrender for some time. A third atomic bomb might be necessary. With news of the Soviet entry into the war, the second bomb on Nagasaki and the offer of surrender, the secretary of war quickly returned to his office in the Pentagon to read the intercept of the Japanese offer. Summoned to the White House, his concern was that further delay would give Russia time to 'get down in reach of the Japanese homeland' and make 'substantial claims to occupy and help rule it'.

It was the Secretary of State, James Byrnes, however, who drafted the Allied response. Concerned about the American public's perception, Byrnes was opposed to agreeing to the one condition and argued for insisting on unconditional surrender. Secretary of the Navy James Forrestal broke the impasse with suggested wording that was ambiguous enough for proponents of unconditional surrender, but might persuade the Japanese that the US agreed to retain the emperor. The Americans offered in their response that Japan's ultimate form of government would be 'established by the freely expressed will of the Japanese people'. In fact, Washington intended to keep the emperor in place to facilitate the occupation.

Truman was no longer concerned about the public's perception of Hirohito—he agreed with acceptance of Japan's single condition—but he was starting to have reservations about the atomic bomb. The day before the Japanese offer of peace, the president had responded to a hawkish telegram from Senator Russell of Georgia.

'I know Japan is a terribly cruel and uncivilized nation in warfare but I can't bring myself to believe that, because they are beasts, we should ourselves act in the same manner,' Truman wrote. 'My object is to save as many American lives as possible but I also have a human feeling for the women and children of Japan.'

At a cabinet meeting on 10 August, Truman ordered that no further atomic bombs be dropped without his express authority. It was the first time he had intervened in the atomic bomb program, the first time that buck had actually stopped there. The day before, generals Spaatz and Twining, with the support of General LeMay and Admiral Nimitz, had urged the third atomic bomb be dropped on Tokyo. Groves called Oppenheimer with the instruction to ease off plutonium production. Heavy incendiary bombing of Japan's cities continued, however.

The US transmitted the Allied reply to Japan through the Swiss on 11 August, reaching Tokyo on 12 August. Forrestal's ambiguity made translation difficult, causing a crisis for the Japanese leaders when cabinet met the following afternoon. Togo believed it meant the imperial institution would be preserved, but others were less sure. Suzuki argued that unless the Allies clarified their position, Japan would have to fight on. Subsequently Togo persuaded him to change his view. Anami's position was that the US had failed to guarantee the national polity and had, in effect, rejected Japan's peace overture. The government was hamstrung once more by its need for unanimous decisions.

At midnight a carrier-based attack by over a thousand navy planes was launched against Tokyo, the largest mission of the war. The following morning, the emperor's principal adviser, Kido, heard that American planes were dropping leaflets with the US and Japanese peace proposals, up to that stage kept secret from the Japanese public. Fearing a backlash by the military, Kido advised the emperor to call another imperial conference. The two military chiefs had refused Suzuki's request for one. The government needed their consent, but the emperor didn't.

Next morning at the conference, Anami, Umezu and Toyoda dismissed the American reply as insufficient. They wanted a more concrete answer. Togo worried that a request to the US for a more 'exact' answer would be construed as a refusal of the terms offered.

The emperor spoke. 'It seems to me there is no other opinion supporting the military's. I shall explain mine. I hope you will all agree with it. My opinion is the same as the one I expressed the other night. The American answer seems to me acceptable.' He asked the government to draft an imperial rescript to stop the war and offered to broadcast the decision to the people. Cabinet reconvened and formally accepted the unconditional surrender.

Later that day, Hirohito recorded his announcement of Japan's surrender for broadcast the next day, 15 August. At the same time, as Kido had feared, a group of junior officers were planning a coup. Some of the group were to steal the recording of the emperor's announcement, while others sought to establish a military government to continue the war. The war minister refused to join the plotters, ordering them instead to respect the emperor's decision.

Running into Togo that night, Anami said, 'I should have given you every assistance in this war, but I'm afraid I've caused you a great deal of trouble instead.' Anami bowed and went to his residence.

After midnight, his brother-in-law visited him to try again to persuade him to join the coup. He found Anami writing what looked like a will. Anami said, 'I'm thinking of committing *seppeku* [ritual suicide].'

They drank a deal of *sake* together. When the police commander came at 4 a.m., Anami sent his brother-in-law to see what he wanted.

While Takeshita was away, Korechika Anami sat on a narrow porchway in front of his bedroom, plunged a dagger into his left side below the waist and drew it across to the right. When Takeshita returned, Anami was feeling his throat, his abdomen cut open. He plunged the dagger into the right side of his throat and fell forward, blood spreading across the floor. The minister was unconscious but not dead. Takeshita grabbed his hand with the dagger and pushed it in deeper to complete the job. A note was left: 'Believing firmly that our sacred land will never perish, I—with my death—humbly apologise to the Emperor for the great crime.'

Korechika Anami was fiercely loyal to both the Imperial Japanese Army and his emperor. He was passionate in his love of his country. Torn by his loyalties, he had nowhere to go but the path he took. Had he not done so, he would no doubt have been tried and executed as a war criminal. Yet, as a firewall between the radicals of the military and the peace faction fumbling through the labyrinth of Japan's decision-making, he probably ensured the Japanese surrender as much as anyone else in its government.

With the rebellion not eventuating, Hirohito's speech was broadcast to the Japanese nation the next day. Most Japanese were hearing the voice of their emperor for the first time. Through crackling static, his words were difficult to grasp. His voice was surprisingly high-pitched and his enunciation stilted. His language was florid and ambiguous. 'The war has developed not necessarily to Japan's advantage,' the emperor said with considerable understatement. 'To pave the way for peace for generations to come we shall have to endure the unendurable and suffer the insufferable.'

Hirohito referred to the atomic bombings: 'Moreover, the enemy has begun to employ a new and most cruel bomb with the power to do incalculable damage and destroy many innocent lives. Should we continue to fight, not only would it result in an ultimate collapse and obliteration of the Japanese nation, but also it would lead to the total extinction of human civilisation.'

This reference is often cited as evidence that the atomic bombs were central to Japan's surrender, thereby justifying their use. However, there was very little reference to the bombs at the time of the decision to surrender. Indeed, the impact of the Nagasaki bomb was greatly understated in the reports that reached the leadership at that time. The extent of the horror of the two bombs would have been much more apparent eight days after Hiroshima, when the speech was written, than three days after, when the decision was made. In his 'Rescript to the soldiers and sailors', delivered on 17 August, the emperor stressed the impact of the Soviet invasion on the decision to surrender, with no reference to the bombs.

◆ ◆ ◆

As the war came to a close, the US government began to give thought to how atomic research should be managed in peacetime. Until the end of 1946, the army's Manhattan Engineer District controlled the nation's nuclear program with General Leslie Groves still in command. But this was a temporary measure in a rapidly changing world.

With no international controls for nuclear research and atomic weapons testing in place at the end of the war, the US tried to introduce them through the newly formed United Nations. However, the Soviet Union was not prepared to accept the terms of the nation with a nuclear monopoly and the US wouldn't modify its terms. In the atmosphere of mutual suspicion, the Cold War set in. In 1949, the Soviet Union tested its first atomic bomb. By the 1950s, the arms race between the two powers was neck and neck.

Groves had difficulty adapting to the post-war role of the Pentagon and Washington politics. Although he had been a highly effective leader of the Manhattan Project, he had made more enemies than friends. His high-handed style during the war years eventually caught up with him. His power and authority were slowly whittled away as it became clear he would not get another project of similar stature. In the end, he was forced into retirement. He left the US Army in 1948.

Groves' scientific director on the Manhattan Project, Robert Oppenheimer, chaired a committee advising on a number of nuclear-related issues and lobbied vigorously for nuclear arms control. His star waned too. Oppenheimer's initial jubilation at the success of Project Alberta faded as reports came in of the dead and the maimed, and of the devastation in the two bombed cities. As the years progressed, the question of whether he regretted his participation got an increasingly evasive answer.

With his connections to the US Communist Party, including his wife and brother, the FBI had been watching Oppenheimer since before the war. Testifying before the House Un-American Activities Committee, he admitted his association with the party in the 1930s but refused to name its members. In 1953, his security clearance was suspended on the basis of a letter from an associate to J Edgar Hoover. In the hearing that followed, some of his eccentric behaviour was used against him, but many scientific, government and military figures testified on his behalf. Leslie Groves wasn't one of them. Under threat by the FBI of examining his role in an earlier cover-up, Groves testified against his former colleague.

One statement Groves made in the hearing is particularly illuminating: 'There was never from about two weeks from the time I took charge of this project any illusion on my part that Russia was our enemy, and that the project was conducted on that basis.'

Oppenheimer's security clearance was never reinstated.

◆　◆　◆

With the war over, *Bockscar* drifted into obscurity, permanently upstaged by *Enola Gay* and ending up in an air force museum in Dayton, Ohio. Like its pilot, *Enola Gay* was not interested in sharing the limelight. Initially the crews of both missions were seen by Americans as saviours who had averted the huge casualties expected in the invasion of Japan, but questions were eventually raised about the morality of atomic weapons and the necessity of dropping the bomb.

Some of the crew of *Bockscar*, like Kermit Beahan, remained in the air force. Others resumed their pre-war lives. None had a crisis of conscience about participation in the Nagasaki bombing, although there was some expression of regret. Beahan, who released the bomb, said he would never apologise for it.

In November 1945, the Nagasaki mission's commander returned to Roswell Army Air Base in New Mexico to train air crews for the atomic tests at Bikini Atoll in the north Pacific. Chuck Sweeney remained in the air force, rising to brigadier-general. He clung steadfastly to the moral justification of the bomb with the slogans of his government: the saving of American lives, the sneak attack on Pearl Harbor, the treatment of POWs. In his later years, Sweeney performed manoeuvres in various air shows as a B-list celebrity.

Colonel Paul Tibbets also remained in the air force. He too rose to brigadier-general. Although Sweeney greatly admired Tibbets, they had little contact after the war. Tibbets waited until Sweeney died before publicly criticising his leadership of the Nagasaki mission. Sweeney, he said, had been a poor choice as mission commander, but gave no reasons.

But Tibbets was also on the receiving end of personal criticism from within his team. Jacob Beser, the electronic countermeasures officer on both missions, has said of his former commander, 'I developed an admiration for him as a pilot, as a co-worker in a cause, but not as an exceptional leader or commander. I saw him as an egocentric, hard driving and selfish individual who played favourites.'

Tibbets became a caricature of a senior American military man, the archetype that inspired the movie Dr Strangelove. In 1976, he re-enacted the bombing of Hiroshima in a restored B-29 at an air show in Texas, complete with a mushroom cloud. A protest by Hiroshima's mayor prompted the US government to apologise to Japan.

In a 2002 interview, Tibbets told an extraordinary story. A couple of days after Nagasaki, he said, he got a phone call from General LeMay wanting to know whether they had 'another of those damn things'. Tibbets said they did but it was in Utah. 'Get it out here,' said LeMay. 'You and your crew are going to fly it.' Tibbets claimed it was loaded on a plane and in California when the war ended. This was after the president's order that there were to be no more atomic bomb missions. The story says a lot about either American military leadership or Paul Tibbets.

In the same interview, Tibbets offered this opinion about war: 'We've never fought a war anywhere in the world where they don't kill innocent people,' he said. 'That's their tough luck for being there.'

It's an attitude that resonates with Curtis LeMay's pooh-poohing of the atomic bombings. 'We scorched and boiled and baked to death more people in Tokyo on that night of March 9–10,' he wrote, 'than went up in vapour at Hiroshima and Nagasaki combined.'

◆ ◆ ◆

In early August 1945 the Russians were in no hurry to end the war. Hostilities in Manchuria continued for over a week, with fierce local clashes but no major battle. Tanks that had crossed the Grand Khingan Mountains rolled over the central Manchurian plain and secured it by 12 August. The eastern front pushed over marshland and through taiga, breaking the Japanese resistance by 14 August. Tanks penetrated and bypassed Japanese positions, and with massive air and artillery support key cities in the region were seized. The Kwantung Army's defences in the east collapsed. The Far Eastern Front linked with the Trans-Baikal force in central Manchuria.

Tokyo had ordered the Kwantung Army to withdraw to a defensive triangle in southern Manchuria. Officers' families were sent south by rail, but 300,000 Japanese civilians were left behind. On 10 August, the Kwantung Army's commander, General Yamada, came back to the palace to tell Pu Yi that the army was withdrawing and moving the capital to Tunghua. With a large household and considerable property, Pu Yi said he needed two days to prepare for the move. The attaché to the Manchukuo Imperial Household suggested respectfully it would be unwise to delay. Pu Yi would surely be among the first to be murdered by the advancing Russians. The puppet emperor left by train the next evening.

The nightmare was just beginning for the Japanese civilians exposed by their military's withdrawal. Tank and air attacks scattered women, children and old men—the young men were mostly in the army—in towns and villages in the path of the Soviet onslaught. In the pandemonium, some were killed fighting, some were drowned desperately trying to cross rivers. There were mass suicides in the retreating bands of civilians. Others were killed by bandits or Chinese irregular forces of the Communist Eighth Route Army that had infiltrated the area. The people of Manchuria turned against the Japanese, taking revenge on their colonial administrators. Many in the Manchukuo National Military changed sides when the Soviet invasion was launched.

On 14 August, Tokyo relayed Emperor Hirohito's ceasefire order to units in the field, but Yamada contradicted the order. Two days later the Kwantung Army was told to cease hostilities and negotiate local truces. The order was difficult to get out to the battle zones. The Kwantung Army had no military communications and used public telephone lines, but they had been disrupted by the Soviet invasion. Fighting continued in some parts, surrender in others, and confusion ruled.

On the nineteenth, the Japanese defenders formally capitulated to the Red Army. Six hundred thousand soldiers of the Kwantung Army were shipped off to the Soviet Union and Outer Mongolia as forced labour. General Yamada was taken as a POW to nearby Khabarovsk and sentenced to twenty-five years in a Soviet labour camp for war crimes.

Amphibious landings on northern Korea on 18 August had supported Soviet land units driving along the north-east coast of Korea. Airborne units were landed in advance around Pyongyang to secure key defensive posts and the north Korean city came under Soviet control. The Russians reached Port Arthur on 22 August.

American forces landed at Incheon in south Korea on 8 September and advanced north to the Thirty-eighth Parallel where a line was drawn in the sand. It's still there.

◆ ◆ ◆

The Pacific War had been Japan's belligerent attempt to rectify a trade difficulty. The US, its main source of oil at the time, had refused to do business while Japan maintained its occupation of China, threatening American economic interests there. The nearest alternative source, the Dutch East Indies, refused also. Japan resorted to invasion as a means of obtaining resources. Except in the short term, it hadn't proved a very productive option.

The economic miracle of post-war Japan is one of the remarkable stories of the modern age. Ironically, it is the product of a stand-off between Japan's former enemies. Japan was fashioned by occupation into a peaceful, pro-Western democracy, but the balance of global power was moving dramatically. The Communists had prevailed in China, and in 1949 the People's Republic of China came into existence. The Cold War with the Soviet Union and by extension China changed Allied economic policy in Japan. The US Under Secretary of the Army was sent to Japan and came back recommending a build-up of industry and trade. Japan was to be a bulwark against communism. In 1947 it was given US$400 million to underwrite an economic plan similar to its wartime plan but without the military component. A proposed purge of the *zaibatsu*, the business conglomerates, was shelved.

With the outbreak of the Korean War in 1950 came $4 billion of orders for Japanese supplies. Prime Minister Yoshida called this war 'a gift from the gods'. Japan's industry surged, restoring its people's income to near-prewar levels. Out of the disaster of the Pacific War and the ashes of Hiroshima and Nagasaki, Japan was able to become the global economic and trading power it had tried to become through conquest.

The survivors of Nagasaki's atomic bomb attack would join their nation's post-war prosperity and all that it would bring in material comforts. Those who were still alive the morning after the attack had no comprehension of a future. What energy they had was spent on just staying alive. For some it would not be enough. The atomic bomb would stalk them with the lingering and deadly radiation left behind on the ground and in their bodies. It would claim many more victims before its threat was gone. Maybe 40,000 died on the day from the blast and 40,000 more from injuries and radiation illness. Nobody knows for sure. But those who survived both blast and radiation would live to see the sun rising on a new Japan.

Chapter 16

Nagasaki, Friday 10 August 1945 and after

Sumiteru Taniguchi woke at dawn in the hills behind Sumiyoshi. The day after the bomb was dropped on Nagasaki, smoke and dust hung over the Urakami valley and down to the city. He lifted himself onto his hands and looked around, realising he was the only one there still alive. It was the first day of the new Japan, but he had no way of knowing that. The wheels to end the war were already in motion.

Sumiteru was intent on staying alive. He dragged himself to a persimmon tree, picked off three hard, unripe fruit and chewed the bitter juice out of them. Far below, the postman could see a relief train coming and going in the valley and survivors lying at the entrance to the torpedo factory tunnels. He tried to call out but his voice was too weak.

Grabbing his mailbag, he wriggled towards a damaged farmhouse and drank water from a bamboo bowl, splashing it over himself. In the shade of a tree, he struggled out of his breeches and puttees, rolled them up as a makeshift pillow and fell asleep. He woke at dusk to find a factory worker standing over him. Without speaking, the man pulled the breeches and leggings from under his head and went away. Sumiteru fell asleep again.

Shockingly burnt, the young postman was found by rescue workers early on 11 August. He asked to be taken to Iwaya-machi, where he dutifully handed over the mailbag to a suburban post office in total chaos, before being taken to Michinoo railway station.

Missing tiles and broken windows was the only damage to Taniguchi's grandparents' house on the slopes of Mount Inasa. Oba-chan had been told by a colleague of her grandson that Sumiteru's battered bicycle and cap had been found at Sumiyoshi. Her husband searched the upper Urakami valley for him by day and slept in a rice field. On the eleventh, he arrived at Iwaya-machi post office. Ji-san was torn between elation and despair when he finally found his badly burnt grandson on his stomach in the shade behind Michinoo station. They went by train to Isahaya, to the emergency centre set up in the school.

Five days after the bomb, Sumiteru's condition deteriorated. His flesh began to bleed and he felt as if he was on fire. The burned flesh began to rot and fall away. Lying on his front, he called out in agony for someone to kill him. No medical aid was available. Ji-san stayed with him all the time. Two days later, they were moved by wooden cart to a temporary hospital set up at Nagayo. There, Sumiteru was treated with a painful concoction of paper ash and maize oil.

Still clinging to life, he was moved again with Ji-san to downtown Nagasaki's emergency hospital at Shinkozen Primary School and treated by experienced doctors for the first time. One day, two American medical corpsmen came in, took flashlight pictures of his wounds without a word, and left.

Finally, ambulance and train took Sumiteru and his grandfather to Omura Naval Hospital where Sumiteru lay stretched face-down on a long bed for eighteen months in pain and hopelessness. His ribcage was burnt and his lung pressed in. Eventually doctors tried two new medications and one of them eased his agony for the first time. By May 1947 he was able to stand up with crutches. A week later he could walk without crutches. Eighteen months after the bomb, Sumiteru caught a train back to Nagasaki and saw the beginnings of rebirth of his city. There were still shanty towns on the hillside, but new buildings were rising from the ashes.

◆   ◆   ◆

The dawning sun revealed to the young girl at the congested shelter entrance the extent of Urakami's devastation. Someone lay on their stomach to drink from a muddy puddle. Sakue's father said, 'Don't drink that water!' and was ignored. The person died and another came crawling out to push him away. Walking around the bodies with a large hook, a man lifted the dead by the shoulders one after the other, looking at their faces. 'This isn't my child,' he sighed after each one. Everywhere, parents were searching for children and children searched for parents.

With Sakue carrying little Tamashii on her back and Ryoko trailing behind, Mr Takigawa crossed the river to Komaba to look for his wife and daughter. Bodies floated downstream under the bridge. Many lay motionless at the water's edge, either dead or waiting to die. They saw a neighbour with face burnt black and a clean cut across her throat. A girl brought her a bowl of soup, but it dribbled out the cut.

Komaba-cho was still burning as they came to the place where their house had once been, where Miwa Takigawa had once held neighbourhood meetings and led national radio exercises. They confirmed its position in the featureless rubble from Mr Matsumoto's dead body in an adjacent gateway, his eyeballs and tongue hanging out.

An incinerated body lay under the broken remains of a cart, so burnt it was unrecognisable. A hand covering the face fell away when the girls' father turned the body over, revealing an unburnt part. Little Ryoko gasped, 'Big sis!' They stared in silent horror at the small section of familiar face like the surviving fragment of a photo that had been torn up.

The three dug around in ashes and debris looking for Mrs Takigawa without success. Neighbours too were searching for missing family when one spotted a plane overhead. 'Run!' she shouted. Everyone was so on edge that the Takigawa family hustled back over the bridge to the safety of their overcrowded shelter. It was still choked with bodies. The family had to camp in front.

That evening, Sakue's older brother, Masuichi, found them. The medical student had been shielded by a pillar in the hospital while those around him were killed by the blast. His clothes were charred and torn, but he appeared not to have any serious external injuries. However, he was vomiting and soon began to bleed from the gums. That night, the Takigawas huddled together shivering in front of the shelter.

Next day, Maseru Takigawa went back to Komaba-cho to look further afield for his wife. Over the road where her close friend Mrs Shimohira lived, he found in the smoking ashes two bodies leaning against each other. He recognised Miwa from the gold crown on one of her teeth.

Sakue and Ryoko returned two days later with their adoptive father, collected broken pieces of timber that had escaped the fires and built a funeral pyre to cremate Mrs Takigawa and Sadako. Too weakened now by illness, Masuichi was unable to move from the shelter entrance. Soon after, he was crying, 'I don't want to die! I don't want to die!'

Maseru and the three little ones were the only members of the Takigawa family to have survived when relatives came in from the country looking for them. Rescued from the stricken city, the young girls' hair started falling out. They suffered nosebleeds and had blood in their faeces. Told they had dysentery, they were taken to hospital for testing, but were found to be dysentery negative and released.

Leaving Tamashii with other relatives, Mr Takigawa went back to Nagasaki with Sakue and Ryoko when their health began recovering. They built a makeshift shanty out of scrap, living there with some of the schoolgirls who had survived in their shelter and the one-legged Korean lady. She would rest her amputated leg on a butcher's chopping block she found somewhere. At dusk each evening, she sang tearful Korean songs until Sakue asked her to stop. The songs reminded her of her missing mother.

Gradually the two girls resumed their lives and went back to school. Ryoko had an appendix operation in her teens, but the incision refused to heal, possibly from a radiation-lowered white blood cell count. The open wound gave off an unpleasant odour, causing such ongoing embarrassment to the young woman that she threw herself in front of a train, ending her short life.

Sakue Kawasaki grew into adult life, working as a spruiker at shopping centres and car sales yards. The son of Miwa Takigawa's close friend, Mrs Shimohira, came to live in the shanty for a while, but he and Sakue never spoke until after Ryoko's death. Now Sakue Kawasaki is Mrs Shimohira.

◆ ◆ ◆

In the morning after the bomb, Dr Nagai woke after a fitful night on their hill to see an ashen landscape spread below. The summer's cicada choir hadn't returned. A group went down to the gutted medical college hospital to see if they could find any useable equipment or medicines, but all they found were the incinerated bodies of their former colleagues and patients. Matron Hisamatsu came running up waving one of the leaflets dropped overnight, warning people to leave the city before it was too late. It *was* too late!

Tsuneo Tomita woke in the Pharmacy Department's shelter under construction nearby and Professor Seiki soon after. Only two of the injured students, Matsumoto and Okamoto, were still alive. Nagai arrived with his assistants to attend to the injured. He showed the American leaflet to Seiki, who read it and gazed into the sky. Meanwhile, Nagai and his team looked at the two seriously injured students, but there was little they could offer. The doctor was starting to feel quite ill himself. The team moved on, looking at the injured nearby, lying about or sitting in groups. All the time American planes came and went overhead, adding to the pervading sense of helplessness.

During the morning in the makeshift dugout, a couple came looking for Matsumoto, their boarder. They brought a basket of fruit, eggplants and cucumbers, but he was unable to eat. Half an hour later, he died. A delirious Okamoto staggered about for a while and collapsed. In a rasping whisper, he begged Tomita to stay with him. As soon as Tomita squatted next to him, Okamoto twisted around and died. In the late morning, the two sole survivors in the dugout cremated the dead in front of the unfinished shelter. The professor and Tomita built wooden markers, inscribing each with a dead student's name in charcoal.

Tsutomu Yamaguchi, the marine draftsman exposed twice to the atomic bomb, lay semi-conscious for a week in another dugout. With the left side of his face and his arm swelling badly, he developed a high fever. The burned area of his skin festered and broke out in boils, discharging blood. He didn't know if it was night or day. As he slowly gathered his faculties, he realised the people around him were crying. They were listening to the emperor's broadcast announcing Japan's surrender. Yamaguchi had no feelings about that. He didn't expect to live.

But he did live. After two months of treatment he returned to the office, physically able to work but in a spiritual vacuum. Yamaguchi was employed for a while by the US occupation force, then as a teacher, but eventually he returned to Mitsubishi's shipworks.

The heavily pregnant Mitsue Tabata was in a vegetative state similar to Yamaguchi. Lying in pain in her parents' house and confused by the sounds of aircraft above, she longed to join her children staying with her husband's family past Michinoo. Her little daughter had gone there the day after the bomb.

The constant care she needed was too demanding for her parents. In the pre-dawn of 15 August, she was put on a sliding door laid across a bicycle-drawn cart. Oblivious to Hirohito announcing the end of the war, she endured a long, rattling journey to join her husband. The pain still didn't subside and the burns remained raw until October. Later that month, Mrs Tabata gave birth to another daughter, a very small baby through lack of nutrition. It was more than two months since she had calculated she was eight months pregnant.

◆ ◆ ◆

Dr Akizuki woke with an uneasy sense of having failed. He'd been disturbed a few times during the night by people wanting to know why they hadn't been given medicine. Nurse Murai, on the other hand, hadn't slept a wink. Adrenalin from the previous day had kept her awake all night. She started the day cooking for the patients.

Noguchi told Akizuki that there were medicines stored in the basement of the Franciscan hospital, put there some time before for safe keeping. Simple medicines like Mercurochrome, zinc oxide ointment and disinfectants, they would provide only limited treatment but they were better than nothing.

A treatment site was set up on the hospital grounds with a desk and cloth hung on green bamboo as an examination area. With his staff,

Akizuki treated mostly burns victims. Apart from the ointment there was little they could offer, except rice and miso soup. Patients were dying at regular intervals. Families came and took some patients home, but others stayed behind. The doctor was frustrated by so little medicine or equipment to treat patients. At times he felt like tossing it in and walking away in defeat, but nurse Murai and the assistants stuck to their task so he couldn't give up. He decided instead that the patients felt comforted just by having a doctor and nurse present.

On that afternoon, Dr Akizuki made his first house call to a small air-raid shelter with about twenty people. He was shocked to find Motohara deserted, just dead trees, charred light poles and hanging wires. Houses were flattened and the residents had gone. In the shelter were the corpses of those who'd been flung violently against a wall by the blast. Most of the others had severe burns. Working into the night by candle-light, Akizuki applied oil with a brush to the burn wounds and removed glass splinters with tweezers.

The next day, men arrived from the garrison, cleared a space on the second floor of the gutted hospital building and laid down straw. They designated it the Motohara Emergency Hospital for the 300 severely wounded patients they brought with them. Their reply, when asked who would treat the patients, was, 'You have a doctor, don't you?'

Apart from Dr Akizuki, the only medical support came from nurse Murai and two female assistants. Brother Iwanaga, Noguchi and a couple of male workers provided non-medical support. The soldiers told Akizuki they would help, but soon drifted away. Later that day, medical teams starting arriving from downtown's Takahara Hospital.

The hospital workers took food at regular intervals from the city council's ration store in the disused gymnasium nearby. The monk and the seminarian also found salt in another store near the cathedral, bringing it back by cart. When council workers arrived several days later to take charge of the storehouse, they could see food had been taken but turned a blind eye. It was never mentioned.

Sugako Murai's uncle arrived on the third day while she was treating a patient. He was surprised and delighted to find her still alive. 'I thought you were dead,' he said, 'and came to collect your bones.' He wanted to take her home, but she said she was needed there, asking him instead to tell everyone she was safe. Temporary nurse Murai didn't go home for several days.

Dr Akizuki encountered symptoms he'd never seen before. Patients were turning black and had severe diarrhoea. Their gums bled and their mouths turned a purplish colour. Some didn't even appear to have been wounded in the bombing. It was most perplexing. The injuries of burns patients were settling after four or five days, but their medical condition deteriorated.

Sugako started feeling heavy and feverish, as if she was floating. Determined not to give in to disease, she kept her symptoms to herself and continued working, assuming she had picked up a night chill. When the fever went down, the diarrhoea and bleeding started. She knew then she had the mysterious disease. Working on in the same blood-stained clothes, she cleaned maggots from patients' wounds, boiled water from the river to wash clothes, cooked food from the council storehouse. Patients she was treating died, but Sugako slowly recovered.

Little news filtered in from the outside world. They didn't hear for two days that the emperor had announced the war was over. For nurse Murai, the overriding feeling was of relief. 'Now I can walk on the street without being threatened by the roar of a propeller.'

◆　◆　◆

Chiyoko Egashira, who had been in the school dispensary so near the hypocentre, remained in the shelter at Tateiwa Shrine the whole day after the bomb. The glass fragments in her back became more painful. She didn't know what had happened to her four children at home with their grandmother or Takashi, her son at work with the transport company. Her only certainty was that baby Naomi had survived, withdrawn but seemingly well.

Ukichi set out at dawn to go home, but the fires were still burning fiercely and he couldn't get close. He tried again several times during the day, on one occasion coming back to the shelter with Takashi. Their son had avoided serious burns, but was listless nonetheless with acute diarrhoea.

In the late afternoon, Ukichi tried again. This time he returned with confirmation in a cooking pot, misshapen by the bomb's heat, of what they knew by now in their hearts. In the pot were the bones of his mother and three of their girls. Of their five children, only Naomi and Takashi had survived.

Next day, Chiyoko was taken on a wooden stretcher to a first-aid station set up in the ruins of Ohashi's weapons factory. As she was carried through her old neighbourhood, she saw a Shiroyama she no longer recognised. All familiar landmarks had been pounded into a layer of burnt rubble. Not one of the cherry trees along the riverside was left standing. The long concrete embankment had been blown over on its side. Corpses were floating, bloated, in the river. Picks were being used to drag them out of the river, as if they were large fish. Bodies were placed in heaps and burned on the river bank. The smell was putrid.

With no beds at the first-aid station, the injured were laid out on straw. Medical staff attended to Chiyoko's back. Her underwear had stuck to her skin and made a rasping sound as it was peeled off so the myriad fragments of glass could be removed. Ukichi lost consciousness and was taken elsewhere in the skeletal factory. Takashi had become so weak that he too was taken away.

With her back treated, Chiyoko left with Ukichi, Takashi and Naomi to stay with relatives. Three days later, the increasingly weak Takashi died. The family moved in with Chiyoko's parents, but Ukichi was starting to show symptoms of radiation illness. Spots appeared on his body and his hair started falling out. Dr Takahara gave him salt injections every day because there was no medicine. In October, Ukichi mumbled that his mother and Takashi had come to meet him. He died soon after.

Chiyoko slowly recovered with blood transfusions and her sister's boiled persimmon leaves. By November she was one of five teachers who borrowed a room at Inasa Primary School to resume classes. Chiyoko Egashira lived to 92. Her daughter, Naomi, lives on.

◆　◆　◆

In the morning after the bomb, others went searching for family and friends, as Ukichi Egashira had done, knowing that finding them alive was improbable, but hoping nonetheless for a miracle to reverse their misery. In any case, there were duties to the spirits of loved ones passing to the world beyond. Warden Minami left Isahaya Prison early on the tenth and made his way back to Urakami. As he neared the prison, shouts and cries gave way to soft groans. By the time he got to where the prison was, there was utter silence . . . and no prison.

All that remained of the three buildings were giant concrete slabs, cracked and blistered, on which the prison once stood. Everyone had been killed, the remains unidentifiable. Minami's wife and small daughter had died instantly. The warden gathered up ash, the remains of anything, once living or inanimate, that had been part of the prison and trudged off with it to hand out to relatives of the dead.

Junji Sato, the Domei News reporter, got through to the munitions factory where his younger sister, Teruko, worked. There was no sign of her, but every indication she had not survived the blast. He never saw her again.

By morning, the Yamawaki brothers' father had still not come to their shelter. The three boys—the eleven-year-old twins and fourteen-year-old Toshihiro—decided to look for him. On their way they found one of the leaflets airdropped during the night by the Americans. EVACUATE YOUR CITIES it said. The paper was good quality but the handwriting was awful. Toshihiro supposed the leaflet had been written by a second-generation Japanese-American.

At the front gate of every police station hung a sign: 'If you find enemy propaganda, it must be reported to police immediately.' As the brothers passed a police station in ruins, Yoshiro became fearful knowing that his older brother had an enemy leaflet in his trouser pocket.

They continued walking towards the Mitsubishi Electric Corporation. The devastation grew worse and worse. Houses along the roadside had burned to the ground. Trees and electric poles stood like oversized used matches. The factories along the river were a mass of crushed metal rods. Only the largest of cement columns remained upright. With swollen faces, arms and legs, the dead bodies among the debris littering the road looked like black rubber dolls. If the boys' shoes accidentally struck against a corpse, skin would peel off revealing white fat underneath.

Bodies floated in the Urakami River. A young woman seemed to have a long white ribbon dragging in the water behind her. On looking closer, the boys saw it was actually her intestine protruding from the side of her abdomen. Nearer their father's factory, Tatsuro let out a scream. At first, it looked like the body of a young boy had vomited up noodles, but on closer inspection the brothers saw roundworms that had been living inside the boy's body now making their escape. The Yamawaki brothers ran away, fighting back their nausea.

The Mitsubishi Electric Corporation was reduced to scorched twisted metal and brick and concrete rubble. Three men were working with shovels inside the demolished walls. Toshihiro called out, 'Our name is Yamawaki. Do you know where our father is?'

One of the men glanced over. 'Your father is over there,' he said, indicating a demolished office building.

The three ran in the direction he pointed, expecting their father would be sitting at his desk. Instead they found his corpse, swollen and scorched like the others. 'If you want to take your father home with you,' one of the workmen said, 'you'd better cremate him. Otherwise, you'll have to bury him here.'

The city's crematoriums had been destroyed. With no alternative they could think of, the brothers collected smouldering pieces of wood from the ruins of the factory. They put their father's body on burnt posts and piled wood pieces on top.

Flames rose high in the air. The Yamawaki boys put their hands together and said prayers for their father. They looked up and saw his feet sticking out from the fire. It was an unbearable sight. The boys were crumbling emotionally. A workman said, 'You'd better go home today. You can come back tomorrow and collect the remains.'

The next morning, the three brothers found a pot and some tongs in the kitchen of their damaged house. They took them to the factory to collect their father's remains. No longer frightened by corpses, now they were just obstacles in their path.

They arrived at the place where they had started their father's cremation, but instead of the small pile of ashes they expected the body lay half-cremated and covered with ash. The fire they had lit the day before had burned out.

A skeleton covered with ash was a more horrifying sight to the boys than the corpses they had seen along the way. Yoshiro could bear no longer to look at his father's body. 'Let's go home and leave his body here,' he said.

Toshihiro stared at the remains. 'We'll just take his skull home and that will be the end of it.'

He put the tongs around his father's skull. It crumbled like old, dry plaster. Half-burned brains flowed out. Toshihiro screamed and threw down the tongs in horror. He raced away with the twins running after him, their father's body abandoned.

The following day the boys' uncle found them in the shelter and took them to join their stepmother and little brothers and sisters in Saga, where they had been evacuated before the bomb. The four walked to Michinoo to be turned away from the trains reserved for the injured. Returning to the family's damaged house, they took the whole of the following night to walk to Isahaya connected by their dead father's black obi so no-one would be lost falling asleep on the way. The boys never told their stepmother what had happened when they tried to retrieve their father's remains.

◆　◆　◆

The day after the bomb, having received a more accurate report from Mayor Okada during the night of the destruction in Urakami, Governor Nagano set about building on the rudimentary emergency response. He wanted fatality numbers and details of the explosion's impact to be reported to the Home Ministry in Tokyo every thirty minutes. Whether there would be sufficient new information for that frequency of reporting and whether Tokyo wanted to hear from them that often wasn't the point. Nagano wanted to be seen to be in charge after his understated report on the day of the attack.

Astonished by Okada's description, the governor headed towards ground zero. The devastating scene he saw was beyond anything imagined. Although smouldering ashes were all that was left of the once flaming fires, the Urakami he saw under the dismal sky had been literally burnt to the ground. Buildings had been lifted off the ground and flattened as they fell back, crushing anyone underneath. Once the blast hit, there had been no time to flee. Fires were like scavenging hyenas after the blast, cleaning the meat off the bones of the district's wreckage.

Charred corpses lay everywhere, as if they were rubbish thrown out in the street. The living were scattered about on the verge of death. Nagano saw a young woman lying face-down calling for water in a voice so small it was 'like a mosquito humming'. Without the strength to say, 'Give me some water,' she could only sigh the word 'water'. The putrid smell of decay clogged the governors' nostrils.

That was the story of Urakami as Nagano observed it the day after the bomb: a district completely gutted by fire, destroyed of all greenery, without shadows and everywhere corpses and the wounded. A first-aid station had been set up out in the open. The wounded were laid out on school grounds, in large houses or on the concrete floors of destroyed factories, waiting until someone came to treat them.

Recovery from the bomb's destruction and the rebuilding of Nagasaki was a long and draining process of endless misery and only a few uplifting moments. It took its toll on Wakamatsu Nagano, a municipal politician of limited ability in the outer reaches of the nation. By January, he asked to be relieved of his duties.

Takejiro Nishioka's career moved in the reverse direction to Nagano's after recovering from the symptoms of radiation illness. It's not clear why Nagasaki prefecture needed a chief of foreign affairs, but that's what the self-important Nakamura was. He claimed that by not briefing officials other than the governor about Hiroshima—officials such as Nakamura— Nishioka added to Nagasaki's death toll.

Nishioka had briefed Nagano, who called a meeting for the time coincidentally of the Nagasaki attack. Nagano had briefed the police chief, who did no more than warn his own family. Nishioka pointed out that had he spoken more widely, as Nakamura proposed, he would have risked arrest for violation of the law against spreading 'wild rumours'.

Subsequently, Takejiro Nishioka turned his interest in the newspaper *Minyu* over to his wife and went into politics. He became Governor of Nagasaki Prefecture.

◆　◆　◆

On 11 August, a makeshift reception centre was set up in front of where the medical college's out-patients clinic had once been. Its purpose was to refer the injured and increasingly the sick to medical staff who were coming from the military and from outside Nagasaki, and to collect information and answer questions about victims and missing people. With a growing stench of death in the summer heat, there was a need as well to dispose of those who were beyond help. Wood was gathered from the slopes to build cremation pyres.

With the arrival of outside doctors and nurses, Nagai was able to look for his wife, already knowing in his heart what the outcome would be. He eventually pinpointed his house in the vast featureless field of broken tiles and white ash, and found Midori, little more than charred bones. He could see she died in her own kitchen. In the powdered bones of her hand, she held the beads, chain and cross of her rosary, melted into a dully glinting blob. Takashi Nagai bowed his head and sobbed. After offering a prayer for her beloved soul, he carefully scooped her bony ashes into a heat-twisted bucket.

On the hill above the medical college, Dean Tsuno was told his family and residence at Nishiyama, on the other side of Mount Konpira, were unharmed, but he refused an offer to be moved there by stretcher. Although feeling a little recovered, he wanted to stay near the hospital ruins for treatment and was carried instead to a nearby shelter. Three days later, his wounds became infected. For over a week, Dr Tsuno battled fever, diarrhoea and all the other symptoms of illness brought on by double exposure to radiation. On 22 August, he died.

Dr Nagai probably had a double dose as well, but it was difficult to separate the effects of atomic radiation from the leukemia already diagnosed. After the war, he was appointed to a professorship at Nagasaki Medical College and started research into atomic radiation illness. Collapsing at Nagasaki station in 1946, he was confined to bed from that point, writing extensively until 1951 when haemorrhaging finally ended his life at forty-three.

◆　◆　◆

Koichi Wada returned to the Hotarujaya terminal of the tram company to assist with rescue activities and the search for missing employees. Walking through the northern sector of Nagasaki, despair was all they could find. Early optimism of survival was often crushed by the lingering effects of radiation.

Koichi's grandparents' house had been damaged by the bomb, tilted out of alignment and much of the tiled roof dislodged. His sister and grandparents moved to Moji while he worked on the house. Japanese tiles are light and easy to work with, but Koichi soon found he was no builder. As summer moved into gusty autumn, the wind blew rain through gaps and into the house. Leaks were revealed in the roof. Koichi stuck to the task though and eventually plugged the holes.

In September his hair started falling out, his gums and bowels bled and he was constantly tired. He became depressed and at times suicidal, but was determined not to let the bomb beat him. His family returned to Nagasaki and moved back into the house. His grandmother brewed a Chinese herbal tea from persimmon leaves she gathered in the hills. The bleeding stopped and by the end of the month the former tram driver began to feel stronger.

One day, men came from the Nagasaki Electric Streetcar Company and offered Koichi a chance to drive trams again if he would help rebuild the tramlines. All along the line from Hamaguchi to Ohashi the tracks had buckled and been lifted up. Koichi worked with a reconstruction crew, replacing sleepers, installing rails into the road and spreading gravel under the tracks. It was hard work, especially as he was still weak from his illness, but he was paid and given a bowl of white rice at the end of each day. He ate half the bowl, wrapping the other half in newspaper to bring home. His grandmother made a watery *okayu* for the rest of the family.

The tramline workers rebuilt seven trams from bomb-damaged street-car parts. On 25 November, the trams began running again. Koichi Wada drove the fourth car out of Hotarujaya. In 1948, he moved from the driving compartment to head office, having completed a night-school course. Eventually he moved into management.

Wada became involved in the *hibakusha* (survivors of the atomic bomb) movement and through this received a telephone call out of the blue from a Mrs Miyahara, a woman with hardened keloid scars over half her body, the typical long-term symptom of burns from the bomb. She said she had worked as a conductor when he was at the tram company in 1945 and wanted advice about government assistance for *hibakusha*. It was Tatsu Noguchi, the older of the two waifs from rural Kyushu, whom Koichi Wada had observed with fascination from a respectable distance sixty-four years before. Now, in 2010, they spoke for the first time.

◆ ◆ ◆

A couple of days after the bomb, Mitsue Takeno felt slightly better. Perhaps the vomiting on the long trek home had cleared some of the toxins from her system. She and Chi-chan went with two school friends to Mezame to find out what had happened to her friend N-san, absent from work on the fateful day. They had crossed the Nakajima River on their way to Urakami when they came across N-san's father, who worked in the commercial area nearby.

'Is Setsuko . . .' started Mitsue, but before she could finish the question, he answered it. Both his daughter and his wife had been crushed to death under the fallen roof of their house. Because he was at work in the downtown area at the time he was saved. His face was haggard and miserable, his head drooped low. The girls stood and watched as he slowly walked away with heavy steps. With no reason to continue to Urakami, they turned back.

Five days after the bomb, Mitsue heard there was a ferry going to the Goto Islands. She rushed to catch it and was met at the port by her mother, who had run the 4 kilometres from the family's home. Mitsue was taken to their village in her uncle's cow-drawn cart. Watching from the verandah, her younger sisters came rushing down the road as soon as they saw cow and cart approaching. The prospect of this loving reunion had sustained the young woman over the last five days. The Takeno family had prepared a large plate of *sashimi* to welcome their daughter home. She was back in the bosom of her own kith and kin.

Her joy didn't last. Almost immediately, red spots appeared all over her body, a sign of radiation illness. Getting thinner over succeeding days, her heart began thumping irregularly and she couldn't stand for any prolonged length of time. By September, her hair was falling out, but at the end of the month the fever began to subside. She began to walk slowly around the house and showed encouraging signs of returning health.

Mitsue's school in Nagasaki reopened in October. She was well enough by then to return to the bombed city and board once again with Mrs Hirai and Chi-chan. Eventually marrying and moving to Kobe, she was there for the devastating earthquake of 1995. She survived that too.

Now a grandmother, the life of Mrs Kubo (as Mitsue now is) has been one of connections and missed connections. Some years after the Nagasaki bomb, a newspaper published a photo of one of the two priests killed in the cathedral by the bomb. Mitsue recognised him instantly, his gentle face imprinted in her memory. It was Father Nishida. He had been the kindly visiting priest who had watched her picking a flower in the church grounds of her island home so many years before.

Before going home to Goto, Mitsue was visited at the shelter by the young man who guided her home over the Mount Konpira ridge. The visitor asked with a broad smile how she was feeling. He now had a patch of gauze on his forehead. It was during the period of her early recovery. Mitsue asked his name. 'That's not important,' he said. 'I'm just relieved to see you're well.'

As they exchanged bows, the sixteen-year-old noticed his name in *sumi* (Japanese ink) on his white canvas shoes: 'Honda'. Over the years she attempted to track him down, with newspaper articles about her search, but she never saw him again.

◆　◆　◆

If many of the citizens of Nagasaki no longer had homes, one group was in the process of returning to theirs after years away. The prisoners of war from Camp 14 came down from their shelters in the hills either side of the valley back to their camp. They were in a state of disbelief, even though it was the same destruction they'd seen the previous afternoon. All that remained of their barracks was flattened and twisted steel girders.

The relationship with their guards now undefined, no longer in custody but not yet freed, the POWs set up a makeshift camp where they had been building the shelters before the bomb. Over the next few days, the uninjured joined working parties cleaning up. They managed to scrounge food and lay out in the open at night. The Dutch medical orderlies provided what assistance they could without instruments, mostly lancing blisters that had formed on burnt skin.

On 13 August, the POWs were moved to a dormitory at Tomashi, south of the city, where Mitsubishi's workers and mobilised students were already living. Some of the Dutch, who had been working bare-chested in the open on the day of the bomb, were horribly burnt and sick. By 29 August, four more Dutchmen had died from injuries or radiation.

Four days after the emperor's broadcast, the prisoners were put on parade and told that Japan had joined the rest of the world to pursue peace. The war was over, the camp commandant said, and they could all go home. They were dumbfounded. There was no shouting, no waving with glee.

Shortly after, American planes flew low over Tomashi. The prisoners made a large sign with the letters 'POW' and lay it on the vacant lot next door to the dormitory. Relief supplies were dropped. On 7 September, a month after the bomb, US reporter George Weller arrived at the new camp with a Red Cross representative. Weller recommended the POWs get themselves to the air base at Kanoye in the south. It had been a Japanese base, but was now a major hub for bringing in occupation personnel and supplies. Forty planes were coming in daily and heading out empty.

The Australian soldiers, including Peter McGrath-Kerr and Allan Chick, found their way to Nagasaki station, and caught the trian to Kanoye. They took with them the ashes of their comrades who had died in Fukuoka Camp 14, retrieved from the foreigners' section of Sakamoto cemetery. Japan was in such turmoil that scruffy, emaciated Westerners raised no interest travelling on the nation's railways.

McGrath-Kerr and John Marshall, who had a broken collarbone, were treated for their injuries in the occupation army hospital at Kanoye. They were airlifted with the other Australians to Okinawa and Manila, where McGrath-Kerr was hospitalised. The other Australians sailed to Sydney on the carrier *Formidable*, arriving 13 October. Dutch and British POWs stayed behind at Tomashi and were handed over to the US Army on 13 September for repatriation.

After discharge from the army, McGrath-Kerr worked in Hobart, then in Launceston as a draftsman–engineer. Chick didn't take discharge when he got back to Australia, but returned instead to Japan with the Australian contingent of the occupation force. He was posted at Kure just out of Hiroshima.

The quiet country boy returned to Tasmania in 1953 with a Japanese wife. Expecting a frosty reception in his home town, he found to his surprise that Haruko was quickly accepted by the people of St Helens. He worked in a timber yard, but after falling out with his boss Allan Chick moved with his wife to Gippsland in rural Victoria. In 2010 they were living there in a nursing home.

◆ ◆ ◆

For weeks after the bomb, Yoshiro Fukuda, the Mitsubishi manager with a stomach ulcer, lay in a bed in Omura Naval Hospital with his white blood cell count falling dramatically. The technician who had covered him on the train journey from Michinoo died after two weeks from the effects of radiation. Doctors gave up hope for Fukuda. Then quite remarkably and suddenly, his condition reversed and he progressed to complete recovery.

Even more remarkably, it was found that his gastric ulcer had been cured by the radiation. It was hard to find an explanation for this, since ulcers were thought to be caused by acids in the stomach. Sixty years later, two Australian scientists won a Nobel Prize with their discovery that peptic ulcers were caused by bacterial infection. Radiation could destroy bacteria even if it couldn't affect acid secretion. Was Fukuda's ulcer that disappeared an opportunity for scientific discovery that went unnoticed?

◆　◆　◆

Dr Yoshioka, the visiting doctor at Urakami Hospital, recovered from the atomic blast's lacerations to her face. Brother Joseph Iwanaga returned as a teacher to the theological college when it was rebuilt. Yoshini Noguchi became a Franciscan priest, Father Felix, and later chaplain at St Francis Hospital, as Urakami Dai-ichi Hospital became after rebuilding.

No sign was ever found of Dr Akizuki's older sister, Suzuko. The doctor eventually moved to the countryside to start his own practice. Taking up a brown rice diet and moving further into the Tara Mountains, the doctor lived in a woodcutter's house and practised medicine in the nearby villages. The newly supplied Urakami Hospital donated some of its medicines to the hermit doctor and asked nurse Murai to take them out to him.

Using Sugako as a go-between to supply medicines and food, Akizuki was able to continue his eccentric existence. He built a small house in the mountains. In 1949, Akizuki asked Sugako to marry him through their mentor in common, Dr Takahara.

Sugako and Tatsuichiro Akizuki were married in two ceremonies. The first, in the woodcutter's house, was for his neighbours in the mountains. They put on a feast for the occasion as is the way in rural areas. Their second ceremony was officiated by the chaplain at St Francis Hospital, a visiting Canadian priest. Sugako couldn't wear a wedding dress. All her kimonos had been burnt or lost and between them they had very few possessions.

The newlyweds lived in the small house Akizuki had built in the mountains, but eventually he was prevailed upon to return to Nagasaki to work in a clinic. Soon after, he was appointed medical director of St Francis Hospital, and Mrs Akizuki became matron at Kwassui Women's College, her old school. The skilled but fastidious doctor, riddled with self-doubt, had found a rock to anchor his life.

◆ ◆ ◆

It is an irony of human existence that out of the most appalling circumstances of suffering sometimes can come small gems of human advancement and happiness. Whether a coincidence or cause and effect, the day after the Nagasaki bombing saw the first steps towards the new Japan and, free from the grasp of militarism that had plagued it, the economic recovery that was the nation's post-war miracle. At the level of everyday life we try to fashion for ourselves, Yoshiro Fukuda was cured by the bomb of his stomach ulcer as if Jesus Christ had passed by, and Tatsuichiro and Sugako Akizuki found each other in the ashes and horror of Nagasaki, eventually forging a life together.

Fate, that drone in the sky, can unfold against us so horrifyingly, but it can also unfold *for* us. It's either in the lap of the gods or in the toss of the dice, depending on how you think the universe got here.

BIBLIOGRAPHY

Books

Akizuki Tatsuichiro—*Nagasaki 1945* (1982) (transl. Keiichi Nagata, ed. Gordon Honeycombe) Quartet Books, London

Allen, Louis—*The End of the War in Asia* (1976) Hart-Davis, MacGibbon, London

Alperovitz, Gar—*Atomic Diplomacy: Hiroshima and Potsdam* (1994) Pluto Press, London

Amrine, Michael—*The Great Decision: The Secret History of the Atomic Bomb* (1959) Heinemann, London

Andressen, Curtis—*A Short History of Japan: From Samurai to Sony* (2002) Allen & Unwin, Sydney

Araki Masato, Aimonoya Tatsuichiro and Takahashi Takao—*Album of Nagasaki, 100 Years—During and After the War (Arubamu Nagasaki Hyakunen—Senchu Sengo-hen)* (1986) Nagasaki Bunken-sha, Nagasaki

Asada Sadao—'The Shock of the Atomic Bomb and Japan's Decision to Surrender—A Reconsideration' in *Hiroshima in History: The Myths of Revisionism* (ed. Robert James Maddox) (2007) University of Missouri Press, Columbia, MI

Ba Maw, U—*Breakthrough in Burma: Memoirs of a Revolution, 1939–1946* (1968) Yale University Press, New Haven, CT

Barnaby, Frank—'The Effects of the Atomic Bombings of Hiroshima and Nagasaki' in *Hiroshima and Nagasaki: Retrospect and Prospect* (eds Douglas Holdstock and Frank Barnaby (1995) Frank Cass, London

Beasley, WG—*The Japanese Experience: A Short History of Japan* (2000) Weidenfeld & Nicholson, London

Beser, Jerome and Jack Spangler—*The Rising Sun Sets: The Complete Story of the Bombing of Nagasaki* (2007) Beser Foundation for Archival Research and Preservation, Baltimore, MD

Bix, Herbert P—*Hirohito and the Making of Modern Japan* (2000) Harper-Collins, New York

Brooks, Lester—*Behind Japan's Surrender: The Secret Struggle That Ended an Empire* (1968) McGraw-Hill, New York

Butow, Robert JC—*Japan's Decision to Surrender* (1954) Stanford University Press, Stanford, CA

Calvocoressi, Peter, Guy Wint and John Pritchard—*Total War: The Causes and Courses of the Second World War*, Volume 2 (1972) Penguin, London

Caron, George R and Charlotte E Meares—*Fire of a Thousand Suns* (1995) Web Publishing, Westminster, CO

Cassidy, David C—*J Robert Oppenheimer and the American Century* (2005) Pi Press, New York

Chinnock, Frank W—*Nagasaki: The Forgotten Bomb* (1970) George Allen & Unwin, London

Clarke, Hugh V—*Last Stop Nagasaki!* (1984) George Allen & Unwin, Sydney

Clarke, Hugh, Colin Burgess and Russell Braddon—*Prisoners of War* (1988) Time-Life Books, Sydney

Coffey, Thomas M—*Imperial Tragedy* (1970) World Publishing, New York

Craig, Campbell and Sergey Radchenko—*The Atomic Bomb and the Origins of the Cold War* (2008) Yale University Press, New Haven, CT

Craig, William—*The Fall of Japan* (1968) Weidenfeld & Nicholson, London

DeGroot, Gerard J—*The Bomb: A Life* (2005) Harvard University Press, Cambridge, MA

Dower, John—*Embracing Defeat: Japan in the Aftermath of World War II* (1999) Penguin Books, London

Feis, Herbert—*The Atomic Bomb and the End of the War in the Pacific* (1966) Princeton University Press, Princeton, NJ

Forbes, Cameron—*Hellfire: The Story of Australia, Japan and the Prisoners of War* (2005) Pan Macmillan, Sydney

Frank, Richard B—*Downfall: The End of the Imperial Japanese Empire* (1999) Random House, New York

Giovannitti, Len and Fred Freed—*The Decision to Drop the Bomb* (1965) Methuen & Co, London

Glantz, David M—*Soviet Tactical and Operational Combat in Manchuria, 1945: 'August Storm'* (2003) Frank Cass, Portland, OR

——*The Soviet Strategic Offensive in Manchuria, 1945: 'August Storm'* (2003) Frank Cass, Portland, OR

Glynn, Paul—*A Song for Nagasaki* (1989) Marist Fathers Books, Sydney

Goldstein, Donald M, Katherine V Dillon and J Michael Wenger—*Rain of Ruin: A Photographic History of Hiroshima and Nagasaki* (1995) Brassey's, Dulles, VA

Gordin, Michael D—*Five Days in August* (2007) Princeton University Press, Princeton, NJ

Gordon, Andrew—*A Modern History of Japan: From Tokugawa Times to the Present* (2003) Oxford University Press, New York

Hasegawa Tsuyoshi—*Racing the Enemy: Stalin, Truman and the Surrender of Japan* (2005) Belknap Press, Cambridge, MA

Henning, Peter—*Doomed Battalion: Mateship and Leadership in War and Captivity* (1995) Allen & Unwin, Sydney

Hirschfeld, Burt—*A Cloud over Hiroshima: The Story of the Atomic Bomb* (1967) Bailey Brothers & Swinfen, Folkestone, UK

Holloway, David—*Stalin and the Bomb: The Soviet Union and Atomic Energy, 1939–1956* (1994) Yale University Press, London

Holman, Robert—*On Paths of Ash* (2009) (ed. Peter Thomson) Pier 9, Sydney

Ibuse Masuji—*Black Rain* (1969) (transl. John Bester) Kodansha International, Tokyo

Ienaga Saburo—*The Pacific War: World War II and the Japanese, 1931–1945* (1978) Pantheon Books, New York

Iriye Akira—*Power and Culture: The Japanese-American War, 1941–1945* (1981) Harvard University Press, Cambridge, MA

Kase Toshikazu—*Journey to the Missouri* (1950) Yale University Press, New Haven, CT

Kato Masuo—*The Lost War: A Japanese Reporter's Inside Story* (1946) Alfred A Knopf, New York

Knebel, Fletcher and Charles Bailey—*No High Ground* (1960) Weidenfeld & Nicholson, London

Kubo Mitsue—*Hibaku: Recollections of A-Bomb Survivors* (1990) (transl. Ryoji Inoue) Mitsue Kubo, Nishinomiya-shi, Japan

——*Sekihyou ni kizamu (Engraving on a Monument)* (2003) Bungeisha, Tokyo

Laurence, William L—*Dawn Over Zero: The Story of the Atomic Bomb* (1947) Museum Press, London

Laures, Johannes—*The Catholic Church in Japan: A Short History* (1954) Charles E Tuttle, Tokyo

MacEachin, Douglas J—*The Final Months of the War with Japan: Signals Intelligence, US Invasion Planning and the A-Bomb Decision* (1998) CSI Publications, Washington, DC, <www.cia.gov/library/center-for-the-study-of-intelligence/csi-publications/books-and-monographs>

Maddox, Robert James—*Weapons for Victory: The Hiroshima Decision Fifty Years Later* (1995) University of Missouri Press, Columbia, MI

Malloy, Sean L—*Atomic Tragedy: Henry Stimson and the Decision to Use the Bomb Against Japan* (2008) Cornell University Press, Ithaca, NY

Manning, Paul—*Hirohito: The War Years* (1986) Bantam Books, New York

Marx, Joseph L—*Seven Hours to Zero* (1967) GP Putnam's Sons, New York

Medvedev, Roy and Zhores Medvedev—*The Unknown Stalin: His Life, Death and Legacy* (2004) (transl. Ellen Dahrendorf) The Overlook Press, Woodstock, NY

Miller, Merle and Abe Spitzer—*We Dropped the A-Bomb* (1946) Thomas Y Crowell, New York

Moskin, J Robert—*Mr Truman's War* (1996) Random House, New York

Nagai Takashi—*We of Nagasaki: The Story of Survivors in an Atomic Waste-land* (1951) (transl. Ichiro Shirato & Herbert BL Silverman) Victor Gollancz, London

——*The Bells of Nagasaki* (1984) (transl. William Johnston) Kodansha International, Tokyo

Nelson, Hank—*POW, Prisoners of War: Australians Under Nippon* (1985) Australian Broadcasting Corporation, Sydney

O'Keefe, Bernard J—*Nuclear Hostages* (1983) Houghton Mifflin, Boston

Oya Soichi—*Japan's Longest Day (Nihon no ichiban nagai hi)* (1968) Kodansha International, Tokyo

Pellegrino, Charles—*The Last Train from Hiroshima: The Survivors Look Back* (2010) Henry Holt & Co, New York

Plutschow, Herbert E—*Historical Nagasaki* (1983) Japan Times, Tokyo

Prange, Gordon W with Donald M Goldstein and Katherine V Dillon—*God's Samurai: Lead Pilot at Pearl Harbor* (1990) Brassey's (US) Inc, McLean, VA

Rappaport, Helen—*Joseph Stalin: A Biographical Companion* (1999) ABC-CLIO, Santa Barbara, CA

Rhodes, Richard—*The Making of the Atomic Bomb* (1986) Simon & Schuster, New York

Robinson, Frank and ER 'Bon' Hall—*Through Hell and Bomb Blast* (1982) Frank Robinson, Waverley, TAS

Rotter, Andrew J—*Hiroshima: The World's Bomb* (2008) Oxford University Press, Oxford

Sanger, SL—*Working on the Bomb* (1995) Continuing Education Press, Portland, OR

Schmitz, David F—*Henry L Stimson: The First Wise Man* (2001) Scholarly Resources, Wilmington, DE

Schoenberger, Walter Smith—*Decision of Destiny* (1969) Ohio University Press, Athens, OH

Sekimori, Gaynor (transl.)—*Hibakusha: Survivors of Hiroshima and Nagasaki* (1986) Kosei Publishing Co, London

Selden, Kyoko and Mark Selden (eds)—*The Atomic Bomb: Voices from Hiroshima and Nagasaki* (1989) ME Sharpe, New York

Shaeffer, Rene—*Oranda heishi Nagasaki hibakuki (Dutch Soldier's Account of the Nagasaki Atomic Bomb)* (1983) (transl. Yasuo Ogata) Sodoshuppan, Nagasaki

Sigal, Leon V—*Fighting to the Finish: The Politics of War Termination in the United States and Japan, 1945* (1988) Cornell University Press, Ithaca, NY

Smith, Jim B and Malcolm McConnell—*The Last Mission: The Secret Story of World War II's Final Battle* (2002) Broadway Books, New York

Spae, Dr Joseph J—*Catholicism in Japan* (1964) ISR, Tokyo

Spector, Ronald H—*Eagle Against the Sun: The American War with Japan* (1985) The Free Press, New York

Sweeney, Charles W with James A Antonucci and Marion K Antonucci—*War's End: An Eyewitness Account of America's Last Atomic Mission* (1997) Avon Books, New York

Takaki, Ronald—*Hiroshima: Why America Dropped the Atomic Bomb* (1995) Little, Brown & Co, Boston

Thomas, Gordon and Max Morgan Witts—*Enola Gay* (1977) Stein & Day, New York

——*Ruin From the Air: the Atomic Mission to Hiroshima* (1978) Sphere, London

Togo Shigenori—*The Cause of Japan* (1956) (transl. Togo Fumihiko & Ben Bruce) Simon & Schuster, New York

Toland, John—*The Rising Sun: The Decline and Fall of the Japanese Empire, 1936–1945* (1970) Penguin Books, London

Townsend, Peter—*The Postman of Nagasaki* (1984) Collins, London

Truman, Harry S—*1945: Year of Decisions* (1955) Konecky & Konecky, New York

Trumbull, Robert—*Nine Who Survived Hiroshima and Nagasaki* (1957) EP Dutton & Co, New York

Volokogonov, Dmitri—*Stalin: Triumph and Tragedy* (1991) (transl. Harold Shukman) Weidenfeld & Nicholson, London

Wainstock, Dennis D—*The Decision to Drop the Atomic Bomb* (1996) Praeger, Westport, CT

Walker, J Samuel—*Prompt and Utter Destruction: Truman and the Use of Atomic Bombs Against Japan* (2004) University of North Carolina Press, Chapel Hill, NC

Walker, Stephen—*Shockwave: The Countdown to Hiroshima* (2005) John Murray, London

Weale, Adrian—*Eye-Witness Hiroshima* (1995) Robinson, London

Weintraub, Stanley—*The Last Great Victory* (1995) Truman Talley Books/ Dutton, New York

Zubok, Vladislav and Constantine Pleshakov—*Inside the Kremlin's Cold War: From Stalin to Khrushchev* (1996) Harvard University Press, Cambridge, MA

Papers, Articles, Webfiles, Diaries, Etc.

Akebiman—YouTube, 2/5/10, <www.youtube.com>

Akizuki Sugako—'My Experience of Exposure to the Atomic Bomb', unpublished MS

Akizuki Tatsuichiro—'Dr Tatsuichiro Akizuki' (1968) in *Testimonies of the Atomic Bomb Survivors* (transl. William Sakovich) Nagasaki Broadcasting Company

Alvarez, Luis—letter to Professor Ryokichi Sagane, 9 August 1945, <www.lettersofnote.com/2009/12/this-rain-of-atomic-bombs-will-increase>

Atomic Heritage Foundation, Washington DC—website at <www.atomicheritage.otg>

Baugher, Joe—*The Atomic Bomb* (2000) <home.att.net/~jbaugher2/b29_11>

Bernstein, Barton J—'Truman at Potsdam: His Secret Diary', *Foreign Service Journal*, July/August 1980 (Burr, Document 38)

Burr, William (ed)—*The Atomic Bomb and the End of World War II* (2005) The National Security Archive, George Washington University, Washington DC, <www.gwu.edu/ ~nsarchiv/NSAEBB/NSAEBB162/index>

Dahl, Linda—*Japanese WWII POW Camp Fukuoka #17*, <www.lindav dahl.com>

Dannen, Gene—*Atomic Bomb: Decision. Documents on the Decision to Use Atomic Bombs on the Cities of Hiroshima and Nagasaki* (2003) <www. dannen.com/decision>

Davies, Joseph E—diary, 29 July 1945 (Burr, Document 43)

Dzirkals, Lilita I—'"Lightning War" in Manchuria: Soviet Military Analysis of the 1945 Far East Campaign' (1976) Rand Corporation, Santa Monica, CA

Egashira Chiyoko—'Ms Chiyoko Egashira' (1970) in *Testimonies of the Atomic Bomb Survivors* (transl. William Sakovich) Nagasaki Broadcasting Company

Eto Jun (ed.)—'Togo's Meetings with the Cabinet and the Emperor, August 7–8, 1945' in *The Historical Records of the End of the War*, volume 4, pp. 57–60 (transl. Toshihiro Higuchi) (1945) (Burr, Document 55a)

Gibbs, John M—'Gibbs Report, Fukuoka #17' (1946) <www.mansell.com/ pow_resources/camplists/fukuoka/Fuku_17/fuku_17_gibbs_report>

Giga-Catholic Information—'The Metropolitan Archdiocese of Nagasaki, Japan', <www.gcatholic.com/diocese/diocese/nago0.>

Gosling, FG—*The Manhattan Project: Making the Atomic Bomb* (1999) History Division, US Department of Energy, Washington, DC

Groves, Major General Leslie R—'Memorandum to the Chief of Staff', 6 August 1945 (Burr, Document 53)

—— 'Memorandum to the Chief of Staff', 10 August 1945 (Burr, Document 67)

Handy, General Thomas T—Order to General Carl Spaatz, US Army Strategic Air Forces, 25 July 1945 (Burr, Document 41e)

Harriman, W Averell—Memorandum of Conversation, 7 August 1945 (Burr, Document 54)

——Memorandum of Conversation, 'Far Eastern War and General Situation', 8 August 1945 (Burr, Document 57)

Harrison, George L—Memorandum to the Secretary of War, 26 June 1945 (Burr, Document 22)

Harry S Truman Library & Museum—'The Decision to Drop the Atomic Bomb', <www.trumanlibrary.org>

Hayashi Saburo—'Study of Strategical and Tactical Peculiarities of Far Eastern Russia and Soviet Far East Forces' (from *Japanese Special Studies on Manchuria*, volume 8) in *War in Asia and the Pacific 1937–1949*, volume 11 (eds, Donald S Detwiler and Charles B Burdick) (1980) Garland Publishing, New York

Hewlett, Thomas D—'Dai ju nana bun sho (Camp #17): Nightmare revisited' in *Japanese WWII POW Camp Fukuoka #17*, Linda Dahl, Lewiston, ID, <www.lindavdahl.com>

Hickley, Lieutenant John, Lieutenant Van Oortmensen, Lieutenant Lance Gibson and Sub-lieutenant Philip Cranefield—Sinking of the *Tamahoku Maru*, <www.mansell.com/pow–resources/camplists/fukuoka/fuk-14-nagasaki/tamahoku-maru>

Hirohito—'Emperor Hirohito, Accepting the Potsdam Declaration, Radio Broadcast', transmitted by Domei & recorded by the Federal Communications Commission, 14 August 1945, <www.myholyoke.edu/acad/intrel/hirohito>

Ikeda Sumihisa—Statement, 23 December 1949, Document No. 54479, Centre for Military History, Washington DC

Kennedy, Thomas—'Nagasaki' in *The Catholic Encyclopaedia*, vol. 10, <www.newadvent.org/cathen/10667c>

Kosuge, Nobuko Margaret—'Prompt and utter destruction: the Nagasaki disaster and the initial medical relief' (2007) *International Review of the Red Cross*, vol. 89, no. 866, pp. 279–303 (June 2007)

Laurence, William L—'Eyewitness Account of Atomic Bomb Over Nagasaki', US War Dept Bureau of Public Relations, 9 September 1945

Long, Doug (ed.)—*Hiroshima: Henry Stimson's Diaries and Papers* (2001) <www.doug-long.com/stimson>

——*Hiroshima: Was it Necessary?* (2005) <www.doug-long.com/hiroshim>

McCurry, Justin—'A little deaf in one ear—meet the Japanese man who survived Hiroshima and Nagasaki', *The Guardian*, 25 March 2009

McGrath-Kerr, Peter—interview by Tim Bowden (13 July 1983) for *Prisoners of War: Australians Under Nippon*, Australian Broadcasting

Corporation, Sydney (held at Australian War Memorial, Canberra, ID #S02898)

Manhattan Engineer District—*The Atomic Bombings of Hiroshima and Nagasaki* (1997) World Wide School, <www.worldwideschool.org/ library/books/hst/northamerica/ The Atomic Bombings of Hiroshi maandNagasaki/toc>

Manhattan Project Heritage Preservation Association (MPHPA)—*Children of the Manhattan Project* (2000–2005), <www.mphpa.org/classic/ COLLECTIONS>

Mansell, Roger—'Fukuoka #14 Nagasaki', Center for Research, Allied POWs Under The Japanese, Palo Alto, CA, <www.mansell.com/ pow_resource/camplists/ fukuoka/fuk–14-nagasaki>

Marine Corps University Command and Staff College (MCUCSC)— *The Soviet Army Offensive: Manchuria, 1945* (1986) GlobalSecurity. org, Alexandria, VA, <www.globalsecurity.org/military/library/ report/1986/RMF>

Miura Masatoshi—*No More Nagasaki*, Nagasaki Institute of Applied Science, <base.mng.nias.ac.jp/Nomore-e>

Nagai Takashi—'Atomic Bomb Rescue and Relief Report' (2000) (transl. Aloysius F Kuo) Nagasaki Association for Hibakushas' Medical Care (NASHIM)

Nagano Wakamatsu—'Mr Wakamatsu Nagano' (1971) in *Testimonies of the Atomic Bomb Survivors* (transl. William Sakovich) Nagasaki Broadcasting Company

Nagasaki Atomic Bomb Museum—*Nagasaki City—Peace & Atomic Bomb: Atomic Bomb Survivors* (2009) <www1.city.nagasaki.nagasaki. jp/peace/English/survivors/ index>

Nagasaki Broadcasting Company (NBC)—*Nagasaki and Peace*, 'Testimonies of the Atomic Bomb Survivors', <www2.nbc-nagasaki.co.jp/ peace/index-en>

National Museum of the US Air Force—Fact Sheets: 'Boeing B-29 Superfortress', <www.nationalmuseum.af.mil/factsheets>

National Science Digital Library (US)—*Hiroshima and Nagasaki Remembered* (2005) <www.hiroshima-remembered.com>

Nihon Hidankyo—*The Witness of Those Two Days: Hiroshima & Nagasaki, August 6 & 9, 1945*, Nihon Gensuibaku Higaisha Dantai Kyogikai (Japan Confederation of Hibakusha Organisations), Tokyo <www.ne.jp/asahi/hidankyo/nihon/rn_page/english/witness>

Office of AC of S, G–2 (US War Department)—'Magic' Diplomatic Summary, No. 1221, 29 July 1945 (Burr, Document 44)

——'Magic' Diplomatic Summary, No. 1226, 3 August 1945 (Burr, Document 48)

——'Magic' Diplomatic Summary, No. 507, 9 August 1945 (Burr, Document 61)

Oregon State University—*Special Collections*, 'Atomic Energy & Nuclear History Collections', <osulibrary.oregonstate.edu/specialcollections.coll/atomic/catalogue/atomic-energy2_1–100>

Parry, Richard Lloyd—'To hell and back', *The Times*, 6 August 2005, <www.times.co.uk/tol/news/world/article766984>

Patterson, Michael Robert—*Arlington National Cemetery*, Biographies: Leslie Richard Groves (2010) <www.arlingtoncemetery.net/lggroves>

Pearlman, Michael D—*Unconditional Surrender, Demobilization, and the Atomic Bomb* (1996) Combat Studies Institute, Fort Leavenworth, KS, <www.cgsc.army.mil/carl/resources/csi/Pearlman/pearlman>

Price, David—'In the Shadow of Hiroshima and Nagasaki' (2004) <www.counterpunch.org>

Rezelman, David—*The Manhattan Project: An Interactive History* (2001) Office of History and Heritage Resources, US Department of Energy, <www.cfo.doe.gov/me70/manhattan>

RIKEN—*Stories from RIKEN's 88 Years* [No. 9], Episode: 'Ryokichi Sagane and "Fat Man"' (2005), <www,riken.jp/r-world/info/release/riken88/text/image/pdf/no09e>

Russell, Richard, telegram to Harry S Truman, 7 August 1945 (Truman Library, Documents, August 1945)

Sasamoto Taeko—Fukuoka 14 bunsho (Nagasakishi Saiwaimachi), POW Research Network, <www.powresearch.jp/jp/pdf_j/research/fk14_saiwai_j>

Scholte, Ronald—'Kamp Fukuoka 14' (transl. Anna Johns) in *Oorlogsherinneringen van militia soldat 8924*, <www.onzeplek.nl/cms/publish/content/showpage.asp?pageid=1592>

Shimohira Sakue—'Experience of A-bomb' in *No More Nagasaki*, 'The Voice of the A-bomb Victims', Nagasaki Institute of Applied Science, <base.mng.nias.ac.jp/Nomore-e>

——'Ms Sakue Shimohira' (1989) in *Testimonies of the Atomic Bomb Survivors* (transl. Brian Burke-Gaffney) Nagasaki Broadcasting Company

——'Plea of Atomic Bomb Survivor', in *Nagasaki City—Peace & Atomic Bomb: Atomic Bomb Survivors* (2009) Nagasaki Atomic Bomb Museum

Shirabe, Dr Raisuke—'My experience and damages' (1986) in *Division of Scientific Data Registry*, Atomic Bomb Disease Institute, Nagasaki University, <www-sdc.med.nagasaki-u.ac.jp/abcenter/shirabe>

Spitzer, Abe—personal diary, 7 January–1 September 1945, <www.mphpa.org/classic/COLLECTIONS/CG-ASPI/ASPI_Gallery_Directory>

Stimson, Henry L—personal diary, 10 & 11 August 1945, (Burr, Document 66)

——'The Decision to Use the Atomic Bomb', *Harper's Magazine*, February 1947, p. 97

Sublette, Corey—*The Nuclear Weapon Archive* (2007) <nuclearweaponarchive.org>

Takagi, Sokichi—'Diary and Documents' (ed. Takashi Itoh) (2000) Misuzu-Shobo, Tokyo (Burr, Documents 37 & 55b)

Taniguchi Sumiteru—'Experience of A-bomb' in *No More Nagasaki*, 'The Voice of the A-bomb Victims', Nagasaki Institute of Applied Science, <base.mng.nias.ac.jp/Nomore-e>

Truman, Harry S, letter to Senator Richard Russell, 9 August 1945, (Truman Library, Documents, August 1945)

United States Strategic Bombing Survey (USSBS)——'The Effects of Atomic Bombs on Hiroshima and Nagasaki' (1946) US Government Printing Office, Washington, <www.ibiblio.org/hyperwar/AAF/USSBS/AtomicEffects>

——*The Effects of Air Attack on the City of Nagasaki* (1947) USSBS Urban Areas Division (15/11–1/12/45)

—'Summary Report (Pacific War)' (1999) HyperWar Foundation, Lafayette, CO, <www.ibiblio.org/hyperwar/AAF/ USSBS-PTO-Summary>

——'Japan's Struggle to End the War' (2006) HyperWar Foundation, Lafayette, CO, <www.ibiblio.org/hyperwar/AAF/USSBS/Japans Struggle>

Wada Koichi—'A Monument to 11:02 a.m.', in *Nagasaki City—Peace & Atomic Bomb: Atomic Bomb Survivors* (2009) Nagasaki Atomic Bomb Museum

Wapedia—'Soviet Invasion of Manchuria, 1945' <wapedia.mobi/en/Soviet_invasion_of_Manchuria_(1945)>

Warner, Denis—'They saw the Fat Man and lived to tell the tale', *The Australian Magazine*, 1–2 July 1995

Weller, George—'A Nagasaki Report', *Mainichi Daily News*, 8 & 9 September 1945

White House press release—'Statement by the President of the United States' (6/8/45) The White House, Washington DC, <www.hiro shima-remembered.com/ documents/PRHiroshima>

Wintz, Jack—'Nagasaki: A Peace Church Rises From the Nuclear Ashes' (2010) in American Catholic.org: 'World War II: 60 Years Later', <www.americancatholic.org/Features/WWII/feature0283>

Yale Law School—'The Atomic Bombings of Hiroshima and Nagasaki' in *The Avalon Project: Documents in Law, History and Diplomacy* (2008), Lillian Goldman Law Library, New Haven, CT, <www.avalon.law.yale.edu>

Yamawaki Yoshiro—'The Unforgettable Experience of the Atomic Bombing', in *Nagasaki City—Peace & Atomic Bomb: Atomic Bomb Survivors* (2009) Nagasaki Atomic Bomb Museum

Zuberi, Matin—'Atomic Bombing of Hiroshima and Nagasaki', *Strategic Analysis*, (August 2001) vol. 25, pp. 623–662

Interviews

Akizuki Sugako, Nagasaki, Japan (April 2010)

Chick, Allan, Heyfield, Australia (January 2010)

Kubo Mitsue, Nishinomiya, Japan (February & April 2010)

McGrath-Kerr, Andrew, Launceston, Australia (November, December 2009)

Shimohira Sakue, Nagasaki, Japan (January & April 2010)

Taniguchi Sumiteru, Nagasaki, Japan (March & April 2010)

Wada Koichi, Nagasaki, Japan (March & April 2010)

Yamawaki Yoshiro, Nagasaki, Japan (March & April 2010)

ACKNOWLEDGEMENTS

This is a story about ordinary people in an extraordinary time. I owe a sincere debt to the people who have shared their lives, their experiences and their thoughts for this book, both in interviews and publications that pre-existed the book. They are listed in the bibliography.

Key to gathering those stories was my team of Hanako Nakano in Nagasaki and Hiroko Moore in Sydney. Hanako found *hibakusha* (atomic bomb survivors) and talked extensively and engagingly with them about daily life so long ago, unearthing fascinating detail. Hiroko not only translated the recordings of those conversations, but followed up with detective work through Japanese websites to clarify and expand the detail we had. Without these two, it would have been a less intimate book.

My thanks therefore to the people in the chain through which I found Hanako and Hiroko: Wakao Koike of the Japan Foundation in Sydney and Professor Yamashita (Nagasaki University), Ms Midori (City of Nagasaki) and Mr Oba (Nagasaki Peace Foundation), through whom I found Hanako; and Mika Nishimura and Tina Koutsogiannis, who pointed me towards Hiroko. Thanks also to Ryoji Inoue and Tomomi Sato, through whom I found, corresponded and lunched with Mrs Mitsue Kubo (nee Takeno).

Thanks also to Sue Briginshaw (History Room, St Helens), Robin Gerster, Ian Bowring and Cameron Forbes, through whom I found Allan Chick in Heyfield, Victoria. Andrew McGrath-Kerr in Launceston shared information about his father and his collection of photos and Tim Bowden his radio interview with Peter McGrath-Kerr. Father

Paul Glynn was a very useful background source about Catholicism in Nagasaki as well as the narrative of Dr Takashi Nagai and his family.

I also owe thanks to Roy 'Kanga' Hogg, Eric 'Pancho' Leadbetter, John Miller and Perce Curvey for sharing their sometimes harrowing experience of Fukuoka Camp 17 at Omuta, across the Ariake Sea from Nagasaki, and to Cyril Gilbert for connecting me to them. For reasons of length, their story has been dropped from this book as the most peripheral to the story of the bomb. Theirs is an engrossing story in itself, but in the end it was a different one to the story I tell here.

I owe much of my understanding of the Japanese people—to the extent that I have any—to those Japanese who have engaged with and assisted me along the path to this and my previous book, but particularly to my co-author of *The Path of Infinite Sorrow*, Hajime Marutani. His friendship is one I value greatly. My initial insights into life in Japan in the dying days of the war came from Yoshi Hosaka in Sydney.

My writing starts off saying too much and saying it woodenly and, if I'm lucky, gets trimmed back with the help of others so it is at least semi-readable. The first person to weed out the prolix, pomposity, ponderousness and general unnecessary and artless verbiage was my wife, Jan Stretton. Then the copy editor, Karen Ward, went through it with disconcerting professionalism. The pair have produced a far more readable work than the one I wrote. That's good news for readers and we should all be grateful to these word police.

Finally my thanks to Allen & Unwin, who have taken a second punt on me as an author and especially to Richard Walsh and Sue Hines for their confidence in the project and feedback on the result, and to Rebecca Kaiser for shepherding (if that's the word) the manuscript through to the bookshop. It all started when Richard said he wondered what the people of Nagasaki were doing after the first bomb and before they got their own. Now he knows.

INDEX

Hotarujaya tram terminal 45, 49, 140,
186, 222, 306–7
Hurley, Patrick 69
Hutou 167

Ikeda, Lieutenant-General Sumihisa
165, 276
imperial conference 187–8, 262,
273–4, 276–9, 284
Imperial Palace 3, 32, 127, 241, 262, 276
Inao, Kazuyo 226
inkan 1, 5, 45, 186
Information and Intelligence Agency
(IIA), Japan 20, 90
Isahaya 96, 121, 140, 184–5,
190–1, 270–1, 301, 303
Ishikawa, Father 196, 212–3
It's a Pleasure 18–19
Ivanov, Colonel-General SP 74
Iwanaga, Akira 2, 5, 10, 14–15, 24–5,
81–2, 103, 120–1, 191, 224–5
Iwanaga, Brother Joseph 47, 135, 172,
196, 211–3, 265, 298, 311
Iwo Jima 145, 151, 158, 161, 181,
183, 230

Japan Broadcasting Corporation
(NHK) 12, 16
Jobling, Gunner Murray 195–6, 216
Johnson, Sergeant Jack 40, 217–8
Junin 35, 170, 252, 269

Kaidaichi 5, 10, 13
kakure kirishitan (hidden Christians)
34, 48

kamikaze (divine wind) 29–30, 45, 93,
226
Kamizaki, Commander 194, 216
Kawabe, Torashiro 169
Kawano, Sakao 243–4, 265
Kawasaki, Sakue 27–30, 45–7, 93–4,
110–1, 140–1, 173–4, 188, 208–9,
267–8, 294–5
Kawasaki, Ryoko 27–9, 45–7, 93–4,
110–1, 140–1, 174, 188, 208–9,
267–8, 294–5
Kawasaki, Tomosaku 110–1
kempeitei 95, 145–6
Kido, Koichi 56, 99, 241, 261–2,
283–4
Kinoshita family 243, 265, 271
Kishi, Tomoyo 226–7
Koba 49, 124, 179
Koga, engineer 189, 193, 221
Koi 82, 103, 120, 125
Kokura 25–6, 60, 119, 138, 147,
151–2, 156, 176–7, 179–82
Kokura's luck 182
Komaba-cho 27, 30, 294–5
Konoye, Fumimaro 57, 67, 115, 169,
241, 261
Korea 66, 272, 290–1
Koura, Mayor 185, 228
Kubo, Isaburo 226–7
Kuharek, Sergeant John 156,
160–1, 167, 181, 163, 230,
234, 241
Kure Naval Base 12–13, 105
Kurile Islands 53, 66
Kuroshima 34–5, 203